Hong Kong at the Handover

edited by
Bruce Herschensohn

LEXINGTON BOOKS
Lanham • Boulder • New York • Oxford

LEXINGTON BOOKS

Published in the United States of America
by Lexington Books
4720 Boston Way, Lanham, Maryland 20706

12 Hid's Copse Road
Cumnor Hill, Oxford OX2 9JJ, England

British Library Cataloguing in Publication Information Available

Library of Congress Cataloging-in-Publication Data

Hong Kong at the handover / [edited by] Bruce Herschensohn.
    p. cm.
    Collection of transcripts of speakers who addressed a Hong Kong conference in
1997, sponsored by The Claremont Institute.
    ISBN 0-7391-0006-8 (alk. paper)
    1. Hong Kong (China)—History—Transfer of Sovereignty from Great Britain,
1997. 2. Hong Kong (China)—Politics and government. 3. China—Politics and
government—1976- I. Herschensohn, Bruce, 1932-   . II. Claremont Institute.
DS796.H757
951.25—dc21   98-45369
                                                        CIP

Printed in the United States of America

The paper used in this publication meets the minimum requirements of American
National Standard for Information Sciences—Permanence of Paper for Printed Library
Materials, ANSI Z39.48–1984.

Contents

Preface

Through the years, The Claremont Institute has had a special interest in Hong Kong. This culminated in the 1995 Hong Kong Conference, in which twenty-five delegates went to Hong Kong to hear the most important speakers on the coming handover of the British Colony to the People's Republic of China.

In 1996 the Institute published *The Last Time I Saw Hong Kong.* In 1977 the Institute published *Chronology of 1996 Events in Hong Kong,* followed by a portable compilation of those two publications.

At the time of the handover in 1997, the Institute had a second conference in Hong Kong, this one with eighty-six delegates. This book is a transcript of the speakers who addressed that conference at that historic time. In addition, particularly for those unfamiliar with Hong Kong, we have included a short history of the former British Colony and a glossary of terms and names.

Acknowledgments

Our gratitude goes to Johnny and Pam Zamrzla, Mr. and Mrs. Paul Hoff, and Mr. and Mrs. Cliff Pratt, whose grants made this book possible.

Our thanks, too, for the voluntary work done by Frank J. Prewoznik II in the preparation of this book.

Introduction

Nothing like the handover from Great Britain to the People's Republic of China has happened in all recorded history: a political entity taken over, not by war or revolution or coup—but by a ninety-nine-year-old treaty between two powers, both having had far different governments when the original agreement was enacted. What the People's Republic of China gained was an entity like no other on earth. Its uniqueness came from three major elements:

1. The people. The inhabitants of Hong Kong proved on a daily basis that no one knew better what to do with liberty than those who once lived under an absence of liberty, and most of the builders of Hong Kong have known such an absence. Their constructions, their creations, their selling, their buying, their trading, their going from one place to another within that small enclave, are journeys that had no daily or nightly horizons of starting and stopping. The only deadline they have ever known since living there has been July 1, 1997. The people of Hong Kong, 94 percent of whom either fled from China or are the children of those who fled, have been caught in an ironic twist of fate with the government from which they fled coming to them. Under the benign government of Great Britain, which has ruled Hong Kong since 1841, the Chinese people of Hong Kong built the world's epitome of free enterprise. Hong Kong has become the combination of the dreams of Adam Smith and Ayn Rand.

2. The British Government. It did very little, which is exactly what any good government should do. Its regulations were few and not stifling of creativity and talent, with almost a relaxed form of anarchy, yet there was little crime on the streets and a general feeling of safety no matter the hour. God-given civil liberties were not threatened. Workers kept most of the fruits of their labor, with only a flat rate tax of 15 percent (with some slight progressively below 15 percent but not enough to mention and often not bothered with by taxpayers); only about two-fifths of the population owed any taxes at all, and tax evasion was minimal. There was a flat corporate tax of 16.5 percent, cut from 17.5 percent. No revenues went to the crown or out of Hong Kong. There were no taxes on dividends and no sales taxes on most merchandise. There was no minimum wage law, yet Hong Kong's citizens possessed one of the highest average incomes in the world, $24,000 a year (surpassing Great Britain), while across the border in China, the average year's wages were $400. And generally the government's annual report showed a surplus. Welfare budgets were low and limited to a fixed percentage of public spending that went up or down depending on the local economy. The World Health Organization listed Hong Kong with the highest life expectancy in the

world (males = 75.1 years, females = 81.4 years). The judicial system, with its established rule of law, was separate from the executive and legislative arms of government based on British common law. For a long time the executive and legislative branches had, in fact, not been separate. There had been an unelected legislature, which was revamped by Governor Christopher Patten who arrived in Hong Kong in 1992, to a democratically elected legislature. The governor, as all governor's before him, was sent to Hong Kong by London. The British were only .003 of the population, but they governed little and well. It is both true and tragic that in the doing of nothing they also did not create a total democracy and left on the 32 large law books of Hong Kong those laws that give government a legal authoritarian status. The laws were not enforced and in most cases were totally ignored by the government, but they gave a legal underpinning to what the People's Republic of China might well want to do.

3. An element that can best be described as the Yixin Teapot. So the old Chinese story goes, an old woman wanted to sell her teapot in the marketplace of Yixin. A traveler came by and, at her invitation, he drank tea she poured from the teapot. It was the best tea he had ever tasted, and he offered to buy the teapot from her for a sum she never expected to be offered. While he went away to get the cash to pay her, she became conscious of the used appearance of the teapot, and because he offered her so much money for it, she scrubbed the teapot inside and out, not realizing that by removing the dross accumulated from years and years of tea leaves used in the pot, that she was removing what made every cup of tea as wonderful as it was. She destroyed the very reason he wanted it. Even a member of the Politburo of the People's Republic of China, Li Ruihuan, told the familiar story of the Yixin Teapot to the Chinese People's Political Consultative Conference in 1995. He did not make any specific parallel, but it was apparent that he was saying Hong Kong was the new Yixin Teapot, and it cannot be fooled with carelessly, or it will be destroyed.

Those three elements; the people, a benign government, and the Yixin Teapot Factor, made Hong Kong, Hong Kong.

A Short History of the British Crown Colony of Hong Kong, 1841-1997

Abraham Lincoln was thirty-two years old and practicing law in Springfield, Illinois, when the history of Hong Kong began. Hong Kong is the only major political entity on earth that has a shorter history than the United States. I suppose Lincoln would have said that our country was threescore and five years old at the time if anyone had asked him. Fortunately they didn't. He could save the line for later.

Prior to 1841, Hong Kong Island off southern China had been a camping ground for pirates and a place for transient fishermen who had either great courage or ignorance to think it was a safe place. Fishermen would often spend their last days in Hong Kong because pirates would slit their throats for their day's catch. Nevertheless, in the years just prior to 1841, British journals say that as many as 5,650 people were scattered there among villages and hamlets and boats.

Two major and frequent biases are obvious in the history books of Hong Kong, depending on whether their authors are British or Chinese. As Americans in the 1990s, we can write a description of events based on those readings without any bias at all since we owe no allegiance to either Queen Victoria or Emperor Ching of the Manchu Dynasty. The histories written by the British do seem to have more credibility since they are generally self-critical and there is no self-criticism in the histories written in China.

Both powers were trading with each other, and it is apparent that both powers had superiority complexes. The British thought of the Chinese as unsophisticated, even uncivilized and primitive, devoted to ancient superstitions and myths, and the Chinese thought of the British as repugnant Europeans who were corrupt and exploitative and smelled of perfumes—or just smelled.

The emperor dictated that the British (as well as any other westerners) could trade only in a "trading season" and only in one small area of China, in the factory area just outside of Canton, with the city of Canton itself off-limits. The British were not allowed to bring their families into China but were ordered to leave them in the Portuguese enclave of Macau, and the British traders were not allowed to learn, read, or speak Chinese, or to go out after dark. In both recorded histories it doesn't sound like the British were having much fun.

To make things worse for the British, the Chinese enjoyed a hefty trade imbalance since the Chinese had little interest or purchasing power for those things the British offered. That was not true for what the Chinese offered the

British. The women of Great Britain had big eyes for Chinese jade and silks and porcelain. And both British women and men could not resist Chinese tea. In return for such British longings, the Chinese would accept nothing less than silver.

But Great Britain was not ready to surrender the trade imbalance to the Chinese. In short time they discovered there was one product many Chinese people wanted that the British could supply. The emperor of China didn't want the product in his nation at all, but there were enough Chinese people who did want it: Opium.

There was plenty of opium in the Bengal area of East India, which was a British colony. Not bad. Not good in obeying the law of the emperor of China but not bad in obeying the law of supply and demand. The trade imbalance gradually shifted in the opposite direction. It seemed as though the Chinese had a greater appetite for bad opium than the British had for good tea.

The emperor of China was infuriated. Opium addicts were replacing China's supply of silver. He appointed a special commissioner whose sole job was to stop the opium trade. He was Lin Tse-Hsu, a name not worth remembering. He had a simple assignment: all Lin had to do was cut off all food supplies to the British. The commander of the British traders, Charles Elliot, had a normal human reaction to Lin's solution. Charles Elliot got hungry. So did all his men. And so Charles Elliot, after six weeks of holding out and having finally run out of anything to eat, produced the chests of opium that had been hidden from the commissioner. Each chest weighed about 150 pounds. There were 20,263 chests. It was an embarrassment.

The commissioner made a nighttime ceremony of burning every one of the chests of opium and demanded the British get off Chinese territory.

They did. They went to Macau but they didn't encounter a welcoming committee of natives. The Portuguese governor of Macau said he couldn't be responsible for their safety and that it would be best if they picked up their families they had previously left in Macau and went somewhere else.

But there was no land close by whose inhabitants would have them. So they went to ships that bounced around what today is Hong Kong Harbor, until the unhappy trick that always works was imposed by the Chinese again. They call it the old Chinese Food-Cut-off-Trick.

The foreign secretary of Great Britain, Lord Palmerston, was enraged at the treatment given the British traders. Lord Palmerston was what we today would call a "hard-liner." He would have made Goldwater in '64 seem like a liberal softy. In retaliation for the treatment of the British, he sent the British fleet to China and bombarded one city after another after another. The emperor's forces couldn't compete with the British who ruled the seas, and the emperor appointed a negotiator named Qishan (whose name is also not worth remembering) who was forced to agree that China would pay for the opium they had burned and would allow the British traders back near Canton.

Commander Charles Elliot was now in the driver's seat and said that wasn't enough. He wanted a trade treaty or a good sized island where the British could camp permanently and bring their families and be safe. Qishan said there was no need for a trade agreement, the British could have Hong Kong Island.

And so on January 26, 1841, the flag of Great Britain was unfurled on what is known today as Possession Point of Hong Kong.

The agreement made no one happy. The emperor was enraged at his negotiator for giving away one inch of Chinese territory and had Qishan brought to Beijing in chains. And Foreign Secretary Palmerston was just as angry at Elliot for accepting a deal that didn't give the British a trade treaty and only gave the British the crummy island of Hong Kong, which Palmerston called "a barren island with hardly a house upon it." He wanted an island like Hainan, not the pirate's hang-out of Hong Kong.

The emperor of China banished Qishan to Tibet. Foreign Secretary Palmerston did practically the same thing to Elliot. He sent Elliot to be consul general to the Republic of Texas.

And Foreign Secretary Palmerston appointed a new commander, Sir Henry Pottinger, to take revenge on China. Pottinger did his job well. He blasted away at Canton, Xiamen, Ninbo, and Shanghai, and threatened Nanking. This time the emperor negotiated by himself or faced the risk of China being under British rule. He signed a trade treaty, and he signed an agreement giving the British Hong Kong Island in perpetuity. Palmerston, who had previously demanded a better island than Hong Kong, had nothing more to say since his Whig government in London had fallen during all of this and the new Tory government had replaced him with a foreign secretary, Lord Aberdeen, who didn't care about Chinese islands.

Within five years there was a population of over fifteen thousand people on Hong Kong Island, both Chinese and British, and practically all men. There was only one career opportunity for women.

In 1847 there was a book published in London entitled *China* which had a chapter that told about the new possession of Great Britain from China. The chapter was called "Hong Kong - Its Position, Prospects, Character and Utter Worthlessness from Every Point of View to England."

Here the history gets murky. The Chinese took a British ship called *The Arrow* imprisoning the British crew and saying the ship was in their waters and it was loaded with pirates. The British history says the ship wasn't in Chinese waters, it was registered in Hong Kong, and it had no pirates. Almost at the same time the first British envoy was en route to be the first colonial secretary of Hong Kong and he was fired on by the Chinese on his way to Beijing to present his credentials. With the *Arrow* incident and the shooting at the new British envoy, another war started. At the conclusion of this war the British secured diplomatic recognition by China, and the British settled across the harbor from Hong Kong Island on Kowloon. They said (with guns loaded) that they were too isolated on an island alone and needed both sides of the harbor for safety, and they needed a military presence on the mainland.

Done. A new treaty. This one gave the British the tip of the Kowloon peninsula to Boundary Street (not much territory) plus Stonecutter's Island. (It's still called Stonecutter's Island although it isn't an island anymore since as a result of reclaimed land it is now part of the mainland.) The new treaty gave the British this additional territory with the same definitive word by which China had given Great Britain Hong Kong Island: perpetuity.

The British who had no appetite for more than one Chinese name, called the whole collection of territory Hong Kong.

Near the end of the century Japan attacked China. No one left China alone. This time Germany, France, and Russia sent enforcement's to protect China. It wasn't out of justice or compassion. They wanted "thank yous" in trade and treaties and money from China. Great Britain was concerned that a terrible European-Asian war was to break out, so they demanded more territory to protect Hong Kong and to protect China itself. Great Britain said that China could use Hong Kong harbor for its warships against foreign powers, but the British had to have more territory to back them up.

This time the Chinese said something like, (the precise words were never recorded) "okay, but this time none of that perpetuity stuff anymore. We'll give you a lease. We'll make it for ninety-nine years and then you give back the new territory since we'll all be dead by then anyway. You can have all the land up to the Sham Chun River for ninety-nine years, and that's it."

The British did it. This parcel of land was called the New Territories, which was huge compared to what they had in Hong Kong and Kowloon. The New Territories, including 235 islands, were 92 percent of the total of all three entities. Since the agreement was signed in 1898 for ninety-nine years, it meant the lease wouldn't be up until 1997, and that was practically forever. Now the British called the whole area, including Hong Kong Island, Kowloon, and the New Territories, Hong Kong. (Hong Kong means "Fragrant Harbor," Kowloon means "Nine Dragons," one for each of eight mountains in Kowloon, plus one for the emperor who, it was assumed, was also a dragon, and the New Territories were called the New Territories because that's what they were for the British.)

When this took place, Franklin Delano Roosevelt was sixteen years old. Throughout his life he would remember the signing of the lease of the New Territories from China to Great Britain. He didn't like it. He was never high on colonialism. This would have an indirect impact in years to come.

The lease was a real one. The British had to pay what was commensurate today with 5,000 Hong Kong dollars a year, which is about 646 American dollars per year. The British have been paying it and the Chinese have been accepting it every year since the lease began without indexing for inflation or opium. The opium traffic went on into the 1930s—when China had a good deal more to worry about than either Great Britain or opium.

In July 1937, Japan attacked China, taking Nanking, Shanghai and Beijing. It was no contest, with Japan the quick conqueror. This was the overture to the Asian theater of World War Two.

The British government of Hong Kong ordered all their men to send their dependents to Australia for safety. Thousands of Chinese streamed into Hong Kong to be protected by the British.

And then came December 7, 1941 (December 8, across the International Date Line in Hong Kong.)

The Japanese attacked Hong Kong simultaneous with its attacks on Pearl Harbor, Malaysia and Singapore, and the Philippines. The Japanese invaded the British territory from the Chinese border into the New Territories and worked their way southward. Prime Minister Winston Churchill gave the order for the British in Hong Kong to hold on. It was an impossible task, but the fight went on for eighteen days and nights through the New Territories, through Kowloon and finally through Hong Kong Island. On Christmas Day 1941, Hong Kong fell to the Japanese. Governor Mark Young had holed himself up at the Peninsula Hotel on Kowloon where the Japanese found him and sent him off to Manchuria as a prisoner.

The atrocities committed during the following three years and eight months are not only well recorded in books authored by victims and witnesses in Hong Kong but are still discussed among so many victims who lived in Hong Kong during those years and still live there.

All subjects of Great Britain other than the very old and ill, were imprisoned, the worst prison being in Shamshuipo on Argyle Street in Kowloon. (The prison is still there and has been more recently used to house Vietnamese refugees. The entire area known as Shamshuipo is now the most densely populated area in the world.)

Hong Kong was liberated in August 1945 and once more recognized as a British Crown Colony.

In 1949, with the fall of China to communism, hundreds of thousands of Chinese poured into Hong Kong, escaping communist rule to live in the small British enclave. It was an influx unparalleled in its history.

The Korean War began in 1951, and with the U.N. embargo of goods from Communist China and the U.S. demanding a Certificate of Origin on any goods sold in Hong Kong to Americans (proving they were not manufactured in Communist China), Hong Kong pushed itself to be a manufacturing center by producing electronics and watches and clocks and printing and engaging in other light industries.

By 1960 (the first travel to Hong Kong by this author) the population of Hong Kong had swelled to three million, almost all refugees from China. The 1960 skyline was nothing more than colonial style buildings with only a few high-rises, practically all buildings capped with squatter-huts on their roofs. The harbor was full of brown canvas-sailed junks, and rickshaws supplied the land transportation for most local residents.

In 1967 came the Cultural Revolution in China with Red Guards and a militia of 300 Chinese soldiers with automatic rifles crossing the border into Hong Kong territory. Governor David Trench had an aircraft at Kai Tak Airport constantly ready to take him and his family to safety should the Red Guards have taken over Hong Kong.

Near the end of 1967 the British Pound Sterling was devalued in Great Britain, with Hong Kong losing one-third of its sterling reserves, so in the same week Hong Kong currency became pegged to the U.S. dollar at a constant value between the two, which still remains: (HK $7.80 = US $1.00)

In 1975, with the fall of South Vietnam, some 57,000 Vietnamese refugees started pouring into Hong Kong on makeshift boats, and they were accepted by Hong Kong, their destination of first refuge.

The twenty-seven governors of Hong Kong representing the Crown from 1843 through 1991 did nothing to bring about self-government. Certainly the laws of British authoritarianism that were on the books, but which were neither used nor abused by Great Britain, should have been removed from those books, rather than be part of the booty of a post-1997 government that wanted to have such an inheritance of authoritarian laws. In 1992, the Hong Kong Journalists Association pinpointed seventeen such authoritarian laws.

But, with little exception, the people of Hong Kong didn't demand, or even appeal for democracy prior to the 1980s. The British had given them a safe refuge in their escape from the People's Republic of China. They knew that most nations did not offer such refuge. And for most Hong Kong people, liberty under the British was so good there appeared to be no pressing need for new law books and self-government. Further, they were grateful to the British for all they did not do that they could have done by taking away their God-given freedoms—and that so many other powers might well have done.

A poll was taken of Hong Kong people in 1982, with 95 percent of the respondents wanting the political status quo of Hong Kong under the British maintained. Demonstrations for democracies were virtually absent until the mid-1980s, and cascading in the last year of the 1980s. The great mass of Hong Kong people were not thinking ahead until "ahead" was on a visible horizon.

London knew the Chinese were looking over the shoulders of their governors of Hong Kong and, unfortunately, the British didn't want to cause the Chinese government apprehensions that could be avoided, so governors remained silent.

In September 1982 Prime Minister Thatcher went to Beijing to negotiate the future of Hong Kong with the People's Republic of China. She felt the time was right since she could deal from a position of strength as well as in a time of necessity. The strength came from her recent victory in the Falkland Islands, and the necessity was that mortgages in the New Territories covered fifteen-year spans, and fifteen years from 1982 was 1997, the year the lease of the New Territories was over. No leases had been granted covering any dates beyond June 27, 1997, three days prior to takeover.

It was the first time a British Prime Minister had ever been to China. Margaret Thatcher met with Deng Xiaoping in Beijing on September 24. Prime Minister Thatcher's position was that Hong Kong Island and Kowloon were the property of Great Britain "in perpetuity" by virtue of the two treaties in which China ceded those lands. The ninety-nine-year lease on the New Territories would be discussed, and Prime Minister Thatcher wanted it extended. (It was also clear that without the New Territories Hong Kong would not be viable. Almost 40 percent of the people live in the New Territories, and it is 92 percent of Hong Kong's territory.)

Deng Xiaoping's position was that the three treaties were "unequal" (meaning signed under duress.) Deng's Foreign Office released the statement, "Hong Kong is part of Chinese territory. The treaties concerning the Hong Kong area between the British Government and the Government of the Manchu Dynasty of China were unequal treaties that have never been accepted by the Chinese people. The consistent position of the Government of the People's Republic of China is not bound by these unequal treaties and that the whole of Hong Kong area will be recovered when conditions are ripe."

Prime Minister Thatcher responded that "If a country will not stand by one treaty, it will not stand by another," and that abrogating the perpetuity clauses of two of the three treaties would be "very serious indeed."

She went from Beijing to Hong Kong where she told the Hong Kong people that Britain had "a moral responsibility" to Hong Kong and that Great Britain took that responsibility "very, very seriously."

And so two years of negotiations began.

They went Deng's way.

Almost two years to the day, on September 26, 1984, a Joint Declaration between Great Britain and the People's Republic of China was released. There was not a new ninety-nine-year lease. The whole of Hong Kong, meaning Hong Kong Island, Kowloon, and the New Territories, would be turned over to the People's Republic of China when the lease on the New Territories ran out. The Joint Declaration called for the People's Republic of China to take over all three entities on July 1, 1997, with those three entities under "one country, two systems" with Hong Kong, Kowloon, and the New Territories able to retain their capitalist system for fifty years more, until 2047, as a Special Administrative Region (SAR) of the People's Republic of China.

The Joint Declaration was filled with guaranteeing language, including guarantees for the people of Hong Kong that the "rights and freedoms, including those of the person, of speech, of the press, of assembly, of association, of travel, of movement, of correspondence, of strike, of choice of occupation, of academic research and of religious belief, will be ensured by law."

But the Constitution of the People's Republic of China, itself, gives nearly all the same guarantees to its own people, and those guarantees are not observed. Article 35 of the Constitution of the People's Republic of China states: "Citizens of the People's Republic of China enjoy freedom of speech, of the press, of assembly, of association, of procession and of demonstration." Article 36 guarantees "freedom of religious belief." Article 34 gives the right to vote and stand for election. None of it means anything.

These kinds of guarantees are not uncommon in constitutions of communist societies. Article 34 in the Constitution of the former Soviet Union stated: "Citizens of the USSR are equal before the law, without distinction of origin, social or property status, race or nationality, sex, education, language, attitude to religion, type and nature of occupation, domicile, or other status. The equal rights of citizens of the USSR are guaranteed in all fields of economic, political, social, and cultural life." Article 49 stated that "persecution for criticism is prohibited" and Article 50 guaranteed "freedom of speech, of the press, and of assembly, meetings, street processions and demonstrations." In all such documents there are caveats, but with or without them, communist societies have simply done those things they wanted to do at the time they wanted to do them.

Many Hong Kong people felt betrayed by Great Britain and were especially resentful that Hong Kong people were given no voice in the negotiations. But they knew, and some admitted, that the People's Republic of China held all the cards, geographically as well as militarily, and in terms of the water and food supplied to Hong Kong by China, Prime Minister Thatcher had few credible threats to give the PRC. With the exception of democracy activists led by Martin Lee Chu-ming and Szeto Wah, most felt they must simply accept the hand they were being dealt—and maybe it would be all right.

But then came June 4, 1989, and the massacre at Tiananmen Square in Beijing. Any optimism was smothered. No event had ever shaken the people of Hong Kong as that one did. Massive demonstrations, unknown in Hong Kong, with somewhere between 500,000 and one million Hong Kong people, protested the massacre. (This was out of a population of about 5.7 million at the time.) A huge replica of the Goddess of Democracy was erected in Victoria Park, shortly after the one built by the students in Beijing was destroyed. The British government would not give it a permanent site. (The People's Republic of China, as expected, objected to a permanent site.) The demonstrations against the People's Republic of China went on and on and on through sunsets and sunrises. (The anniversary of the massacre has been observed in Hong Kong in every year since 1989.)

Four months after Tiananmen Square, with protests against the People's Republic of China still on high, Governor David Wilson advised Hong Kong people to use their rights and freedoms "with self-restraint."

On April 4, 1990, The Basic Law (a Constitution for Hong Kong) was established by the People's Republic of China for the years 1997-2047. It is a document of 160 articles, which is a more detailed and somewhat changed itemized guarantee of the freedoms and autonomy promised Hong Kong in the Joint Declaration written by Great Britain and the PRC. It has been referred to by democracy advocates not as "The Basic Law" but as "The Basic Flaw."

There was a striking similarity between The Basic Law written for Hong Kong in 1990 by the People's Republic of China, and the Seventeen Point Declaration written for Tibet in 1951 by the People's Republic of China.

On July 9, 1992, a new governor came to Hong Kong. He was the twenty-eighth sent by the Crown: The Right Honourable Christopher Francis Patten. He started a surprising and unparalleled administration. He was the most outspoken of any governor of Hong Kong while walking a tightrope stretched between the people of Hong Kong, his home government, and the People's Republic of China. He was the first governor of Hong Kong to attempt to bring about a democratic framework for Hong Kong. The framework was coming too late, but it still took courage.

Governor Patten introduced bills to replace the appointment of local council members by the governor, with elected members; to lower the voting age from twenty-one to eighteen; to increase the number of elected members of the Legislative Council; and to expand electoral participation for those seats in the Council that had been indirectly elected by business and professional constituencies. The proposals were modest in terms of democracy, but for Hong Kong they were explosive. And the fact that he proposed important changes without first seeking the approval of the People's Republic of China was something that had never been done since the PRC came to power in 1949.

Democracy advocates celebrated that they finally seemed to have an ally in Government House, while the government of the People's Republic of China was outraged at his "outlandish, audacious and criminal behavior," and much of the business community of Hong Kong placed itself on China's side, scared to death of the displeasure of that government.

Governor Patten hit back at the business community; "This is one of the most sophisticated economic communities in the world, well traveled, well educated, hugely successful economically. There are some people who think it's outlandish that they want to decide how their kids should be educated, who should collect the dustbins, how much of their taxes should go on housing rather than health service. I mean it's crazy. What we have to do now is to try and convince the business community that accountable government and the beginnings of democratization aren't a threat to five and one half percent growth, low taxes, big surpluses, and a pro-business ethic in government. I, too, hope we will be able to make at least some progress in convincing Chinese leaders that this hugely precious community, representing as it does twenty-three percent of Chinese GNP, succeeds not just because of some capitalist equation but because its way of life helps to sustain its prosperity as well as its prosperity helping to sustain its way of life."

The government of the People's Republic of China's voice was loud and clear. It announced that come July 1, 1997, they may well not honor contracts made with Hong Kong prior to the takeover and they would abolish all three tiers of Hong Kong government established before July 1, 1997.

It did not go unnoticed that Governor Patten was advocating policies that London did not invent and, in some cases, did not even endorse. Governor Patten was walking the highest wire in Asia without a net. There was no way some element wouldn't attempt to push him, as those five elements measured his every step: his own government in London, the democracy advocates of Hong Kong, the business community of Hong Kong, the People's Republic of China that would take over no matter what he might do, and his own conscience, which was on the side of the democracy advocates.

Beijing, never subtle with language, continually called Governor Patten a criminal and decided not to deal with him but rather to deal with his second in command, Hong Kong's Chief Secretary Anson Chan. She was much more palatable to Beijing. In time, representatives from the People's Republic of China would not even shake hands with the governor, and any invitation to Beijing was addressed not to the governor but to Anson Chan. By such treatment they were attempting to send a message to the people of Hong Kong that the governor had no authority with the Beijing government.

Following his conscience, Governor Patten continued to advocate democratic changes that challenged the People's Republic of China, challenged the business community of Hong Kong, and at times, challenged London. In his quest of ensuring more confidence for the people of Hong Kong in their future, he advocated that the Court of Final Appeal, the highest court of the Hong Kong Judiciary (replacing the Privy Council of Great Britain as Hong Kong's highest court), should run as a "through train" starting prior to 1997 going right through the takeover date into the future. He also publicly advocated that the Court of Final Appeal should have two overseas judges out of its five members, so that at least two would be knowledgeable and experienced in the common law. Further he said that he wanted it established that Beijing would not have the ability to go above the decisions of the Court of Final Appeal other than in acts of state, and those acts of state would be defined by Great Britain's common law, already identified as those acts solely involving foreign affairs and defense.

Back in the United States, the 102nd Congress passed and President Bush signed into law, the United States-Hong Kong Policy Act of 1992 that established U.S. recognition that Hong Kong would be dealt with as the autonomous region agreed upon in the Joint Declaration and Basic Law. The 1992 act also established that all previous agreements with Hong Kong would remain in full force, and the U.S. would treat Hong Kong as a separate and distinct entity. The Act also emphasized U.S. support for democratization and human rights. The reaction of Hong Kong was one of relief, but the act had no effect on the PRC.

On February 25, 1994, the PRC vowed to disband any and all elected bodies in Hong Kong when they took control. In June 1995 an agreement was reached between the PRC and Great Britain regarding the Court of Final Appeal, with Great Britain giving in to every demand of the PRC.

Chris Patten won none of those things he advocated. But he defended the orders of Beijing. The Court of Final Appeal would not be established until after the takeover on July 1, 1997, there would only be, at most, one foreign judge rather than two, and Beijing would have jurisdiction over and above the Court of Final Appeal in acts of state "such as" foreign affairs and defense. The words "such as" permitted a wide scope of unknowns. "Such as" could mean anything the People's Republic of China would say it would mean—case by case. Unfortunately those were the words that were used in Article 19 of The Basic Law, although the earlier Joint Declaration, upon which the Basic Law was supposed to be based, had read "the Hong Kong Special Administrative Region will enjoy a high degree of autonomy, except foreign and defense affairs which are the responsibilities of the Central People's Government." Someone in Beijing made a quick change from the Joint Declaration to the Basic Law and carried it through to the decision of the Court of Final Appeal.

Governor Patten said of the Court of Final Appeal, "I think it was a good deal on both sides. Not every deal with China is a sellout or bad for Hong Kong."

The democracy advocates of Hong Kong were outraged at Governor Patten's defense of such a decision, calling it a "betrayal" after he publicly advocated exactly the opposite of what Beijing decided. There was a no-confidence vote in Patten held in the Legislative Council. He survived it thirty-five to seventeen, but not before powerful voices let be it known that he was no longer their champion. The most respected voice in Hong Kong, the voice of legislator Martin Lee Chu-ming, said the governor had kowtowed to the People's Republic of China and "it must be painfully obvious to all that this Court of Final Appeal agreement was wholly in Britain's interests and Governor Patten has now abdicated all his principles and responsibilities to Hong Kong...It's a calculated condemnation of the Hong Kong people to the grimmest possible future...Hong Kong people will never be able to challenge the Beijing Government....the capitulation (of the governor on the Court of Final Appeal) opens the door to all political or sensitive cases being deemed 'acts of state' by the Beijing central government."

Governor Patten answered back that "there is a middle-ground between confrontation and kowtowing" and, "I spent three years being lambasted for being too aggressive, too assertive in standing up for Hong Kong...One deal with China and suddenly, Martin Lee and others are saying 'It's all over, the game is up.'"

On September 17, 1995, an election for four-year seats in the Legislative Council was held. For the first time in Hong Kong's history, due to Governor Patten's plan, all sixty members were elected, with none appointed by the governor. The electoral system was a combination of three tiers: twenty seats to be decided by geographical constituencies (by residents of districts), thirty seats to be decided by functional constituencies (by profession or craft), and ten seats to be decided by election committee (by electors).

The results of the September 17 election were not what Beijing wanted—or expected, as Beijing had mounted a serious campaign for their candidates. The election results caused the business community even more fear than before. By and large, democracy advocates enjoyed massive victories. Martin Lee Chu-ming proclaimed, "Hong Kong people voted with their hearts and minds for freedom and genuine democracy." They did.

Exhibiting the strength of the elected Pro-Democracy coalition, on November 15, 1995, forty members of the Legislative Council voted to "strongly object" to China's plan to weaken Hong Hong's Bill of Rights, while fifteen voted against the motion and five abstained.

Gary Cheng Kai Nam of the pro-Beijing party, The Democratic Alliance for Betterment of Hong Kong, (who lost his election) said that the colony's six million people would "have to pay" for their choice.

Cheng Shousan, deputy director-general of the Hong Kong and Macau Affairs Office (a front for the People's Republic of China) said that future candidates for local offices in Hong Kong would have to be proven loyal to Beijing and that freedom in Hong Kong would not be unrestricted but come with "some limits and bounds."

A Foreign Ministry spokesman for the People's Republic of China, Chen Jian, gave his government's view: "We don't think this election truly reflects the will of the Hong Kong people." Without any logic or basis, a spokesman for the Xinhua News Agency (which acts as the "embassy" of the People's Republic of China in Hong Kong) said, "The results showed that hope for a smooth transition and love of the motherland and Hong Kong remain the main trend in Hong Kong."

Deng Xiaoping didn't make a statement, but the ninety-one-year-old "paramount leader" hadn't made a statement on anything in some time. In the absence of a fresh statement, *Ta King Pao*, the Beijing-run Hong Kong newspaper, dusted off a 1987 statement of Deng Xiaoping. *Ta King Pao* ran an article stating that Deng believes that popularly elected officials wouldn't be the best choice to administer Hong Kong and instead it should be run by "Hong Kong people who love Hong Kong and China."

The PRC said it made no difference as they had already announced the Legislative Council would be dissolved on July 1, 1997. The fact that the elections placed the winners in office for four-year terms that should take them to 1999 in the "autonomous" region of Hong Kong was immaterial to the PRC. The PRC announced that the PRC-appointed Preparatory Committee would replace the elected Legislative Council with a provisional body until elections were held under PRC-approved rules.

Democracy advocates in the legislature reminded Beijing that they had just been elected for four-year terms. Reality, however, was not bright. Beijing immediately repeated that the Legislative Council would be dissolved on July 1, 1997, no matter that the winners were elected to four-year terms. They would serve only through June 30, 1997.

Results of the Election of September 17, 1995, for the Hong Kong Legislative Council

	Geographical Constituencies	Functional Constituencies	Election Committee	Total
Democratic Party (Pro-Democracy)	12	5	2	19
Liberal Party (Business People)	1	9	0	10
Democratic Alliance for the Betterment of Hong Kong (Pro-Beijing) combined with Federation of Trade Unions	2	3	2	7
Association for Democracy & People's Livelihood (Social Welfare)	2	1	1	4
Independents (No Party, Generally Pro-Democracy)	3	10	2	15
Others (Minor Parties)	0	2	3	5

Note: Most political parties and independents did not participate in all elections or for all seats.

Governor Patten said, "It seems to be an astonishing way of trying to win the hearts and minds in Hong Kong to say, at the moment when the people of Hong Kong are taking part in the most credible and democratic election in our history, that you are going to give the whole thing thumbs down."

In some respects it was also a tough election for the governor because through the remainder of his term he would be faced with a Legislative Council that would fight him on every measure that might be conciliatory to Beijing but that he might be ordered to endorse by London. But he was the one who reformed the electoral process so that he couldn't appoint members, as governors previously did. The reforms that were his own invention were in effect through the remander of his administration, and he took pained pride in living with them.

One of the most unexpected events in the pre-1997 chronology occurred in October 1995 with Governor Christopher Patten calling on his nation, Great Britain, to give the right of abode to all the 3.3 million Hong Kong residents who qualify for passports. Home Secretary Michael Howard quickly said it would not be done.

Governor Patten answered, "I don't think that three million Hong Kong citizens are suddenly going to arrive at Heathrow. Nobody seriously supposes that and, if they did, they certainly wouldn't be living on the welfare state." What he wanted was the Chinese government to be more sensitive in their treatment of Hong Kong, knowing the people there could leave if they so choose. The governor called it a "Passport Wagon."

John Carlisle of Great Britain's Parliament said, "Britain should not become a dumping ground for every traveling China man."

With the scorn of so many of his countrymen, Governor Patten received at least the temporary praise of many Hong Kong people represented by the democracy leaders, Martin Lee and Szeto Wah, who claimed both surprise and pleasure at Governor Patten's advocacy. There was no praise from most of the business community who gave the governor their disapproval for such a suggestion, and there were new epithets given him from the People's Republic of China who, even more markedly, turned their back on him with the claim that he is "irrelevant."

On December 19, 1995, the PRC announced that during the transition period "the last colonial governor cannot represent Britain."

Governor Patten said, "After this is over (July 1, 1997), I'm certain I'm going to have earned some time with a good book under a tree."

No one fought him on that one.

One hour away from Hong Kong by hydrofoil, forty miles to Hong Kong's northeast, is Macau with its gambling casinos, its tradition of strange things going on, and its Portuguese government that has reigned there since 1557. Macau doesn't take up much room. The entire territory is only six square miles, which means it's about seventy times smaller than Hong Kong.

It's going to be taken over by the People's Republic of China, too, as a Special Administrative Region (SAR) on December 20, 1999, and the takeover is accepted in Macau with a yawn. No one seems to care. After all, out of its population of 500,000, 140,000 Macanese are Portuguese passport holders and Portugal has offered a passport with the right of abode to anyone born in Macau before 1981 (anyone who will be eighteen or older at the time of the takeover.) Ironically enough, they will even have the right to live in Great Britain after European unification, while Hong Kong's old British National Overseas (BNO) passport holders had no such entitlement.

China has not been in a hurry to take over Macau, and the Portuguese have not been trying to hold on to it. It's the last Portuguese colony and it's a nuisance. Portugal was willing to give it up in 1975, but Mao Zedong and Chou En-lai wanted to wait. They simply weren't ready for it, not quite knowing what to do with it. Unlike Hong Kong, Macau has been perceived as merely being under the "caretaker" administration of Portugal at the behest of Beijing; a slice of Chinese territory under an agreed-upon temporary administration of Portugal.

Just like Hong Kong, Macau has also been promised fifty years of "a high degree of autonomy" and can continue the "existing capitalist system and way of life." But since it hasn't been totally autonomous, having been an ally of the People's Republic of China even to the point of refusing to accept any of the escaping dissidents from Tiananmen Square (there were some brave voices of opposition among the citizenry, particularly Reverend Pedro Chung and Ng Kuok Cheong), and since no one is quite sure exactly what system Macau truly has, few are pressing for guarantees. Only 3 percent of the population is Portuguese, and with all laws written only in Portuguese, few local Chinese understand the laws under which they live. They have lived under what is called the "traditional force," which is composed of the main Chinese business communities. Those communities generally side with Beijing, because that is where they get their money.

The casinos will undoubtedly remain (gambling accounts for approximately 40 percent of the government's revenue), and quite probably Macau will be absorbed into a greater area of China as a suburb of Zhuhai, which is across the border that will soon be erased.

There are indications that Macau could be used by China as a competitor to Hong Kong to keep Hong Kong democracy advocates at bay. With Macau's new international airport already opened in December 1995, with Macau's economy being diversified with textile and garment manufacturing, with a new railway line to Guangzhou, with new land reclamations adding about four square miles to Macau, with a new passenger ferry and a new deep-water container terminal, there is a plan that is being enacted to make much more of Macau than it has been. The Chinese government has a long memory and deep wounds. That government well recognizes that Macau was once the most prosperous trading center in the Far East—before Hong Kong became a British Crown Colony.

On Thursday, December 28, 1995, the People's Republic of China's Standing Committee of the National People's Congress endorsed a panel to establish the government that would take over Hong Kong on July 1, 1997. The panel would be administered by the PRC's Vice Premier and Foreign Minister Qian Qichen, with Lu Ping, director of the PRC's Hong Kong and Macau Affairs Department as general secretary. It was announced that the panel would consist of fifty-six officials from the PRC and ninety-four members from Hong Kong. None of the Hong Kong members were to be affiliated with the Democratic Party. eleven were to be politicians, sixteen social, rural and religious leaders, thirty-three professionals and academics, and thirty-four business people. There was immediate opposition to the list from Hong Kong democracy advocates, charging the list of Hong Kong people were those who did not represent the majority view of the citizens of Hong Kong. David Chau, who was one of the Hong Kong business people on the list justified the choices by saying, "We have to understand the reality that the Chinese government appoints only those who they think can work with China. China has to consider its own interest."

With eighteen months to go, 1996 began an escalation in the chronology of one handover event after another:

Great Britain's foreign secretary, Malcolm Rifkind, met with Qian Qichen, (the PRC's vice premier and foreign minister), on January 9, 1996. They announced the PRC had agreed to allow permanent residents to stay in Hong Kong after the takeover: "I am pleased that Qian said that all those with current permanent residence status will continue to keep it, and he did not qualify this in any way." This was in reference to ethnic-Chinese permanent residents. That good news was tempered when Secretary Rifkind stated, "It is no use my suggesting to you or to the people of Hong Kong that the United Kingdom can suddenly produce some formula which will deal with the determined Chinese desire to dismantle institutions." He also stated that Britain cannot force the PRC to submit regular reports to the United Nations on Hong Kong's human rights after the takeover. Regarding the continuation of the Legislative Council's members already elected by Hong Kong people and the PRC's decision to abolish the Legislative Council, Secretary Rifkind said, "This is a closed case. China's stand will not change."

On January 10 an opinion poll by the Chinese University of Hong Kong reported that 43 percent of young people want to leave Hong Kong, fearing less freedom and fewer jobs and more corruption after the PRC's takeover.

Governor Patten said on radio, January 15, that "No one, no one, should keep silent. This is a time, if ever there was one, for speaking up and saying what one wants to happen, and what one expects to happen, to preserve Hong Kong." Although the statement was not necessarily connected, it was made on the same day that the PRC ordered all places of worship in China to register with the government, and the PRC announced that some adherents of permitted faiths were trying to subvert the state.

On January 17, the PRC announced that 6,000 People's Liberation Army troops from the First Regiment will be stationed in Hong Kong after takeover, noting it was below peak British troops strength. The PRC's Major General Liu Zhenwu will be the commander. Two thousand more People's Liberation Army troops will be based in Shenzhen across the border, for rotation and replacement in Hong Kong. (There are fourteen defense sites in Hong Kong.) It was announced that the troops would be accomplished karaoke singers whose favorite song is "I Love You, Hong Kong." (I'm not kidding.)

On January 26, the Preparatory Committee was officially appointed in Beijing's Great Hall of the People. The committee's business would be conducted in secret, conforming to what the PRC calls "collective responsibility." Jiang Zemin, president of the PRC, said the committee faces a "heavy task....In terms of reunification, the return of Hong Kong to the motherland is the first station in our Long March. After that there is Macau and, finally, Taiwan."

Governor Patten said the British government and the Hong Kong Legislative Council should form a partnership with the Preparatory Committee to ease the transition.

Great Britain's Prime Minister John Major visited Hong Kong on March 3, and promised that "Britain's commitment to Hong Kong will continue well beyond the summer of 1997. If, in the future, there would be any suggestion of a breach of the Joint Declaration, we would mobilize the international community and pursue every legal or other avenue available to us." He challenged the PRC not to dismantle the Hong Kong Legislative Council and said that laws should not be altered by decree after July 1, 1997, urging that human rights be respected. He then said that Hong Kong's ethnic minorities (Indians, Pakistanis, etc.) would not be left stateless but were guaranteed the right to live in Britain after the turnover if they came "under pressure to leave Hong Kong."

The following day, an editorial in the PRC-backed newspaper in Hong Kong, *Ta Kung Pao*, said "For Major to say such a thing at this time at this place is extremely unwise, and could put improving Sino-British relations under a cloud." Governor Patten responded, "The most effective way in which Chinese officials could meet what they say is their aim of boosting confidence in Hong Kong would be by making it absolutely clear that they stand by the promises that have been made to Hong Kong on both human rights and their safeguarding, and as well on the development of representative institutions and the development of democracy in Hong Kong."

Governor Patten said on March 21, "I think if the Preparatory Committee and Chinese officials insist on tearing out the roots of democracy in Hong Kong, they will have to justify that to the people of Hong Kong. I think the view in the community is there is only one purpose which Chinese officials are seeking: that is to exclude from the legislature some of the politicians in Hong Kong who most clearly represent the majority view of Hong Kong....Let them categorically deny they will put forward any arrangements designed to exclude some of those politicians in Hong Kong who have demonstrated that they clearly represent majority opinion."

Five days later, the Preparatory Committee voted 148 to 1 to disband Hong Kong's elected Legislative Council and its elected leaders when the PRC took over and to install an appointed body to run Hong Kong. The lone dissenter was Frederick Fung, the chairman of the Hong Kong Democracy and People's Livelihood. For doing that, he was immediately stripped of the right to vote for the chief executive of Hong Kong and was told he would not be eligible to be part of the provisional legislature. Governor Patten called the 148 to 1 vote "a black day for democracy in Hong Kong....A Chinese appointed body of Chinese government officials and handpicked Hong Kong advisers have voted to tear down a legislature which was freely, fairly, and openly elected by the people of Hong Kong in the most democratic election in our history." The governor praised Frederick Fung, saying Hong Kong would "salute him."

Chen Ziyan, the deputy director of China's Hong Kong and Macau Affairs Office said that Hong Kong officials who serve beyond the transfer of power must support the provisional legislature that China would establish and that civil servants would have to declare their loyalty to the new provisional legislature to be announced by China. Anson Chan, Governor Patten's chief secretary (and previously speculated to be a prime candidate for the first chief executive position appointed by the PRC) warned that the PRC's statement would jeopardize the morale of Hong Kong's 180,000 civil servants.

To beat a midnight deadline to obtain British-issued travel documents on March 31, 54,178 Hong Kong people who were not born in Hong Kong lined up outside Immigration Tower for applications. (There were 34,500 applicants in 1995.) A sports field was opened to accommodate the waiting people. The travel documents, British National Overseas Passports, do not confer British citizenship or right of abode but allow residents of British and former British territories to travel without a visa to Great Britain. (Approximately 200,000 applications were received in March.) Simultaneously, there was a demonstration of 800 people carrying red balloons (which serve as "a symbol of PRC lies") chanting, "Silence is not golden, it's fatal." The demonstrators went outside the Xinhua News Agency, which is the PRC's de-facto Embassy, singing "Freedom Flower." Martin Lee told the demonstrators, "we are the legitimate body and we will not be replaced by a rubber-stamp legislature appointed by Beijing....We will fight to the end."

On April 14, the Preparatory Committee met at the Hong Kong Club and announced ten demands to the British government:

1. Air time on government-owned radio and TV.
2. Security and travel arrangements for the Preparatory Committee members.
3. Information on professional bodies and functional constituencies to help the Preparatory Committee in forming the Selection Committee which will choose Hong Kong's chief executive.
4. Facilitate the activities of the Selection Committee.
5. Provide office accommodation and information to the chief executive after he is selected.
6. A venue and other help for the provisional legislature.
7. A list of all ordinances and regulations enacted since 1984.
8. Assist in establishing Hong Kong's Court of Final Appeal.
9. Information on government departments including recent changes in their functions.
10. Any other assistance required by the Preparatory Committee as its work progresses.

In addition, there was a call for the British government to support a China-appointed body to replace the elected Legislative Council. Governor Patten answered that his government would "do nothing whatsoever, that's nothing, spelled N.O.T.H.I.N.G. Nothing whatsoever" to undermine the elected Legislative Council.

Vietnamese refugees rioted in a New Territories Refugee Camp over forced repatriation to Vietnam. On May 30, approximately 120 escaped with eighty caught. (On this date some 18,000 Vietnamese refugees were left in Hong Kong camps.) The PRC insisted that all go back to Vietnam before the takeover date of July 1, 1997. The riots involved some 3,000 at a holding center of 8,600 scheduled to be forced back to Vietnam. Twenty-six buildings and fifty-three cars were burned. For a brief period fifteen prison wardens were held hostage.

On May 20, President Lee of the Republic of China on Taiwan said that the ROC was prepared to help citizens of Hong Kong and Macau "to maintain democracy, freedom, and prosperity."

All nations that had consulates in Hong Kong were told by the PRC on May 30, to re-apply for approval to have a consulate in Hong Kong after June 30, 1997.

On June 4, the traditional demonstration protesting the 1989 Tiananmen Massacre took place with between 15,000 and 20,000 gathering in Victoria Park for a candlelight vigil for those killed in the massacre.

In a series of June speeches, Lu Ping, director of the Chinese State Council's Hong Kong and Macau Affairs Office, addressed the subject of freedom of the press in Hong Kong. "Freedom of the press has to be regulated by law...advocacy is not part of the freedom of the press." He suggested that those areas outside of freedom of the press would be advocating independence for Hong Kong and/or Taiwan. "Anyone found guilty would serve their prison term in Hong Kong." He said that even in the United States journalists would not be allowed to advocate independence for Hawaii.

In July, eight Democrats were forced to leave Beijing airport when they attempted to present to PRC officials, a 60,000-name petition, opposing the prospective PRC-appointed provisional legislature to replace the elected Legislative Council.

On August 10, the PRC's foreign minister, Qian Qichen, offered talks to those in Hong Kong who "hold different views" providing they support the handover itself. The Democratic Party immediately requested such a meeting to discuss the future of Hong Kong. It was rejected with the justification that "the Democratic Party does not agree that the elected Legislative Council should be abolished while the Democratic Party claims to support the handover. The two beliefs are incompatible."

Beijing announced that after the handover, it would close down the consulates in Hong Kong of the thirteen countries that might still maintain diplomatic relations with the Republic of China on Taiwan. Should they choose to break such relations, they could stay. South Africa agreed to cut relations with the ROC on Taiwan.

In an interview of France's Le Figaro, PRC President Jiang Zemin said that "Hong Kong's prosperity in the past cannot be attributed, as some have suggested, to an independent judiciary and a free system of the press, but mainly to the creativity of the Hong Kong people themselves." (Was he then suggesting the Chinese living on the mainland were not as creative?)

As November began, the Preparatory Committee chose the 400-member Selection Committee who would decide who would be Hong Kong's chief executive and those to be on the provisional legislature. Both the Preparatory Committee and 400-member Selection Committee were PRC-approved in a labyrinth of rules that insured the PRC's choice. Two Hong Kong democratic politicians were evicted from Beijing for "disturbing public order."

Former Prime Minister of Great Britain Margaret Thatcher announced she would be in Hong Kong at the time of handover (at the Peninsula Hotel).

On December 11, Tung Chee-hwa was named by the Selection Committee as the new chief executive to take over on July 1, 1997. (Tung was fifty-nine years old, was born in Shanghai and, with his parents, escaped to Hong Kong from the mainland during the 1949 communist revolution there. He studied in Great Britain and lived in the United States for a decade, known as a powerful shipping and business tycoon. He served for four years in the cabinet of Governor Patten. So why on earth did the PRC want him to be the chief executive of Hong Kong? The following might be important to know:

He had said that anyone advocating independence for Tibet or Taiwan would not be allowed to remain in Hong Kong after the PRC takes over. He warned foreigners not to use Hong Kong as a base to sow dissent in China after the handover. He promised to reinstate anti-subversion laws being dismantled by the British government. "Our society has become too politicized in recent years." He believed in the need to roll back Governor Patten's democratic changes, to abolish the elected legislature, and to enforce a more authoritarian executive government. He has stated that the Democratic Party is "anti-China on all issues"...The press should remain free but shouldn't "go stirring up all that muck"...The Communist Party should be legalized in Hong Kong...Hong Kong "should be prepared to make sacrifices for China"...The 1989 Tiananmen Square Massacre should be forgotten and the verdict on the massacre "dealt with by historians"...Dissent in Hong Kong should be dealt with "according to the laws" passed by a PRC appointed legislature. He called for "an emphasis on obligations to the community rather than rights of the individual."

Despite all this, Tung appeared to be liked, on a personal basis, even by his political opponents.

Martin Lee expressed "hope that Mr. Tung can prove himself better than the unrepresentative system that produced him. To that end we are prepared and willing to help him come up with the right answers to many of our pressing problems...Hong Kong people expect him to be able to defend our system...

Though by all accounts he is a good man, the unacceptable system he now joins and China's demands of him may cause Mr. Tung to allow the erosion of Hong Kong's freedoms....The new Chief Executive can empower Hong Kong people to defend our system—or he can be the agent of its destruction. The choice is his to make, and the world is watching."

On December 12, it was announced that the 400-member Selection Committee (hand-picked by the PRC) would now go about the business of selecting a provisional legislature of sixty members, the names to be announced on December 21. It would replace the elected Legislative Council. It started its work in January 1997 to be ready for the handover on July 1, 1997. (No mention of this was made in the Joint Declaration or the Basic Law.) Many of the "candidates" for the provisional legislature were Pro-PRC people who lost the Hong Kong elections of September 17, 1995, for the Legislative Council.

(The Basic Law called for a sixty-person Legislative Council with thirty chosen by functional elections, twenty by democratic elections, and ten by an election committee. Even if the PRC regarded their Selection Committee as an election committee, then they would only have the right to choose ten rather than all sixty.)

Governor Patten said: "We will have nothing to do with it [the provisional legislature] in any form because it is reprehensible and unjustified....All that is very sad for Hong Kong."

On December 18, the Heritage Foundation listed Hong Kong, for the third consecutive year, as the most free economic area in the world. (The PRC is rated as number 125 in the economic index.)

On December 20, Great Britain's Foreign Secretary Malcolm Rifkind threatened to bring the decision of the PRC for a provisional legislature to the International Court of Justice. The next day, the 400-member Selection Committee named those to serve on the provisional legislature, including ten Pro-Beijing people who had run for the Legislative Council in Hong Kong in 1995 and lost.

Governor Patten called the selection of those on the provisional legislature a "bizarre farce" and a "stomach churning" process.

Referring to the pledge of Britain's Foreign Secretary Malcolm Rifkind for international monitoring over the future of Hong Kong, the PRC's Vice Premier and Foreign Secretary Qian Qichen said that after July 1, "it is China's internal affair."

1997 began with Jeng Zemin, president of the People's Republic of China, giving a New Year address in which he stated that "the return of Hong Kong to the motherland will wash away a century-old national disgrace and signal a significant victory in the Chinese people's struggle towards national reunification."

On January 25 was the first meeting of the Provisional Legislature across the border from Hong Kong, in Shenzhen, PRC. They recommended that Hong Kong's Bill of Rights, written in 1991, be rewritten with repeal of twenty-five provisions. Among other items, the repeals would mean that no longer would any group of thirty or more people have the ability to hold demonstrations without first obtaining permission of no objection from the police, "in the interest of national security," and political parties would not be able to accept financial help from foreign political groups, with the PRC exempted since it would no longer be foreign. (Therefore this would leave a channel open for pro-PRC political parties in Hong Kong but not from anti-PRC political parties.) The vote in the Provisional Legislature was 140 to one. The one was Fredrick Fung. Chung Tee-hwa agreed with the recommendations saying, "I believe it is important to get the right balance between individual rights and social order." (The Preparatory Committee approved these recommendations on April 9.)

On February 19, Deng Xiaoping died at the age of ninety-two. (Undoubtedly from chain-smoking since he was a kid, as well as breathing in secondary smoke on a daily basis for over nine decades.)

Qian Qichen, the foreign minister of the PRC, announced on March 10, that when the PRC takes over Hong Kong, some of the textbooks in Hong Kong schools would need to be revised as they "have some contents that do not form with history and reality and won't suit the changes" in Hong Kong under Chinese rule.

On April 12, the *South China Post* announced it had hired Feng Xiliang as a consultant. Feng had founded the PRC's *China Daily*, and worked for the PRC's magazine, *Windows.*

An advance contingent of forty unarmed PLA troops arrived in Hong Kong on April 21.

June 4, was the last anniversary of the Tiananmen Square before Hong Kong's handover to the PRC, and in Victoria Park, 50,000 Hong Kong people assembled to commemorate the Tiananmen Square Massacre, in memory of those who lost their lives or were imprisoned. Tung Chee-hwa said that such demonstrations would still be permitted after the PRC takes over Hong Kong, but Hong Kong people should "put aside the baggage of June 4 and move on with building the country."

On June 23, Great Britain compromised with the PRC in allowing some 509 troops of the PLA into Hong Kong with pistols and rifles three hours prior to midnight of June 30.

The Claremont Institute's Hong Kong Handover Conference began on June 8, 1997, at the Hyatt Regency. The following transcripts of the conference take the history of Hong Kong through the handover from Great Britain to the People's Republic of China.

Delegates to The Claremont Institute's Hong Kong Handover Conference

Adams, Thomas
Ahmanson, David
Ahmanson, Howard
Ahmanson, Roberta
Anton, Marily
Anton, Mike
Anton, Thomas
Armstrong, Laurie
Arnn, Larry
Balazs, Fernando
Balazs, Melissa
Baldwin, James
Baldwin, Jason
Baldwin, Nancy
Bendetti, Don
Bendetti, Dorothy
Bennett, Brian O'Leary
Burge, Ann
Burge, Robert
Chacon, Victoria
Childers, Victor
Clark, Colin
Crosby, Jane
Crosby, William
Culbertson, Todd
Cullen, William

Danielson, Beverly
Dorres, Christina
Driscoll, Audrey
Dykema, Dale
Dykema, Suzanne
Finch, Michael
Francoeur, Eve
Gaffney, Frank
Gates, Nancy Tuggle
Gates, Vern
Greenberg, Dan
Grubbs, Jr., Kenneth E.
Haines, Shirley
Hannah, Helen (Campbell)
Herschensohn, Bruce
Hoff, Gwyneth
Hoff, Paul
Hume, George
Hume, Jerry
Hume, Lucy
Hume, Patti
Jacobs, Carl
Jacobs, Elizabeth
Keystone, David
Keystone, Dolly
Kranz, Thomas

Kranz, Travis

Linkletter, Ransom

Lion, Harold

Mah, Diane

Mah, Kevin

Mah, Vivan

Martin, James

McIver, David

Mulgrew, David

Myles, Jeffrey

Myles, Michele

Naftzger, Pauline Crowe

Parker, Patrick

Parler, Sally

Peschong, John Allan

Pratt, Cliff

Pratt, Pat

Robinson, John

Robinson, Roger

Scherer, Jr., Ernest J.

Scherer, III, Ernest F. (Skip)

Seavey, Todd

Smoot, Jean

Sutnar, Elaine

Sutnar, Radoslav

Tunney, John

Tunney, Katinka

Tunney, Tara

Wagner, Rick

Warder, Michael

White, Dorothy

Winchell, Steve

Zamrzla, Johnny

Zamrzla, Pam

Speakers at The Claremont Institute's
Hong Kong Handover Conference

June 28

Richard Boucher, Consul General of the United States
Bruce Herschensohn, Distinguished Fellow of The Claremont Institute
Larry Arnn, President of The Claremont Institute

June 29

Ada Wong, Panelist from the Hong Kong Policy Institute
Dr. Jane Lee, Panelist from the Hong Kong Policy Institute
Wudy Heng, Panelist from the Hong Kong Policy Institute
Martin Lee Chu Ming
Leader of the Democratic Party, Legislative Council

June 30

Journalists' Panel:
Bill McGurn, Senior Editor of the *Far Eastern Economic Review*
Jesse Wong, *Asian Wall Street Journal*
Frank Ching, Senior Editor of the *Far Eastern Economic Review*
Frank Shakespeare, Former Ambassador
Edwin J. Feulner, Jr., President of the Heritage Foundation

July 2

David Dodwell, Director of Group Corporate Communications of Jardine Fleming
Hugh Davies, Senior British Representative of the Joint Liaison Group
Frank Martin, President of the American Chamber of Commerce in Hong Kong
Joe Zhang, Writer, speaking for the positions of the People's Republic of China
Larry Arnn, President of The Claremont Institute

July 3

Roy Huang, Assistant Director of Listing of the Hong Kong Stock Exchange
Open Forum of All Delegates

Consul General Richard Boucher

Conference Speaker
June 28, 1997 - 4:00 p.m.

Bruce Herschensohn: This didn't happen by design, but I'm glad that it did happen this way, because it's more than appropriate that we have as our first speaker the consul general from our country, from the United States, Consul General Richard Boucher. I'm positive that even if you haven't kept up with government and political activities—although most of you have—Consul General Boucher is familiar to you through television, radio, and the press. He has been the deputy press secretary and the press secretary to three secretaries of state. Tonight he's meeting with our current secretary of state, Madeleine Albright.

He served twenty years in the foreign service of the United States. I call him Mr. Ambassador because he was ambassador to Cyprus, probably one of the most difficult posts because two NATO allies, Turkey and Greece, have had a conflict over Cyprus for so many years. Of course, because Hong Kong is not a sovereign state, he is not our Ambassador here—there isn't one—he is, however, the highest-ranking official American officer, consul general. A few months after he received this post, I talked to a number of people I respect very much in Hong Kong and asked how they liked the new consul general. They all have the highest regard for him. One of the persons that I talked to, and I won't give names at this point of history because I don't know who's afraid and who isn't, but one of the persons that I talked to said, "You guys have sent over a lot of different kinds of people, some of them I didn't like so much, some of them were very good, and Richard Boucher's certainly one of the best." So I'm delighted to present to you Ambassador Boucher.

U.S. Consul General Richard Boucher: Those are very kind words. I appreciate them very much. Obviously you haven't been reading the newspapers around here in the last few days where one of my good friends, Emily Lau, has called us disgusting and contemptible. I've had an ongoing discussion with my British colleague as to whether he's disgusting and I'm contemptible or whether I'm disgusting and he's contemptible. When we figure it out we'll tell you. But I did talk to Emily the other day, and I think she doesn't really agree with our action, but she understands it a little better.

I'll be glad to talk about that later, but first let me thank everybody for making your time available to see me today. We originally, months ago, scheduled this for eleven o'clock on Sunday, and I figured there's no way the secretary of state will arrive on Saturday, but now she's landing here in about an hour and a half. So I'll go from here to the airport and then I've got activities with her all day tomorrow. So, first of all thanks for your flexibility on changing the time and it is good to see you.

What I'd like to do is just talk for a few minutes, give you an overview of things and how we see them here, and then just take any questions. I'd like to hear any comments you might have about things.

If you look, in recent weeks and months you've had President Clinton, Vice President Gore, Secretary of State Albright, a small army of senators and congresspersons, talking about U.S. policy and U.S. interests in Hong Kong. Many of those in Congress have been here to visit in person. We have some more coming in tonight at around midnight. I get to go to the airport and meet them as well. And then, of course, we have Secretary of State Albright coming in just a few hours to participate in the hand-over ceremony. She said she's here to emphasize America's continued interest and American support for the Hong Kong people as they enter China. All this interest is sincere on our part, and some of it has to do with the visions of China, and the implications of Hong Kong for China, and for some of the broader things happening in Asia. I'd like to talk a little bit about the reasons for our interest.

The one point I want you to keep in mind as we go through this is that we believe our interests, in fact, are the same as the interests of China and the interests of the people of Hong Kong, themselves. We want the transition to succeed. Like the people in Hong Kong and China, we want this thing called "One country—two systems," we want that to work. And like the people here and in China, we want Hong Kong to keep on going as a prosperous and open city. So our interests are not necessarily in conflict with anybody else's.

We do have a special role, a special involvement here. We've been involved for a long time; we're one of the major investors in Hong Kong; we have over 40,000 Americans here; we're Hong Kong's second largest trading partner; we have over 1,100 U.S. companies that are based here and over 400 of those do business beyond China and Hong Kong, they are regional operations. U.S. and Hong Kong law enforcement officials cooperate to make life safer for us and for people in the region. We are involved in anti-drug smuggling, anti-alien smuggling; we have counterfeit cases that we pursue out here; we've had cases of stolen cars from California that ended up on the docks here in containers on their way to China that we've been able to bust here. We've had lots of fraud— money laundering type things to follow up on; we've had kidnappings in the United States where ransom notes were sent out here. So, we have very effective and very good law enforcement cooperation with the Hong Kong government and authorities.

Another major interest is the U.S. Navy visits. We've had an average of about sixty-five U.S. Navy ships that come every year. They come in large carrier battle groups, and Hong Kong is really one of the most convenient, one of the safest, one of the nicest places for them to visit, and 3,000 men and women can get off the ships and get absorbed into the town and have a good time. Some of the families come down, people shop, they mail stuff back from the fleet post office. It's just a very good place to visit.

We have Americans going back and forth. We have people studying at colleges and universities, people sharing art, acting, and personal and professional ties. These things constitute the interests that we want to see preserved here, and that we want to see prosper in the future.

We believe, basically, that we do have in place the arrangements and the agreements that are necessary for these activities to continue and grow. Whether they, in fact, do continue and grow depends on how much Hong Kong keeps on being Hong Kong.

Hong Kong's social, economic, and political mechanisms operate on information, on discussion, on debate, and on all legal mechanisms. Hong Kong has a unique genius in the business world: it's ability to put together complicated deals with different inputs, technologies and areas, it's ability to trade in fast moving markets, it's ability to do flexible, quick manufacturing so that McDonalds can order up a new toy and get it delivered within thirty days, whatever it happens to be, from toys to power plants. Hong Kong can do it, do it quickly, do it right, and do it involving a lot of complicated things. But this ability depends on a basic foundation of the rule of law, of open information, and a clean, efficient government. Without those things you wouldn't have the same business ability, you wouldn't have the same business environment here.

President Clinton and the Heritage Foundation have both called Hong Kong the freest economy in the world. It might be one of the few things that they both agree on.

I think perhaps no place better than Hong Kong demonstrates the intimate relationship between political openness and economic prosperity. We sign contracts in Hong Kong because the rule of law means they'll be implemented and, if necessary, adjudicated fairly. We trade, we put together deals in Hong Kong because we believe that we have all the information that's necessary that make the markets efficient. We bid on major contracts here because we think the field is basically level, and if it stays level, we'll keep doing it. Now, these are not new insights, this relationship. It's quite clear from the Joint Declaration, which the British and the Chinese signed in 1984, and even from the Basic Law, which is the Chinese law that will constitute the Constitution for Hong Kong that was passed in 1990, that the pledges of economic and political continuity, in fact, belong together. Preserving Hong Kong's important economic role for China and for Asia, preserving Hong Kong's status as a free port and an international center, and preserving Hong Kong's way of life, including open government and fundamental freedoms, do go hand in hand. That was recognized by China and the United Kingdom when they put together the Joint Declaration and the elements that were necessary to implement "One country—two systems," the approach that they adopted.

They agreed that Hong Kong would retain its autonomy for judicial matters, for administrative matters, for financial matters, and indeed for all other matters except for foreign affairs and defense. The border is to remain between Hong Kong and China; the currency and the reserves are to remain in the hands of the Hong Kong government; the Civil Service is to remain purely Hong Kong. Civil liberties are guaranteed in these documents, and the judicial system is to remain an independent common law judicial system. It's easier to see, first of all, that full implementation of these agreements will, in fact, preserve U.S. interests in Hong Kong, just as it will protect the interests of China, and the people of Hong Kong themselves, and their own future.

Our view, I think, if you had to summarize the policy, is very simple, and the president did this a couple times in the last month or so. The framework for Hong Kong's reversion to China is a good one. We said it was a good one in 1984 when it was signed, and we expect to see it implemented. We believe that, in fact, any compromise in this framework could potentially harm Hong Kong's overall prospects. So we've been pretty active in trying to see that the entire framework is maintained.

When we look at the factors that are necessary to guarantee the continuity, to actually implement the framework, I think the omens are generally good. First, the legal framework is, in fact, complete. The economic indicators are positive; judicial autonomy is being reinforced by some of the appointments that have been made recently; anti-corruption efforts are continuing; the Hong Kong Civil Service is staying on the job; the international environment augurs well and the interest of the parties themselves push them to meet their commitments. Hong Kong, finally, remains bound up in a set of international practices of standards and agreements which help keep it to a level of meeting international commitments.

We do have some very serious concerns about some key areas, and we often raise these. Let me go over them. We want to see that a new legislature is elected as soon as possible under rules that do, in fact, adhere to widely accepted democratic standards. Second, we want to see that the Hong Kong press goes on reporting and editorializing in a forthright and unfettered manner. We also want to see that new laws on civil liberties are not used to stifle legitimate freedom of expression. Our intention is to play an active role here. We'll be watching developments in these areas very closely as the transition continues. We'll be using our influence where we can, since the outcome on these issues will, in fact, determine Hong Kong's prospects for all of us.

So, in sum, Americans are heavily committed to Hong Kong, commercially, professionally and, in fact, personally. We believe that the principles which underlie the transition of sovereignty, and which provide for continued cooperation with the United States, give us an opportunity to advance our interests in the coming period. We intend to do everything in our power to contribute to a successful transition, so that Americans can go on participating in and sharing in the prosperity and dynamism of this wonderful, modern Chinese city.

That's the overview. I'm happy to hear any comments, and take any questions. Thank you.

Question: Prior to coming here I've been getting a lot of media reports, TV—

Boucher: Well that's your mistake right there. (Laughter)

Question: Are the Chinese people in Hong Kong and the Chinese around the world happy about this transition, or do they wish it would stay the way that it has been?

Boucher: The polls show things like most Americans believe the people in Hong Kong don't want this to happen, and most polls in Hong Kong show that people do, in fact, want this to happen. Americans think—4 percent, I think, or some number like that—that Hong Kong people want to be part of China, whereas 60 percent of the Hong Kong people say they want to be part of China. There's this sort of the bias of media reporting, and depending on the audience, I too will sometimes rant and rave about media reporting on Hong Kong, because frankly I think it fails to capture the complexity and the interesting nature of what's going on here. And in doing that it fails to capture what our interests are and how we pursue them.

If it's simply a question of the communists coming and everybody's going to roll over and play dead, then you have to deal with things quite differently than if you have a vibrant and an active society that has a lot of different currents cutting across it right now, but which will, in the end, probably be more important to its own fate than outside factors. So that's one thing.

I think the reporting in some ways is bad. It fails to capture the historic nature and the complexity of what's going on here.

However, I do defend our friends in the journalist trade and the people in the press, because there are, in fact, political changes being made here. And if you don't want the press to keep reporting that you're making political changes, there's one simple way of stopping them, and that's to stop making all these damn political changes. The problem in some ways is that—it's when you're 12,000 miles away and you read the newspapers which tell you what's new— you read about the political changes being made. When you're in Hong Kong and you read about the political changes being made, you also know that the driver's license that you hold is not changing, that the cop on the street is not changing, that the person you just had lunch with yesterday, who's a judge, is not changing, that the legal system is not changing. I mean, you just know because you're here, you're part of this. You see all around you everything that's not going to change, and then you see within that context the things that are. So that's the distortion of news and the distortion of distance. But if it disturbs people in Hong Kong who complain about Western press coverage, really the answer is stop making all the political changes.

There's a lot of polling done—let's say you have your web site up—there's something called the Hong Kong Transition Project that's been doing polling for eight or ten years, and they've got a web site as well. If you look up the Hong Kong Transition Project, you can find them. Their polling generally shows that a goodly number, I think it's something like 60 percent of Hong Kong people want to be part of China. But a goodly number also have pretty serious misgivings about whether they want to be part of this particular China at this particular moment, particularly among younger people. It's a very odd situation actually. The polling shows that older people, most of whom came to Hong Kong as refugees, people that came out in '49—some of them are swimmers, people that swam through shark infested waters to get here, many of them are people who were persecuted in the cultural revolution for having ties overseas, people who escaped from China to get here—they're more inclined to say, "Well, that was then, and this is now. China's different now and we are Chinese, we want to be part of China and this is okay." Whereas younger people, who are more Westernized and whose lives are maybe more affected by Tiananmen Square, are much more reticent about being a part of this particular China. And then you get a chunk that would just as soon stay, either as a British colony or part of the commonwealth—or, you know why change it? And you've got a very small group that wants to be independent.

There's one guy that sits across from the U.S. Consulate on sunny days, and he's a nice old guy. He's got a sign, he's got flags, and he's the only guy I know that's in favor of the independence of Hong Kong. So that sentiment is really very, very small. There are then maybe another group of 20 percent or so that really want to be part of this China—The People's Republic of China. They feel that they got a raw deal under the British and now it's their turn.

And so some of the things that are going on in Hong Kong society you have to understand, and sort them in the different groups that are coming and going, depending on the power structure. I'd say, by and large, you poke your average guy on the street and he'll say, "Yeah, I'm Chinese, I deserve to be part of China, and there's this historical period that's been good for us all but it's coming to an end. It needs to come to an end but, you know, if I had my druthers, I wouldn't be part of this particular China right now." I think most people, though, say, "It's happening, let's make the best of it." Kind of a complicated explanation of what I think is a complicated situation.

Senator John Tunney: What do you think the impact of the 4,000 troops stationed on the border will be? They, apparently, are going to be coming across at the time of hand-over. What is the message to the world that they're trying to convey? And what's the reaction in Hong Kong? Is it that they just don't care? Is it of concern to them?

Boucher: I haven't had a chance to read too much of the reaction in the papers today. What I've been briefed on is that, more or less, we knew they were coming. When the first 200 in the advance party came in without weapons, subject to customs and visa search, et cetera, in jeeps and drove downtown, the *New York Times* reported that under ashen skies the PLA marched into Hong Kong over streets where seven years before a million demonstrators had protested their actions in Tiananmen Square. That's not reporting when they write that it's a dark and stormy night. So I suppose you'll get some dark and stormy night reporting at 6:00 a.m. on July 1st as well. The British garrison has averaged about 10 to 12,000 troops. They have had some of their best troops out here. They frequently invite reporters out to run around the bush with them in camouflage and take pictures on exercises and things like that. The Chinese garrison will have about 10,000 troops, we think, of whom about 4,000 will actually be in Hong Kong and 5,000 or 6,000 will be just across the border. There have been various scenarios for their arrival discussed over the past several months. I don't particularly like this scenario, but it's about the fourth or fifth worst on the list. They discarded the top three or four, of even worse scenarios. But I guess they've got to come in some way. The reaction of the few people that I've talked to so far is, "We knew they were coming, now we know how they're coming." Once they get here, they'll pretty much disappear. They're not going to be on the streets; they have no public security order role, and they're apparently not going to be very visible. The Chinese that I've talked to say, "You know, we're going to lock those guys up in the barracks basically." So I think they'll end up not being a major presence in town.

Larry Arnn: There's a specific legal controversy about the terms of the Basic Law and the Joint Declaration, and I want you to correct me if I'm wrong about this, but I think it's the Chinese position that the 1995 election of the Legislative Council was illegal, and it's the British position that the Provisional Legislative Council that's been appointed is illegal. And so there are specific allegations of a breach of the law against one another. I wonder if you could comment on that, and state what our official view is on that—the United States view.

Boucher: Neither one quite get to the point of breach. There are people here that have pushed the British, and us for that matter, to declare the Chinese in breach or in violation of the Joint Declaration. But the British have resisted that, and have not done it for a variety of reasons. Mostly it's that they don't think this needs to be argued as a judicial matter, but that this is a political matter. The Joint Declaration and the Basic Law say that Hong Kong's legislature shall be constituted by elections. The Joint Declaration says that neither party, neither the British nor the Chinese, will make any significant or major changes in Hong Kong without consulting with the other. The British say that the reforms that Governor Patten introduced in 1992 and that led to the 1995 election, were entirely consistent with that, that they led to a legislature constituted by elections. And there were a series of discussions over 1993 and 1994 with the Chinese about the form the elections should take, and they never reached agreement. The British felt they were in their rights because it says, the British will run Hong Kong until July 1, 1997. The Chinese say: "Come on! This is a major and significant change to introduce a level of democracy in Hong Kong that you haven't had for 151 years of colonial rule, and now, suddenly, you're going to introduce a much broader democratic franchise in Hong Kong! If that's not a significant change, then tell us what is? And you can't do that without our consent. You're changing the terms of the deal, we're not going to allow you to, it ain't fitting, it ain't fitting, it ain't fitting, and we're going to get rid of it when July 1st comes around."

So, true to their word the British introduced democracy in the 1995 elections, and true to their word, the Chinese will get rid of it. They have the right to abolish laws on July 1st. So they'll abolish the procedures for electing the legislature. The Chinese then say: "Well, there we are. What are we going to do? We have to have an elected legislature. The British won't put people at our service to prepare for an election on July 2nd, so we can't start working on new legislative laws, nor the preparations for elections until the beginning of July. Therefore, we promise we'll have an election within a year, but in the meantime we've got to have some legislative authority, so we are setting up the Provisional Legislature, and we, as the sovereign power, have a right to do that.

Our view is that the establishment of the Provisional Legislature is unjustified, it's unnecessary, we've said it's just plain a bad idea. It's clear to us, I think—our basic view is that democracy, once given, can't be taken away. And that whatever the disputes over the election in 1995, it was a broad and democratic election, such as Hong Kong has not had before. And once people have that right, you shouldn't take it away. Therefore, we have not endorsed the Provisional Legislature as a body. We've put a lot of emphasis on having early and open elections. We've been pushing very hard in public, but also in private, telling Tung Chee-hwa [the new chief executive replacing the British governor] to have those elections as early as possible. He's made quite clear he wants to do it as early as possible. In fact the holdup at this point has been the people in the Hong Kong government. The civil servants that I said were most admirable and efficient have come back and said it takes them almost a year to prepare for an election. My response has been that we did it in nine months in Bosnia, and you can do better than that in Hong Kong. That may become one of the elements of how soon the election happens. But, the point is, I think we should see that there will be an election by next April, May—probably May—that it will be open to all the parties, that it's basically fair to all the parties, and that Hong Kong ends up with the elected legislature that was promised. At that point a lot of this will become history: the democrats will be back in the legislature, and the voices in Hong Kong that are needed to run this place will be there. The essential function that the legislature performs of supervision, of oversight, of approval, will be reconstituted in a good manner in Hong Kong. That, we see as being part of the process of keeping the system honest—to have that kind of legislature, and that's where our emphasis is.

Herschensohn: Mr. Ambassador, originally the United States was not going to have any official at the swearing-in of the Provisional Legislature. That received the applause of a lot of people in Hong Kong, and I know Great Britain wasn't going to do it either. Now you are going, although Secretary Albright isn't. You're going to attend. In doing that, the response here in Hong Kong among many people is that President Clinton is waffling. Originally he held a rigid position that we don't recognize the Provisional Legislature. What changed his mind?

Boucher: I don't think anything changed his mind. With my background in press relations I should have seen this one coming, and I'm afraid I didn't. We left ourselves this option right from the start. We said the secretary of state will not attend in order to make a point. The secretary of state is our biggest gun in this fight, and we make, I think, a very clear point by saying the secretary of state will not attend because this is, in some ways, a tainted ceremony. We left ourselves the option of deciding to send somebody at a lower level, depending on how the ceremony worked out and depending on what the other events were that we would be invited to. One of the things was finding out where, in fact, some of the other executive parts of the government were going to be sworn in. It was reported in the press that we were boycotting, that nobody was going and, therefore, when we announced that, in fact, our consul general was going to go, people took that somehow as a change of position. In fact, it was an option that we left ourselves all along. We were waiting to see how some of these things came out. We've been discussing this with the British for several weeks in order to coordinate our positions, so that we and the British would end up doing the same thing.

I guess I describe where we came out as this: it's an attempt to send two messages, which maybe, therein lies the problem. But, it's an attempt to send two messages: one is we do not endorse a Provisional Legislature, and the secretary of state, herself, is not going to attend a ceremony that involves their swearing-in. As a representative of the United States of America, with an elected legislature, with our form of government and values, it's inappropriate for her to be there, at the swearing-in of this legislature. At the same time, you have to recognize there is something fundamental going on at this event that is important to us, and it's that Hong Kong is getting a government of Hong Kong people to run Hong Kong. That is something that we fundamentally support and that we fundamentally look forward to. So our guy on the ground who is going to work with those people is going to witness their swearing-in.

If it were simply the swearing-in of the Provisional Legislature, frankly it would be easy, none of us would go. If it were simply the swearing-in of the new chief executive and his cabinet in Hong Kong, that's easy, all of us would go enthusiastically. As it is, the event is mixed, and our response is somewhat mixed. The response in Hong Kong, my good friends, Emily Lau and Martin Lee, are—how can I say this—some of the most vocal but also some of the most quotable people in Hong Kong are opposed to any attendance as the Provisional Legislature is sworn in. And Emily, you know, called it disgusting and contemptible. I called her up on the phone and we talked about it and she didn't agree, but she made a point that we should have announced it all as a package at once, and said the secretary is not going, the consul general is. But factually, we wanted to leave ourselves a little while to figure out exactly what was going to happen during the middle of the night.

Herschensohn: I see why you were press secretary to three secretaries of state. (Laughter)

Boucher: Well, I didn't learn anything did I?

Question: How much of the rhetoric that's going on here in Hong Kong is really aimed at the position of the United States regarding China's takeover of Tibet and possibly Taiwan?

Boucher: I don't think in policy terms that there's a whole lot about Taiwan and Tibet involved in what we're doing here. In Chinese terms, in terms of what this means to the Chinese leaders, Taiwan is a very important factor. I think, basically, they know that if they mess things up here, they can kiss Taiwan good-bye. I think they also understand that there's nothing they could do here that they could do so well and so incredibly wonderfully, that people in Taiwan would say, "Oh yeah, me too!" So there's a big down-side and not much of an up-side, but they've got to do it right in Hong Kong. They've got to respect their commitments, they've got to show that "One country—two systems" works if they're ever going to attract Taiwan with a better deal than that. They've got to keep Hong Kong as a viable place for the contacts and the trade and the business that goes on between the mainland and Taiwan. So if you ask, "What are the incentives in the Chinese mind to do this right, to respect their commitments on 'One country—two systems'?" I would list Taiwan way ahead of everything else, at the top. Now, they also have a lot of money tied up in this. They also have a lot of questions of international reputation showing they can do this as well as the British. Also, some of the Chinese leaders have a personal stake in showing that they can have a successful return of Hong Kong. So a lot of this does come through a lot in the Chinese rhetoric, in the Chinese minds. But when we look at it from the U.S. side, we don't see that Hong Kong would become a model that folks in Taiwan would embrace, I don't think we see too many implications in terms of how we handle this for what Taiwan may or may not eventually decide to do.

Herschensohn: Because of the Ambassador's time, let's have one more question if we may.

Question: A follow-up question, quickly, on the transition from the elected Legislative Council to the Provisional Legislature, and where that might lead. I just read that the Legislative Council, on its way out the door, passed a package of bills to create collective bargaining rights and a mini-NLRB here for the first time to protect union organizers, which is a radical transformation in labor relations in the colony. My specific question is why did they do that and will that not poison the atmosphere here for returning to a democratically elected sort of body?

Boucher: Hong Kong politics is kind of funny. You have, basically, the pro-communists and the pro-business groups aligned against the democrats and some of the trade union groups, some of which are left and some of which are right. When I talk to the people in Beijing about democracy and Hong Kong, their answer on sort of too much democracy too quickly in Hong Kong is the same one you get out of some of the tycoons in Hong Kong; some of the billionaires down here, and that is, "My God, if we have too much democracy, all those democrats are going to get elected, and they're going to spend all the money on poor people, and we're going to have a welfare state just like in Europe or the United States, and that would be awful." So it's a strange alignment of forces when you have basically pro-communists telling a conservative British politician that he's trying to spend too much on old age pensions. But that's something that happens in Hong Kong.

So what you had in the legislature is the democrats and some of the others, some of the pro-labor union people, supporting better workers' rights. It's going to be very interesting to watch, because the legislation that presently exists in Hong Kong is valid through the transition. They have prepared a bill that explicitly makes it all valid, with the exception of the pieces of the election ordinances and the other things that were invalidated by the National People's Congress. This power to invalidate laws by the National People's Congress basically, I think, expires on July 1st, but the new legislature, if it was duly constituted, could amend all these laws once again. The Provisional Legislature may try, but one of the things they're committed to is that it will do the minimum possible, because they said it was established by virtue of necessity, it will only take up legislation that's absolutely necessary. And there is, I think, a willingness on the part of some of the people involved in seeing a strong chief executive. We've talked to him quite a bit about keeping to that commitment and not to expand the list of things that the Provisional Legislature has to do.

So they're in a quandary right now. Do they allow this legislation to be applied? Do they try to revise it in the Provisional Legislature and thereby sort of expand the mandate? Do they wait for the newly elected legislature a year from now? So it's going to be interesting to see what happens on that point. I don't know what the answer will be.

If you look at the system that's been designed by the Basic Law, you'll find that it's based on the British model. It's very firmly based on the model that we have in Hong Kong now, the model that existed in 1984 of executive-led government, where the legislature plays a role of supervision and approval of budgets, and investigation, but not so much initiating legislation. And, in fact, the ability of people in the legislature—apologies to former Senators [referring to Senator Tunney]—but their ability here in any case to actually do something and initiate something is severely constricted. The power that you had in the U.S. Senate to introduce legislation is very restricted here, and is going to be even more restricted under the new framework that's been laid down and agreed to by everybody. But one of the reasons that exists is that they don't want people coming up with worker's rights laws and stuff like that. They want initiatives to be on the part of the Executive Branch. This gets then to the kind of election system—this is the last question so I'm sort of throwing everything you might want to know into the last answer—this gets to the kind of election system that's being devised.

The difference between the Governor Patten reforms, which took the basic structure of the legislature but broadened the franchise so that you had more voters in each of the different areas of the legislature, the difference between that and the kind of system that is probably going to be put in place, where you have fewer voters in some of these areas, is going to mean that it will be more difficult for any particular political party to dominate the legislature. That is not just because the democrats are the most likely to be dominant, and they might do things like pass worker's rights laws, but also because the chief executive, who sees himself as a chief executive like he was in his corporation, doesn't particularly want to have to put up with these ornery people down there in the legislature, and to have to put up with a strong political power base within the legislature.

Now, he recognizes that as we go toward the next election and the one beyond that, and then the eventual review of the whole system to go toward universal suffrage, which is promised in the Basic Law—that political parties will probably grow and that political parties won't be content getting some seats in the legislature where their powers are restricted, but they'll want the prize, which is the chief executive. So I think he recognizes that over time we will end up in Hong Kong with political parties trying to get a majority in the legislature, and get their guy into the chief executive slot. But for the moment, in order to emphasize executive-led government in a way that the power of the legislature is limited to what I said—supervision, approval of budgets, and investigation—they'll come up with an election system that makes it more difficult to have these crazy things like tough worker's rights thrown in at the last minute, and have to deal with them. But how they'll deal with them this time, I don't know. It will be interesting. Thank you. I'm going to have to run off to the airport.

Herschensohn: Thanks so much for coming this afternoon, Mr. Ambassador. I realize this is a time, a busy time for you. Thanks.

Welcome to Hong Kong Dinner

Bruce Herschensohn
Conference Speaker
June 28, 1997 - 9:00 p.m.

Bruce Herschensohn: Senator Tunney and I made a pledge to each other decades ago that we would be here together in 1997, and we are. Thanks for being here, John, Katinka, and Tara.

This afternoon we heard from the consul general. I was very impressed with him. I disagree with many of the things he said, but as a foreign service officer, he supports the president of the United States. I would not respect him if he said everything that I believe, because he wouldn't be doing his job. The foreign service is like the military in that you back the president. I'm not a member of government at this time, so I can ethically speak my own mind.

I read so often in the press and hear on television that the reason that Hong Kong is reverting back to China is because of a treaty that places that reversion at this time. Not true. There were three treaties. One of them for Hong Kong Island, that's where you see the skyline, the most magnificent skyline in the world. That treaty, in 1842, ceded the island to Great Britain, by treaty in perpetuity—forever. Where we are right now, Kowloon, was ceded to Great Britain in 1860 in perpetuity—forever. Now, the third treaty, the one of 1898, was the one in which the emperor said something to mean, "No! You can't have this one forever. This is going to be a ninety-nine-year lease, and we're all going to be dead by the time this thing is up, so it's a pretty good deal for you and it's okay for us." And that's what we're talking about. That was the treaty for what the British called the New Territories. If you were here a few decades back, the New Territories were nothing. There were rice paddies and a walled city, and that was about it. But in the last couple of decades, the New Territories became an integral part of what we call Hong Kong, which are the three entities. In terms of the land, the New Territories have 92 percent of the land of what we call Hong Kong, and 40 percent of the people live there now. So the possibility of returning the New Territories alone isn't even worth talking about, it's too much a part of Hong Kong.

A lot of people blame Margaret Thatcher for coming to Beijing in 1982 and negotiating with Deng Xiaoping about all this, as though Deng Xiaoping would have forgotten about all this. I think she did exactly the right thing. She did it for two reasons. One of them is that there are fifteen-year leases that the government of Great Britain gives, and 1982 plus fifteen in 1997, and she wouldn't be able to negotiate those leases if there was an unknown after 1997. Secondly, three months previous to the time she went to Beijing, she won the Falklands War, so she was coming in a position of strength, real strength. So she went to Beijing.

Deng Xiaoping just said, "No." Period. "No." He was going to take all three entities. She said, "But a treaty is a treaty"—meaning that, "Look, there are two other treaties!" He said they were unequal treaties. What he meant was that they were signed under duress because of what's called the Opium Wars, and "Too bad, we're taking them!" So then for two years, from 1982 to 1984, they worked out what we call the Joint Declaration. The Joint Declaration said "One Country —Two Systems." I think it's "One Country—Two Systems—One Tragedy."

I want to tell you what I believe is a misinterpretation of two systems. Obviously people refer to it as the system of communism for the mainland and capitalism here. But the system of Hong Kong is liberty, not capitalism. Capitalism is a part of liberty, it's the economic dimension of liberty, but it isn't the whole thing. The system is liberty. It's true that you cannot have liberty without capitalism, but you certainly can have capitalism without liberty. That's what the People's Republic of China has right now, and I am convinced that's what they want to eventually bring to Hong Kong.

Secondly, Hong Kong will be called an S.A.R., a Special Administrative Region. A lot of people think the "A" designates the word "Autonomous" for a Special Autonomous Region. That isn't what it stands for. The reason that Deng Xiaoping didn't want to make it a Special Autonomous Region, even though they promised autonomy in the Joint Declaration, is because the term, "Special Autonomous Region" was given to Tibet, and there was a seventeen point plan that read very much like the Joint Declaration about what the People's Republic of China was going to do with Tibet, as far as its autonomy was concerned. The People's Republic of China didn't keep its word. So this is a Special Administrative Region and it's supposed to be for fifty years, until the year 2047, when we have to go through this celebration again, and John and I have pledged not to come back for that one.

The tragedy as I see it—and these are opinions, but I think they're valid opinions—is this: It isn't that it isn't worth a celebration that Hong Kong is going to China; the tragedy is that it's going to the People's Republic of China. It's this particular government of China. So when people say, "Gee, it's right that Hong Kong should go to China," I have no argument with that. Neither do the British.

Deng Xiaoping said, "We have been humiliated by the Opium Wars," and now Jiang Zemin and Li Peng say the same thing about China's humiliation and shame. I've never seen a government or any person so proud to be ashamed. They keep on talking about the shame of this. If I was ashamed of something, I would shut up about it. They talk about it continually. I think the humiliation is the fact that Hong Kong is what it is, in comparison to other urban areas of the mainland. That's the humiliation that's the shame. The Chinese people did all this in Hong Kong without the chains of the P.R.C. Hong Kong, to me, is China without chains. It is what all of China could be without chains. I can't help but feel that a lot of this celebration is done out of fear. How could they celebrate unification when they or their parents risked their lives to disunify? A lot of people are afraid not to celebrate.

Some of the businesspeople—and the consul general hinted about this, although he didn't say it specifically—the businesspeople have been, in my opinion, the worst, the very worst regarding all of this. In a sense, they've been prostitutes, thinking more of their own wallets than the liberty of the people of Hong Kong. And they regard human rights and civil liberties, at times, as nuisances rather than as something that they should fight for or try to preserve.

Now, what should we do about it? What should we, as America, do? There's only three ways that a government can influence another government: economically, diplomatically, and militarily. Let me just go through those very briefly. Obviously you don't want to use military means until a very, very last course, but we have to have a much stronger military than we do, to be credible for that option. If we, in any sense, want to influence the People's Republic of China or any power, we can't afford to diminish our military. We did this after World War I and after World War II and after Korea and after Vietnam and now after the Cold War. And the people, who keep arguing for less defense keep on saying, "Well look—the Cold War is over." They're the same people who were arguing for less defense when the Cold War was at its height. It's just a new justification for an old advocacy. I would like to see the defense budget go back to what it was during the Reagan Administration, because we never know what we'll need. Unlike any other budget item, we don't know what's going to happen.

Secondly, on April 23, 1993, President Clinton said—and I'm saying this statement with precision—he said, "The United States should not be involved as a partisan in a war." Not as a partisan? It must mean that he wants the military to be a uniformed Peace Corps or a uniformed Agency for International Development, and I'm afraid that that's what it's becoming. Now, diplomatically, what could we do? Very little, since we already screwed-up diplomatically—we screwed up when President Carter, on December 15, 1978, gave diplomatic relations to the People's Republic of China. President Nixon was asked for diplomatic relations when he went to Beijing in '72, and they made three demands for such normality of relations: that we break diplomatic relations with the Republic of China on Taiwan, that we take our troops out of there and abrogate a mutual defense treaty that we had since 1954 with them. President Nixon said, "No." They asked President Ford in '75. He said, "No." They asked President Carter in '78. He said, "Yes." We didn't get anything in return. President Carter could have said, "Yes, if you promise that you'll never take Taiwan by force, and yes, if you guarantee civil liberties to Hong Kong in

1997 and beyond when 1997 comes." But there were no demands made on our side. Absolutely nothing. We simply gave up diplomatic relations with the Republic of China on Taiwan and accepted them with the People's Republic of China.

Third, economically. We're afraid to do anything, economically. Last week we voted for retaining M.F.N., most favored nation status. I'm very much opposed to most favored nation status. Most people say, and President Clinton says, the reason that we want to have most favored nation status is because that's the way you bring about civil liberties—our trade, our integration with them, that's the way you bring about democracy. How come he was arguing on the other side when it came to South Africa? We had total economic isolation there. The Reagan Administration called it constructive engagement, which is what we're calling the policy with China. I argued on behalf of constructive engagement with South Africa and I was wrong. It was successful. Look what South Africa is today. It is becoming a democracy. There is no revenge against those who practiced apartheid, those who did some terrible, terrible things. And I have to say, as much as I didn't like Nelson Mandela, I now think he's a great man. He is avoiding future centuries of revenge that would go back and forth, and he's stopping it. He's stopping it by saying, "Confess what you did and there will be no prejudice, there will be no retribution taken." He's so much of a leader that he's able to influence his people not to take revenge. I think that's great. And I apologize for having taken the wrong side in that. Economic sanctions had a large role in the transition of South Africa.

Moreover, we know that the Soviet Union rejected communism because of economic failure. Why do we think economic health will bring about the same rejection to the People's Republic of China? I don't think that's logical. What is it that the P.R.C. is going to do with all this money that they receive from the United States in trade? I know what they're doing; building up their military. They're buying missiles from what was the Soviet Union; they're sending missiles to Iran; they're sending nuclear material to Pakistan; they're building up the People's Liberation Army; they're building up their navy. When I was a little kid, there was a book, which I still have, called, *You Can't Do Business with Hitler.* It was warning the business people of America not to do business with Hitler. I'm going to read you one sentence from it: "We must get this straight once and for all, there is no such thing as having purely economic relations with the totalitarian States. Every business deal carries with it political, military, social and propaganda implications." That book was written before we entered the war.

There's going to be a toast that's going to be given—it was already printed in the *South China Morning Post*—it will be given in two nights; Tung Chee-hwa and Li Peng will toast the continued stability and prosperity of Hong Kong. Where's the word "liberty"? Patrick Henry didn't say, "give me stability or give me death" or "give me prosperity or give me death." He said, "give me liberty," and that's what this place thrives on.

The greatest foreign policy statement, I believe, in contemporary times, was said by President Kennedy. It was in his inaugural address. If you would, just listen to these words that he said: "Let every nation know, whether it wishes us well or ill, that we will pay any price, bear any burden, meet any hardship, support any friend, oppose any foe, to assure the survival and the success of liberty." He said we'd do all of that for liberty. He didn't say the survival and the success of stability nor did he say the survival and the success of prosperity. It was liberty. Whenever we think of what Hong Kong is, and what I hope it's destiny will be, the word is liberty.

Welcome to Hong Kong Dinner

Larry Arnn
President of The Claremont Institute
Conference Speaker
June 28, 1997 - 9:15 p.m.

Michael Warder: We are not here by accident. The Claremont Institute exists to serve a mission, and many of you here in this room have helped us. That mission is to restore the founding principles of the United States to their preeminent authority in public life. The leader of The Claremont Institute since 1985 is a remarkable man, Larry Arnn. He was one of the original incorporators, back in 1979, when the organization was first conceived.

I have worked for four different think tanks, one of which is the Heritage Foundation, another is the Ethics and Public Policy Center, and I've never encountered a person who is as devoted and dedicated to those founding principles, and has an ability to explain them and relate them to contemporary problems, as Larry Arnn. It is a great pleasure and a great joy—mainly because Larry has also an excellent sense of humor and keeps the troops animated that way—it's a great pleasure and joy to work with him in this project, which I hope you will all agree is very, very important. It's my pleasure to welcome him to the podium, Larry Arnn.

Larry Arnn: Thank you very much. Welcome all of you. I have the advantage on you as I've been here a few days and I'm getting adjusted. I will speak briefly.

I was here for a conference of journalists for a few days. It was organized by Roberta Ahmanson, who is a journalist, and by Howard Ahmanson, who is not, but who is a thinker. And it put me in mind of some themes, and the themes can explain to us why we are here. We're a big group—this is many more people than we imagined would come—and it's a special group here, of which we know, that will set out to accomplish the mission I'm going to state.

The world is assembled here. Foreign ministers and prime ministers from most of the major countries and all of the minor countries are here—the minor countries seeing an opportunity for a junket. The world press is here in massive numbers. This is a moment of grand and wonderful success for the government of the People's Republic of China, and they are not stupid people; they are very intelligent and purposeful people. And they have chosen to engage in an ongoing argument, most recently with the British government, about a three hour time period in which they wanted to have Chinese soldiers carrying weapons, on Hong Kong soil. They asked for armored columns to come into town about two months ago and were turned down. They have made incessant demands over and over again that soldiers be allowed to come, until finally in the culminating meetings on the transition they said, "Give us three hours," and generated headlines. In the press they explained this on several fronts. They used the Chinese explanation that the Chinese are concerned about security, especially for their own dignitaries who will be here, and they used the explanation that the garrison will be smaller, and ultimately the same size, as the British garrison, when the garrison is full size. Understand, by the way, that the purpose of the British garrison was to be a trip-wire against an invasion from China, which is the only obvious threat to Hong Kong in the neighborhood. So what is the Chinese garrison here to do? Stop the British from invading, I suppose. Is the entire British navy across the harbor over there?

Then finally, they do sometimes suggest another thing, but they never define what it is. Ask yourself the question, what point? What is the point that they are here to make? The point is someone might get shot, that's the point. Think about that. In the midst of all of this, in a moment of great glory, fireworks going off and celebrations everywhere, they want to make the point that someone might get shot.

In today's *South China Morning Post* there is an article about the handover and about how it's going to go, and whether it's going to be good for Hong Kong. And there's an extensive and interesting interview with an academic scholar from the mainland. I invite you to read it. It's a very interesting document. Read it when you're not sleepy. It reads as if someone is squeezing the last piece of information out of a reluctant witness. The man makes very plain, but only by implication, that Hong Kong has a lot of things about it that are better than things in China, but he never comes out and says that in so many words. Then he gets asked a question. He is asked, "Is it better that Hong Kong is going to China instead of Britain?" Now if he had answered that question, "No," that would be a crime. And people are often arrested and sometimes tried, and sometimes they disappear, for committing such crimes as that. And in response to that question this man speaks really clearly. "The shame of the Opium War must be effaced." Now if you read that and think about it for just a minute, you can see that that man is watching what he says with great care because he knows he's one of the people who might get shot. But think about this, the Hong Kong paper, whoever is the journalist who wrote that story, does not say that. This is a place where there is a free press, but no one says out loud that plain point.

And that brings me to our mission here. We Americans have a special heritage. We believe that every human being born has a right to choose the government under which he lives. We believe if a person is arrested for going to church, as is common all over China, and if it does not make any difference when that happens, and it does not make any difference where that happens, that is wrong. Our purpose in being here is to observe these facts for ourselves, as a group, and to think about them together. The reason it is good to come here is because we can be confident that not everything will be properly reported either here or perhaps at home. So if we do observe these facts and learn them ourselves and see their significance, perhaps we can be better able to govern ourselves at home, and to prepare our fellow citizens to do what they must do to preserve their liberty. It's good to be here.

Szeto Wah

Conference Speaker
June 29, 1997 - 9:00 a.m.

Bruce Herschensohn: Years ago, after the Tiananmen Square massacre, Szeto Wah organized an organization called the Hong Kong Alliance to support the Patriotic Democratic Movement in China. Listen to those words, "to support the Patriotic Democratic Movement in China." In China! In support of those who demonstrated in Tiananmen Square. And in Hong Kong, he organized a demonstration in which over one million people participated. This was at a time when the population of Hong Kong was 5.8 million. Therefore, it was more than 1/6 of the entire population that came out for this demonstration. That's one of the biggest crowds in history. As a consequence of Szeto Wah's organization and leadership, Beijing kicked him off the Basic Law Drafting Committee, and they labeled him a subversive. Szeto Wah won in a landslide in the September 17, 1995, election. He's with the Democratic Party.

If you have been following the news magazines lately, practically every international news magazine has had a cover story about Hong Kong, and every one of them give prominence to Szeto Wah. *Time Magazine* has a special edition listing the twenty-five most influential people in Hong Kong and, of course, Szeto Wah was in that group.

Szeto Wah's occupation, his career, is teaching. At one time I sent for his biography, I asked his office for a biography and I received a handwritten biography that mentioned nothing other than teaching and those things that he devoted his life to without any mention of awards or honors received. He has one of the most unique characteristics of anyone I have ever known in political life and that is humility. So many people say that you can't get ahead in politics if you're humble. To prove them wrong, in the United States I point to Abraham Lincoln. In Hong Kong I point to Szeto Wah. Wah?

Szeto Wah (with interpreter): Good morning, ladies and gentlemen. Thirty-nine hours from now Hong Kong will be in the hands of China. On the streets you can see lights. On the streets you can see people walking leisurely. In the next two days you'll be expecting to see lots of extravagant activities. You will also expect to hear from some people who have worries about the future. Can you explain it all as to how the people react to the future of Hong Kong? How can you anticipate what Hong Kong will be like in the future? You have to understand yesterday in order to understand today. And you have to understand today in order to anticipate tomorrow.

First of all, let's understand yesterday's Hong Kong. I will talk about the last year until the previous month. China has elected Mr. Tung Chee-hwa as the chief executive of Hong Kong. The P.R.C. devised a Provisional Legislature instead of our own Legco (Legislative Council) and two urban councils and a district board. They have reinstated the security provisions of the old law, and it's a loss to society and the democracy and freedom of Hong Kong's people in the future. Also, the P.R.C. will change the election law. Currently, the members of the Democratic Party get over 30 percent of the majority votes. After the election in May next year, we expect to receive only 10 to 15 percent of the votes because of the new arrangement in voting jurisdictions.

In the recent month, the atmosphere has been a little bit relaxed compared to before. The reason is that they know everyone in the world is very aware of the handover. That's why they have devised so many activities to celebrate the event—in order to influence the people over the world, as well as people in China. Jiang Zemin has to make sure that there will be a very smooth takeover, and that's why the atmosphere in Hong Kong in the past month has been relaxed. He has approved of our June 30th, as well the July 1st, demonstration and meeting. Yesterday the stock index went to a record high. I anticipate this kind of relaxed atmosphere to last for anywhere between one to three years. However, Hong Kong, I expect, will be entering quite a serious moment. There are a few things that they need to do in order to effectively rule Hong Kong. The first thing is that Mr. Jiang Zemin, in the upcoming fifteenth annual meeting, must be very secure in terms of his position. And secondly, in April and May of '98 they will hold an election for new Legco members. Although they have not devised a very democratic way of electing, it's more preferable than the Provisional Legislature. And certainly among the people who work for the government of Hong Kong they will probably re-hire people whom they think are trustworthier. Fourthly, there will be more control over the media. Upon achieving these, then Hong Kong will be more tightly controlled.

So how is Hong Kong going to be in light of all this within the next one to three years? In terms of finance they can achieve an open attitude. However, politically speaking it may be a monopoly system. A lot of people ask, "Will there be the existence of the Communist Party of China in Hong Kong?" In fact, the Communist Party has always existed here in Hong Kong. The first Communist Party member was here in Hong Kong in 1992. Therefore, it's natural for us to expect to find the Communist Party in Hong Kong. However, I expect that in the future it will not be disclosed. I expect that this Communist Party will be an underground organization that controls Hong Kong's politics and the society in general. Similarly in China, the Communist Party has existed for fourty years without being disclosed. The vice president of Xinhua News Agency was not disclosed until after he was searched in the Cultural Revolution, disclosed by the Red Guard. In the future it can spread throughout the government via this underground organization. At the present in China a lot of "democratic members" are also members of the Communist Party, and in Hong Kong in the future we can expect the same thing. Similarly, they will regulate the laws.

So after these things have been achieved, I expect the relaxed atmosphere in Hong Kong to disintegrate. Therefore, we're not optimistic about Hong Kong's future. My view is that if there are no changes made in China, then Hong Kong has to make some changes. Only if China changes itself can Hong Kong remain unchanged. What are we democratic members going to do? The first thing we need to do is to be in next year's legislative election. We have to be involved even though it's not a democratic election. We will then be a minority in the legislature, but we still have to use our voice for Hong Kong's people. The voice of us minorities in the legislature have to work very closely together with the people of Hong Kong in order to achieve stability. The first problem we encounter is the financial problem. The money right now comes from funding from the nineteen members of the Legco Committee. Because those members will no longer be there is why we no longer will have funding from them. The second problem is that we expect to have less and less exposure on the media side, in terms of television and newspaper exposure. Also, on the government side, we expect less cooperation with us.

Based on these problems we have done a few things. In the first part of this year we have raised over seven million Hong Kong dollars, both local and overseas. But this money is only sufficient for the activities carried out within the Democratic Party. It's not enough for the spending needed for the next election. Secondly, we have formed a shadow cabinet organization. That is, although we no longer are in a Legco Committee, the provisional legislative activities can still be monitored. We have to let the people of Hong Kong continue to hear our voices.

We are often asked by our friends overseas, what can we do here? We think that the overseas media is tremendously important. They have importance for Hong Kong's media. This way the news can be transferred from overseas media to the Hong Kong media. Secondly, I think other countries' governments are important. In the Joint Declaration between Britain and China they have requested support from the other countries' governments, and at that time these countries expressed that they were willing to support the Declaration. If China violates any of the Declaration, then the foreign countries are responsible to point out what they have done to violate it. And I would urge you to keep a close eye on the new laws and regulations, and if they are non-democratic, and if they slack from the current election system, then you should be able to criticize it. And in the next April and May election, bring people in to monitor the election process. Also, I would like to urge you to support our friends overseas. People who have migrated to other parts of the world from Hong Kong are very concerned about the future here, but because they have not spent a whole lot of time overseas, their power is quite limited. Therefore, I urge our friends internationally to support our friends overseas so that they can support democracy in Hong Kong. We thank our friends overseas very much for caring about Hong Kong, but we know that we have to rely on ourselves. We have the courage to survive on our own.

Lastly, I have a few more points to make. If there are no improvements in China, then there is no future for Hong Kong. If there is no future for Hong Kong, then there's no hope for China. So we can say that if we do not allow Hong Kong to be democratic, then how do we expect to achieve democracy in China? We can say that the future of Hong Kong is China's biggest test. If the freedom of Hong Kong can be maintained, that means there will be positive changes made to the monopoly communist system of China.

Herschensohn: During the translation process, there were a couple of areas that were a little tough, and because they were important, I just want to clarify them. I think most of you know that Legco is an abbreviation for the Legislative Council, which is commensurate with the United States Congress and will be abolished as of tomorrow at midnight. The Provisional Legislature is the one that was appointed by a selection committee, who were appointed by Beijing, and is illegal by virtue of the Joint Declaration and by the Basic Law. And when he was talking about the changes of election laws, what he means is that next April or May, when there is supposed to be a free election, the rules will undoubtedly be changed—correct me if I am wrong, Wah—that the rules will undoubtedly be changed so that the Democratic Party cannot receive the massive majority that it enjoys; in a sense it will be an extreme gerrymandering, as we would call it in the United States, to ensure that the Democrats do not have that majority. When he talks of the Xinhua News Agency, that's the de facto embassy of the People's Republic of China that's been here. It isn't a real news agency, they call it a news agency. It's massive. The two laws that he was referring to were the Public Order Ordinance and the Securities Ordinance. Prior to Tiananmen Square, the British had on the law books some pretty tough laws but they never enforced them except in 1967 during the Red Guard Cultural Revolution Crisis. Then after the Tiananmen Square massacre those laws were changed so that anyone could demonstrate in any way demonstrators wanted, unless they were interfering with the obvious—the traffic flow and so on. These are being changed back; the Bill of Rights is being changed; those areas are being abolished so that once again demonstrations will not be permitted without a police permit of "no objection," as it's called. Also—just one other point and then we'll get to the questions, but it's important to understand—the P.R.C. is cutting off funding from foreign countries for political parties. That may seem okay to us because of political parties regarding funding in our own country. The problem with that here is that China, under "One Country—Two Systems," is not a foreign country. That means that the Communist Party, and anyone else who opposes the democrats, will be able to get plenty of money from China, whereas the democrats, who would ordinarily get funds from people in free countries including people of the United States, will not be able to. So they've sort of taken care of their own political base while excluding the possibility for the democrats. I think that we touched on the things that may not have been clear through the translation process, so if you have any questions for Wah, please go ahead.

Question: You mentioned how non-Hong Kong entities will not be able to contribute to Hong Kong political parties, but you did not mention Taiwan. Since Taiwan is such an important part of this whole handover because everyone says China's ultimate goal is to have Taiwan become part of China as a whole, what part will Taiwan play in Hong Kong after the handover?

Szeto: There's not a whole lot that Taiwan can do. First of all, there's a movement for Taiwan to become independent, apart from the mother country, therefore, they will not be very concerned about Hong Kong. And also, the power of Taiwan within Hong Kong is completely disintegrated. Their organization in Hong Kong has completely cracked down, divided into separate parts. Some are in favor and some are against Mr. Tung Chee-hwa, so there will not be a whole lot of influence from them in Hong Kong. Also, Taiwan worries that with more influence over Hong Kong, Taiwan will be too inviting to China. Therefore, in reality there's not a whole lot that Taiwan can do.

Question: Do you think that there is enough concern among the people of Hong Kong to seriously resist the infringement of their freedoms?

Szeto: A lot of people say that Hong Kong is politically cold, but I don't feel so. I just feel that there's a very limited amount that Hong Kong can do, because of the limited power of Hong Kong. Over half of the current population, which is 6.4 million Hong Kong people, came to Hong Kong after 1949, and they are aware of how the communists deal with things, and they know that the communists will never change. They know that, at best, if they voice objections, the communists will just ignore them. Therefore, the people know that under communism, they can never change their own fate. Therefore, they are not very enthusiastic about speaking out for democracy and freedom. Secondly, those who can leave have already left, and for those who are more financially secure, they already have foreign passports. And for a lot of businessmen, all they care about is if they make profits, and they're not very concerned about democracy, about freedom. Therefore, that's why you see people on the streets of Hong Kong walking leisurely, without any worries, it seems. The voting percentage of Hong Kong is not high, it's anywhere between 30 and 40 percent. Partly it's because the registration process for the voters is not very sufficient, many people have moved, but the government has never bothered to change their address. Also, for those who do go and vote, they have no right to vote for the chief executive of Hong Kong and they have only the right to vote for over one-third of the Legco members. Because they realize that their votes don't have a huge influence, they are not enthusiastic to vote. Therefore, some people ask the question, in reality are people in Hong Kong concerned about their democratic freedom? And as I've said before, over half of the population in Hong Kong came from China, so they are concerned about democracy and freedom. They are very aware of the past history of China, meaning how they deal with things. Therefore, I can say that they're not unconcerned about their own freedom, but they are very limited in what they can do for themselves. There are people who are willing to stand up and protect the people of Hong Kong, and for those who don't stand up, they are willing to support those democrats who have stood up for them. Therefore, democrats have been shown to be the most popular as a result of the surveys done in Hong Kong. Between 1991 and 1995 the Democratic Party has won the majority in the direct elections. In the past two elections they achieved getting over 65 percent of the votes. You can see that we are having support from the Hong Kong people. That's why some people termed us Hong Kong's future hope.

Herschensohn: One more question, and that's it, if I may, and that's out of respect for Mr. Szeto's time. He has been up for twenty-six hours now, which is really something. The session of Legco ended at something like 8:00 a.m., so let's have one more question if we may, please.

Mrs. Roberta Ahmanson: Mr. Szeto, I understand that in China there has been in the last few years a major crackdown on those who practice the Christian faith. About 10 percent of the Hong Kong people are Christians, and I wonder if you expect the Chinese government to further crackdown in China itself, and what the Christians in Hong Kong can expect for their future.

Szeto: I believe that the Christians in Hong Kong are not the first ones to be suppressed, and if there's a line-up of the suppressed, they'll be pretty well at the back of the line. That's because there are more important things that the government has to deal with. For example, people have asked me if there will be any changes that will be made to the education system, the government workers, the police force. I have to mention an incident about a press conference recently held by five very high ranked police officers, and they declared that they were not willing to work for the S.A.R. government, and requested that the British government allow them to resign within the next two days. They have already made the request of Mr. Chris Patten, but their resignations were rejected by him. Therefore, we can see the type of control that the S.A.R. government will be exerting over the government workers, especially in the police force. Secondly comes the control over the media, and next would probably be the education system. I expect that religion would probably be further to the back of the line. However, we can see that if there's control over the Legislative Council and also over the education system and government workers, we are sure to expect limitations to the religions. Therefore, I hope that for those involved in religious work in Hong Kong, be also concerned about anything not to do with religion. If they keep silent to the lack of democratic freedom, and then if they need the voice of the people of Hong Kong in the future, they will not have it. I quote a common example that Mr. Martin Lee always mentions: In the Nazi government system in Germany, the Nazi's caught the communists, and one

Christian said, "I'm not a communist, therefore I don't care." When the Nazis caught the unionist, he said the same, "I'm not a unionist and I don't care." When the Nazis caught the Jews, he said the same, "I'm not a Jew and I don't care." And when the Nazi's finally caught him, nobody said anything for him. Therefore, I think the Christians here in Hong Kong should learn a lesson from this.

Herschensohn: Next week, July 6th, Szeto Wah is getting an award in Prague from the Czech Republic for freedom. (Applause) I just want to say, as Americans, you are tremendously inspiring both for your courage and your wisdom. It means a lot to us, and we hope we can repay you and repay Hong Kong in some way.

Szeto: I am very sorry, I only speak very little English.

Panelists from the Hong Kong Policy Research Institute

Ada Wong, Dr. Jane Lee, and Wudy Heung
Conference Speakers
June 29, 1997 - 2:00 p.m.

Bruce Herschensohn: All three of our panelists are part of the Hong Kong Policy Research Institute, which, in American terms, we would describe as a think tank. They also have a close association with Tung Chee-hwa, maybe in the same way that Heritage had with President Reagan. And Tung Chee-hwa, as you know, is the new chief executive as of midnight tomorrow.

To my right is Ada Wong, born in Hong Kong. She went to Pomona College, just a couple of miles from The Claremont Institute. She's an elected member of the Urban Council here, which is what the name implies, and has authority over everything from garbage collection to the Cultural Center. It's a big job. She's elected as an Independent, but she was one of the founders of the Liberal Party. The Liberal Party generally is described as pro-business, and a lot of business people within it veer, more than the Democratic Party or the Frontier Party, to some of the statements of the People's Republic of China. Fair or not fair? Not fair probably. That's all right; I'd say more than the Democratic Party and more than Frontier, anyway. She's a very prolific writer; she writes for the *Oriental Daily News* and for the *Oriental Weekly* and for *Apple Daily*. She's certainly done a tremendous amount for her age.

Dr. Jane Lee is the chief executive of the Institute. She was the director of Public Affairs with Burson-Marsteller. Burson-Marsteller, I'm sure you know, is an American public relations firm. I'm very familiar with them because they handle the public affairs of the National Smokers Alliance, so they're okay with me.

The third member of the panel, who will arrive very shortly, is Wudy Heung. He was born in Hong Kong, but he spent sixteen years in the United States. He studied at Georgetown University and is a member of the District of Columbia Bar Association, and a member of the American Bar Association, but I see no reason to hold those three things against him; he's probably a fine man. (Laughter)

Why don't we go first to you, Dr. Lee, if you would?

Dr. Jane Lee: Good afternoon ladies and gentlemen. It is very nice today to have this chance to share with you the experience of the Hong Kong Policy

Research Institute. Today we have three of us here. I think we shall, first of all, each of us, spend about fifteen minutes to give our views, and I shall, first of all explain to you what this institute is about and how a think tank like ours operates in Hong Kong. Ada is going to share with you her experience, because she is the elected member. She will share with you her views about "One country—two systems." Mr. Wudy Heung is a contributor to our research on U.S./Hong Kong relations, and he's going to share his views with you about the importance, from Hong Kong's point of view, of our relations with the United States after July 1.

To start with, about the institute: We started in June 1995, so exactly two years ago. When the Institute started, it was at a time when Britain and China had a lot of disagreements about Hong Kong's political reforms. At that time we felt the atmosphere was actually not very promising in the sense that the Preliminary Working Group, which was the body before they set up the Preparatory Committee, was in general seen by the liberals or many Hong Kong people as a very conservative, pro-China committee, which would prepare for Hong Kong's transition. Perhaps the democrats, Martin Lee, Szeto Wah, saw themselves as being suppressed; the future looked very bad. When our institute started we thought, it is really important for Hong Kong, after July 1, to have a very rational and good atmosphere for Hong Kong.

What do we mean by a rational and good atmosphere? It does not mean that some of the rules and the important elements, which existed before July 1, should be eliminated. So we promoted a concept, in political terms, to maintain all of Hong Kong's views, whether you're pro-China, you are pro-Democrat, you're a liberal, or you're conservative, we have to learn the diverse nature in society. We have very diversified opinions and we think all these views should be preserved. The other thing is about economic diversity. This, of course, is important for Hong Kong after July 1 because we are a free economic system. We are a very competitive city in the world, and so we think the free market is important. We also believe in maintaining the Legco and beginning the "One country—two systems."

Now how do we realize this? We had a membership system. Members are mainly the professionals in all different fields. In general our ages are above thirty or forty, it's not very young, but it's because they are all experienced. We also have members of different political parties, and that is very unusual for Hong Kong. When we started in June 1995, we had just about seventeen members and now we have more than sixty members. At that time we started off with at least about eight or nine of them from the Democrats. Now we have Ada, she has the Liberal Party member background. Then we also have some pro-China individuals. Our Chairman is Mr. Paul Yip, who in general is very well known as a pro-China candidate. So we have very diversified backgrounds, and members with very diverse political opinions.

We are generally seen as a very balanced organization, but, of course, when we started many thought, well you are a separate party in Hong Kong, is this something to do with the united plan of the Communist Party? And, of course, since I started the Institute myself, I know there is no such hidden agenda. In fact, when we started we were somehow facing a lot of skepticism from the pro-China background people. They thought, "Why do you have such close relations with the Democratic Party, who are not acceptable to us?" We operated like this for more than one year, and during that period we tried a lot of efforts to include members from very diverse political backgrounds and political opinions and also professional backgrounds. Then we started field research. At that time we started, first of all, researching Hong Kong and Taiwan's relations, and for that research we made a lot of effort to get participation from China, and from the Taiwan's Affairs Institute and the Academy of Social Sciences. Now the Taiwan government has a very close relationship with the research project. So this is the forum where they communicate and discuss to make thinks work out.

Another project we started was about nationality, and the right to vote for Hong Kong. That was not very easy, although it's resolved now, because there were a lot of controversies about who should be eligible and who should not be eligible for maintaining both foreign passports as well as Chinese nationality.

We also worked on some important issues about the linkage in the Exchange Rate System—the Hong Kong dollar linked with the U.S. dollar. At that time I thought there was a lot of skepticism from the Chinese government, especially in the financial sector; people who were skeptical whether the Hong Kong government had a conspiracy about doing something. Our research suggested to them that if even there is a crisis, assuming even a war between Taiwan and China, what you have to do is to make all efforts to maintain this link.

So we've been working on a lot of things, to try and tell them status quo is important; maintaining the best things of the British-rule administration is important. So it was with this background that we ran for one-half year, and it was when Mr. Tung Chee-hwa started his campaign for the chief executive. He contacted us. About eight months ago we started to get involved in helping him, to warm him up to understand Hong Kong's policy issues because he said, "Well, I've been a businessman for sixty years, I know a lot about economics, but I know very little about politics and public policies, especially social policies." So we started with that. Then in January our Chairman, Mr. Paul Yip, was appointed by him as a special adviser. I think one difficulty for us is that when Mr. Tung appointed Mr. Yip, he announced his appointment together on the same day—actually in the same announcement—with his appointment of the other eleven Executive Council members. He is not part of the system, and so he was given the title of special advisor. And that gave us some difficulties since then when many people started to speculate why is he so special? What is his role in the system? What are his duties? Mr. Tung did not openly explain how special this was.

But I can perhaps explain a little bit on behalf of Mr. Yip, about his job in the past six months. I think it is necessary to have this role, which is not part of the system. He does not receive any salaries or allowance from Mr. Tung, but he is to maintain his business background and to maintain his full-time relationship with the Hong Kong Policy Research Institute. It is important to allow him to be very flexible in helping Mr. Tung on a number of very difficult internal political issues. So in the past few months he has been basically handling the very difficult problems of the Democratic Party in a communications dialogue with the Chinese government. Now he is handling the Taiwan issues, that is Hong Kong's relations with Taiwan; what should be the S.A.R.'s policies toward Taiwan? He's also been making a lot of efforts about arranging the Hong Kong Alliance, which has been holding a lot of demonstrations. And much of the attention has come from overseas and especially from the U.S. media. In the past week he has been handling issues concerning the Democratic Party members, and whether they should enter into the Legislative Council on the morning of July 1, at 1:00 a.m. and then give a speech up there in the balcony. Even on that small issue there were a lot of dialogues, discussions, and communications between the S.A.R. government, Mr. Tung, the legislature, and the Democratic Party. So this is the time when we are in a very sensitive situation.

I could, in general, explain to you about the atmosphere here. I think perhaps from the United States point of view you would focus a lot on how much democracy we have, whether we have freedom of speech and expression and freedom of information flow. From our point of view, we find that we should not neglect the fact that in the past ninety-nine years or so, the so-called pro-China organizations felt suppressed by the colonial government. For example, Mr. Yip graduated from a pro-China leftist secondary school. He was not allowed to join the Civil Service. He was not even allowed to teach in the normal government secondary schools, so finally he decided to go into business. So he has the British to thank. In fact, a lot of the pro-China organizations in these regions have this feeling of being oppressed for ninety-nine years. On the other hand, we must also not neglect the fact that the British government has cultivated people like us, who graduated in Anglo-Saxon schools, having the opportunity to study overseas, and have the orientation to understand the world outside, and we think that this system is good.

So the whole point is how to make this balance work—to make the transition, the emotions calmer, more acceptable to each other. We have been doing confidence studies, and in the last months we have made these studies more frequent, and we've found that in April, May and June, the political confidence in general has been going up. In the past year, for the whole year, the political confidence went up, and the main reason was very much related to a significant improvement in China-Hong Kong relations—that was the major factor in our findings. On that factor alone, the increasing confidence was about 76 percent. So that was very important, I feel. Of course we still have a little of the other things we have to pay attention to; these include concerns about corruption, expression of freedom, whether we can still participate in demonstrations, all these things.

So this, perhaps, gives you a background from our Institute's point of view, and how we analyze the changes in the political atmosphere, and the general issues. I think Ada would be in a much better position to explain, from her point of view, "One country—two systems," and what she expects of it, and how it's going to work. Ada?

Ada Wong: Thank you very much for giving me the opportunity to speak to you and to share with you some of my thoughts on the handover and beyond. As Bruce has introduced me, I spent four years in Claremont, and those were really happy days, and so I am very happy to see all of you because it sort of brings back a lot of happy memories.

I had a phone call from a very good friend in the United States last night. She was very concerned because apparently Dan Rather said something quite exaggerated in the news—he said the P.L.A. troops, with tanks, are now marching in, are now moving in. And this very good friend of mine asked me, "Are you leaving now or what?" You know, now you're in Hong Kong and you feel the carnival mood, everybody's happy, people are taking pictures of all these decorations. I think thirteen years ago, when I first came back to Hong Kong, I would never have believed that this would be actually happening two days before the transition because my parents told me, "Look, we've got to leave in 1995." In those days I had an American permanent residency, I had a green card, and they said, "You've got to emigrate." So we bought a house in Los Angeles, and I thought I'd leave Hong Kong in 1995 and I would never come back here, because this would not be a safe place anymore. But we never left, and my father is now a Selection Committee member, and I am an elected member of the Urban Council, and my brother is actually a member of the Provisional Legislative Council.

In 1982 through 1984 we had a confidence crisis, and in thirteen years this confidence crisis turned into a carnival. So I think this is a great achievement if we look at it from this angle. Then if the handover is smooth, peaceful, and fun, this will probably be something quite unique in history: turning a British colony to China. But friends who have emigrated are still scared because they haven't caught up. So I think people in the West have different perspectives of things. But I am very glad that you are now in Hong Kong because you can see for yourselves whether we have a smooth transition or not, and I hope that when you go back you will be able to tell your friends and families in the United States.

I was elected to the Urban Council in 1995. I am a lawyer by profession. The reason I chose to enter a direct election is because I saw that Hong Kong has changed a lot. In my younger days I would say Hong Kong was still a very colonial and authoritarian society. And I would say that we don't really have a civic education in schools, we are only taught the basics, we are only taught skills, and we are never taught to think who we are and what we are and that we are Chinese. Those things are never mentioned because it will make ruling by the British very difficult. So we just go on, and the most important value is money; how to learn so that we can make money and be prosperous. So Hong Kong was like this. But I came back in 1984 and I saw that a lot had changed. People began to speak up, especially in the last six or seven years. This has really changed a lot. We now have a local culture.

First let me tell you a little bit about what I think is the local culture. We have phone-in programs on the radio—those probably are very popular in the United States as well, but certainly not popular in the P.R.C.—and in the phone-in programs the ordinary person can call the radio and talk to the people, talk to the commentators, and really express their views. In the past we have not been able to do so. In 1991 we started to have real elections. Back in 1985 and 1988 we only started to have indirect elections and functional constituencies, and in 1991 we finally had the elections, and that really changed the culture. We have rallies, we have assemblies, we are able to see films—at the Hong Kong International Film Festival, for example, we are able to see underground Chinese films that were banned in China, but we were able to show these films in Hong Kong. So this is a very unique culture, which has eastern values as well as western values emphasizing freedom of expression.

A question that is most often asked by the West is, "Will the S.A.R. government be able to retain a high degree of autonomy?" Mr. Tung's answer is an emphatic yes. In fact he said at an Asia Society dinner that the leadership of China is very much committed to Hong Kong people governing Hong Kong principles. In the five months since I assumed my responsibility, my confidence level in this respect is has been rising higher as each day goes by. Indeed it is in China's national interest to ensure Hong Kong will continue to be successful in "One country—two systems." A prosperous and successful Hong Kong will contribute to China's modernization. A prosperous and successful Hong Kong will be an excellent example to Taiwan for the country's eventual reunification. I would like to qualify that a bit. I believe that economically we will probably get to do things our own way because the essential thing understood is that we are keeping a capitalist system and a socialist system. But I always ask myself, will this two systems idea extend to the cultures here? The cultures, including the things I just talked to you about: the ability to see films, to call into the radio and speak-out, or to log on to the Internet and get access to all sorts of information.

In Singapore for example—Mr. Tung likes to talk about Singapore a lot—I went to Singapore and I couldn't find a single book in the bookstores criticizing Lee Kwan Yew. But nowadays in the bookstores in Hong Kong we can still find books published in Taiwan. Can we still do that after the first of July, in 48 hours?

What I do in the Urban Council has a lot of relationship to that cultural sphere. We manage all the cultural venues in Hong Kong, we have the biggest arts budget, we spent—I think in U.S. dollars terms—we spent about forty million U.S. dollars last year just on bringing the best cultural events to Hong Kong. That is quite a big budget considering that we are only a small territory of about six million people. A forty million dollar budget just on programs, not on a running cost.

Apart from that, we manage all the public places like the plaza outside the Cultural Center, the Victoria Parkway where all the rallies are held, and we have the power to decide whether public assemblies and rallies, commemorating June 4th for example, can be held. I mean, if Mr. Szeto Wah's association applies to the Urban Council for the use of Victoria Park for a commemorative event or a candlelight vigil on June 4th, the councilors, fifty of us, have the power to say yes or no.

We also have the powers to—well not powers—we also manage the libraries and museums in Hong Kong. In our public libraries we don't really have, yet, a lot of books on the governmental system, we only have novels and magazines and newspapers. The colonial government has been putting some books there but it is not computerized enough. There aren't computer stations there. We also manage all the museums in Hong Kong. We are building a history museum, which will be finished next year. We think that in the history museum, we want to emphasize natural history, i.e., what was Hong Kong like six thousand years ago? So we have the fossils and rocks and things, but I am more interested in how we tell our youngsters what Hong Kong has achieved in the last 150 years.

But whether we have enough room—whether we want to have enough room—in the new museum, is something that will have to be debated. We don't know what will be in there. How will we describe the Opium War? How would we describe the last 150 years of British rule? We don't know yet. These are things that we are in charge of and, in essence, it's like displaying a way of life, a quality of life, and things that we are used to seeing like the freedom of expression, et cetera.

From the first of July the Urban Council will also become provisional. This is something that has not been reported by the international newspapers. We will be appointed, so I won't be able to call myself elected. I have another thirty-six hours and then I'm an appointed member. I have been appointed by Mr. Tung, together with Mr. Szeto Wah, whom you met this morning. He's a colleague of mine, also in the Urban Council, with forty-eight others in the Council.

So what will we do next year? Next year we will still have the International Festival but will we allow Chinese underground films to participate in the Festival? Will we still invite them or will we have to only show Chinese produced films in this Festival? This Festival will lose its standing internationally if we do so, because the American film critics are coming to Hong Kong because they believe that at the International Film Festival we can see films from Taiwan, from the P.R.C., and from Hong Kong. It's a window for Chinese films. Will the new Urban Council, with all the appointed members, decide to change what we put in the libraries and what we put in the museums and what we put on the stages of all our cultural venues? I certainly hope not. I hope the cultural life we have been experiencing will not change, but this is something we have to speak-out for and to really fight for.

Maybe I should just say one or two words about elections, since I am an elected member. I think elections have to be fair and open in Hong Kong, and I am confident that there will also be fair and open elections in 1998 and 1999. But you may not realize that there are a lot of constitutional limitations in the elections. We are getting votes without that much meaning because the political parties in Hong Kong cannot form the government, like in the West. We will always be the opposition, we will always take the role of the monitoring body. When a councilor moves a debate in the Council, the government does not have to follow, the government can turn a blind eye and just ignore what the councilors have just said.

The second limitation, I think, is because the government here is pro-active, is non-interfering. It makes a pro-business political party very difficult to survive because you are seen as endorsing the government all the time, you're not opposing the government all the time. The Democratic Party is more labor oriented or socially oriented, welfare oriented. They just passed a bill in Legco, putting a ceiling on the increase of rent for all publicly subsidized housing in Hong Kong. They put a ceiling on the increase, and this is something—free lunches and welfare, this is something that they always stand for, and that is why, apart from the political stance, they always get the attention of the masses. As a founder of the Liberal Party, we realized that, and we thought that by giving people an alternative, maybe the people will opt for a pro-business party, a bit like the Republican Party in the United States. But since forming the party—I have left the party already—the party is now going nowhere because the party is saying yes to government decisions all the time. Why do you want to vote for a politician who says yes to government all the time? So the Liberal Party is really having a difficulty time. Because we cannot form the government, we're elected with no responsibility, but with a lot to say—so everything is up in the air.

So these are some of the constitutional limitations. I think the year 2007 is the year to watch for. The year 2007, according to the Basic Law, is the year when we decide whether we have more democracy, universal suffrage, for the election of the chief executive. At the moment, as you know, the chief executive, Mr. Tung Chee-hwa, has been elected by a group of 400. Whether we can do so by popular vote in ten years time is something that I would like to see. If we have a chief executive who is democratically elected, then I think the whole picture of elections will change.

I think I've said too much, although I want to say a bit about Shanghai — maybe I just could do that quickly. Hong Kong will change in the next years, and Shanghai is already changing. So when Hong Kong is part of China, will Hong Kong still get the competitive edge? Shanghai is already doing a lot to catch up. It has now got a fairly good infrastructure, it has got all the roads, and even the mobile phones are working. The people are very hard working. They are building a new opera house and they are getting this French architect to build the new opera house, which will be, I think, the best opera house in Asia. Shanghai has cultural ambitions. We have competition from other cities in China, but I think Shanghai has one thing which means they will never be able to catch up with Hong Kong—they don't really have autonomous decision making power; everything will still be controlled by the central government.

So the key to the future of Hong Kong is how autonomous can we be? Not only economically but culturally, the way of life, the way we do things. In the future, in civic education in schools, the children will be singing the national anthem every day, according to Mr. Tung, and they will be raising the national flag just like in America. Apart from these things, in civic education will we teach our kids what is meant by the rule of law? What is meant by human rights? And what is meant by all the personal freedoms and responsibilities as a citizen of Hong Kong and Hong Kong S.A.R.? These are the challenges ahead.

I think I'll just stop here and hand this on to Wudy. Thank you.

Wudy Heung: Good afternoon. My name is Wudy Heung. I was born some forty-six, forty-seven years ago in Hong Kong, and at that time my name was Heung Chuk-wu, so Wudy is really a nickname that I adopted because Wu is one of my given names and I'm Dee's brother. So at home I was called Wu-dee. So I'm Wudy now. After high school here in Hong Kong, I went to Taiwan to study law. I was twenty then. After one year I went to the United States and I finished my undergraduate and graduate studies and received a law degree. So I'm a U.S. attorney at law. Same profession but different jurisdiction. Then I became a citizen of the United States and I came back to Hong Kong in 1986. Since then I have been spending about 60 to 70 percent of my time in China, in and out, and working basically with clients on matters related to China.

So with that background I'm sure that it's not difficult for you to appreciate my confusion of mind, my state of confusion because in a couple days Hong Kong will be Chinese, a Chinese territory. But what am I? I'm an American citizen, I was born in Hong Kong, spent half of my time in the United States, and then in the last ten years or so I spent 70 percent of my time in China. Maybe this state of confusion is why the Policy Research Institute asked if perhaps I could focus on Hong Kong/U.S. relations. Then I started to think, what does Hong Kong/U.S. relations mean? Because in a few hours the British will be retreating, we will no longer have the British government here. However, the American interest must still be here. The Americans have been the largest investor in Hong Kong. Maybe that has been changing in recent days, because a lot of Chinese money is pouring into Hong Kong. And the British have been retreating. I think when I came back in 1986 there were already reports saying that there were more American passport holders in Hong Kong than British passport holders.

So what does it mean to all these Americans and to all these American interests, and what does it mean for the future of Hong Kong? We really do feel that with the British retreating—and then you look around—who is there to balance, if there is such a thing, to balance the influence of Beijing? Who's strong enough? Is it Tokyo? No, I don't think that the Japanese would ever come out against China. Would it be Taiwan? No, I think they're too small. Well, do you think the European community? Probably not, because there is a history of their sort of independent dealing with China, and China has been very skillful in dealing with them one by one. So it's very easy to see that after 1997 the American role most likely, almost certainly, will increase, because there will really be a vacuum here, and in my opinion, whether the U.S. government likes it or not, they will be sucked into it. They will be the only existing balancing influence to Beijing.

Is that bad or is it good? Right now you have all kinds of philosophies, all kinds of thoughts, and schools talking about how to deal with China in the next two or three or four decades from the American point of view. With China growing very rapidly with unprecedented economic growth, still with the memory of Tiananmen Square, it's very complex, it's very difficult to see a very clear path to take. That's why I thought that although I am confused I think this is a very healthy confusion. I think it's also a very healthy confusion between the United States and China because this means that they really need to try to understand each other better, and to find a path. What does that mean to Hong Kong? What does it mean to this little ant under U.S./China relations? If those relations fall, we'll be crushed. If it doesn't fall, we're happy. Or is there something better that we can do? That is really the most fundamental question for the Institute, for the Hong Kong/U.S. relations focus.

We feel that with Hong Kong changing sovereignty, with China coming in, we have a choice of sitting back, taking what is given to us, or we may have to manage the relationship. What does it mean by "manage the relationship?" Within Hong Kong/U.S. relations you have this broader U.S./China relations and you have this side issue of Beijing/Taipei relations and Taiwan/U.S. relations. So it is not a very clear situation. Management of U.S./China relations, if it is done well, will serve the purpose of Hong Kong. Hong Kong has been dealt with as somewhat outside and different from all of China. When we say managing, what is our objective? Our objective really is communications, because we really appreciate all of you who are here today to witness this handover transition of sovereignty. But unfortunately there are millions of Americans sitting at home just watching television and listening to Dan Rather. We don't say that he's right or wrong. My family lives in the United States, so I go back to the United States on the average of about twice a month, and I can see—I can read in the newspaper the reports and so on, and I can compare them with what I know here. You can say that they're all right, all the facts are correct, but then the picture painted is really far from the reality.

One example: some months ago when forty-seven of the P.L.A., the Peoples Liberation Army, came into Hong Kong—these are some of the advanced personnel for the arrangement—and I remember reading in the newspaper that the P.L.A. are arriving in Hong Kong, and that it intensified the jittery feeling of the Hong Kong people, that it reminds people of June 4th. And it said that during this time of press self-censorship, and during this time of further limitation of democracy, this makes the Hong Kong people even more worried and more concerned about July the 1st. If you look at all that—every single fact is correct. People are concerned of course; people remember June 4th. The P.L.A. representatives are coming, yes they are coming in, but the whole picture that's painted to people is very negative, whereas in Hong Kong I doubt if too many people even knew that they were coming in. They were just really coming in and doing a lot of preparation for the transition.

So we are hoping that maybe through communications, we can present a more comprehensive picture. I mean, obviously, we cannot make a decision for people, and we cannot put things in people's minds, but we can try to relay the facts and relate parts of the facts that are not very clearly related, and that the press did not have interest in relating. We feel that through communication, through understanding, we hope that we will come to a point where we have a very healthy concern of the international community—a concern that is based on facts and understanding, and we hope, some compassion.

When people talk about Hong Kong, when they think about Hong Kong, when they discuss Hong Kong, perhaps they will have a little bit more understanding of our feelings, the feelings of the people who actually live in Hong Kong. And in that case, the understanding would be more sympathetic and more positive for the future of Hong Kong.

We know that our concern will start actually from the day after tomorrow. We understand that there will be a lot of work to be done, and the focus of the Hong Kong/U.S. relations group will not be on trying to lobby or trying to change people's perception. Let's try to forget people's perception, and hope through communications we can have a healthy concern for Hong Kong from the international community.

And again I'd like to thank you for your interest in Hong Kong, the fact that you are here today, and we will be happy to answer any questions you might have.

Question: I'd like to ask a question about Taiwan. As I understand the situation, Taiwan now has a freely elected government, and as I look at politicians once they're in power they really don't like to give up power. What would cause the Taiwanese politicians to change their mind and come under the authority of the P.R.C.?

Mr. Heung: Okay, again some confusion. I think, from our point of view, we do not believe that we are trying to, and I don't think it's possible to try to change the mind of the rulers—let's say, the leaders of Taiwan. But my feeling is that there are a lot of conditions that are surrounding what you alluded to, which is re-unification. I think that your experience of Hong Kong does shed a little bit of light on that relationship. For a long time people—including people in Hong Kong—tend to look at this transition as something negative, a lot of concern, a lot of reservation, a lot of doubts and so on and so forth. But as time progressed and as the relationship—I mean the commercial relationship, the political relationship—interactions between Hong Kong and the United States increased, and with China increased, then this concern has basically or gradually subsided.

I remember in 1972 at the time of Nixon's trip to China, I was in Washington, D.C. At that time there were a lot of questions about exactly what was going to happen to Taiwan, how the United States would deal with Taiwan, and how Taiwan would deal with this situation. And behold, in the mid '80s suddenly you found Taiwanese all over China and you found counters almost everywhere saying "Special Counter for Taiwanese Compatriots," and so on and so forth. We, who are non-Taiwanese, almost become resentful of the fact that they were so pro-Taiwanese. The fact is that Taiwanese investment and Taiwanese business in China has been very substantial. I think it would not be a situation of twisting arms and saying you have to come and become part of China but, perhaps, as history progresses, there will be some mutual benefits that can be gained from a closer tie or closer relationship. That would be a more constructive outcome.

Question: Next fall there will be a party conference in Beijing, a Communist Party Congress, and the outcome and the decisions made and who ascends and who declines will undoubtedly have consequences for what happens here in Hong Kong. So my question is, do you have any means to formally or informally influence government decisions in Beijing?

Dr. Lee: Well, I think we have a number of channels to influence decisions in Beijing. In the past twelve years we've had so many delegations from Hong Kong to Beijing, different levels of leaders, from the very top to the intermediate and lower levels. I think Hong Kong has tremendous impact on the decisions of Beijing. First, of course, is the tremendous economic importance of Hong Kong business in China and vice versa. We now have more than 1,800 businesses from China in Hong Kong, so I think from an economic point of view we have a tremendous impact. From a political point of view, Hong Kong must stand upwardly, and it will be important for China's relations with Taiwan in the long run, and even in the near future. The "One country—two systems" achievement for Hong Kong is the invention of Mr. Deng Xiaoping. What is the next most important issue to China? That is Taiwan's relations. So the success of "One country—two systems" in Hong Kong is obviously an important showcase. The success of maintaining this relationship is important. So from this political/economic point of view, I think Hong Kong's influence on Beijing's position is tremendous.

Question: About the language difference between the Mandarin and Cantonese: Do you foresee any requirement for using Mandarin here in Hong Kong? How might that adaptation take place?

Dr. Lee: My feeling is that we've been starting since 1985, late '86. I think we have improved a lot.

Ms. Wong: I think this is part of two systems. We just have to be tri-lingual. Most people in Hong Kong are bilingual, Cantonese and English. And now we have a nine-year free education. We just have to try to be tri-lingual. More and more people are, and I don't think that will be a problem. On the mainland they use a simplified form of characters now but we still use the original version of the characters. We use the most complicated version. We have to learn the simplified characters. But basically the characters are the same.

Question: Since you are concerned about the relationships with the United States and the People's Republic of China, certainly one thing that you must convey is that what happened over the past couple of years where transshipments of arms from China and North Korea came through Hong Kong, and were only discovered because of the Crown Colony's diligence. Now the administrators of the Crown Colony will not be administrating the situation. That could have an enormous effect on American policy, and it would be most dangerous if the People's Republic of China was to transship arms into the Middle East. It could threaten Israel, and America's relationship with Israel is implacable, cannot be estranged, and it could cause mischief in the Middle East generally. Such a repeat of that would create profound problems in the United States.

Mr. Heung: If that is the case, I certainly agree. I don't know what else I can say because, you know, it's a concern of the United States, it is a concern of the international community, it would be an issue that we certainly should be working on. Yes, I agree.

Question: I have a question for Jane Lee about the Policy Research Institute's support of free market policies. Can you tell me a little bit about whether your Institute has a position on Tung Chee-hwa's views of industrial policies—his support of preferences for high technology industries here in the future? Have you or anyone you know of, advised him on this?

Dr. Lee: Well, in general I think we believe Mr. Tung is quite determined to maintain a free market system in Hong Kong. By "free market" we are not saying the government should not have proactive policies on certain areas of economic development. In fact, in the past we did not have a very free and proactive industrial policy, and the existing Hong Kong government strongly argued for the case of supply and demand. But I personally don't have special views from Mr. Tung on how he looks at industrial policies. Maybe I could explain briefly to you about the research we've been working on. Just last month we launched a free market index research. This free market study—this is quite interesting—came from an American organization called C.I.P.E. and I think you possibly know them, the Center for International Private Enterprise. We had much discussions with members there, and the original idea was to work on a study question which would monitor Hong Kong's development of economic freedom before and after 1997. Then I developed an idea to make it become an index that would trace Hong Kong's maintenance of the free market index before and after July 1. That will be a longitudinal study. This will be a little bit similar to that of the Heritage indexing of economic freedom, but the difference is that they are working on country comparisons and we are working just on Hong Kong internally.

Ms. Wong: Henry Tang, who is a Liberal Party member and is a member of his 11 member cabinet, is chairing a group and studying whether there should be an industrial policy—not to intervene, but to see whether the government can do more to facilitate—whether the infrastructure is already sufficient for Hong Kong's industry to change from a manufacturing base to a high tech and a more sophisticated sort of value-added industry. This, I think will be one of the key things for the S.A.R. government to look at, because the manufacturing based industries have been shifted to southern China. So do we have an industrial future or not? Henry Tang and his group are looking into that.

Question: Szeto Wah said today an important thing, I thought. He mentioned that Hong Kong would like one China, except he'd be happier if the government would change in China. But I see that the infrastructure in China is filling very rapidly and I see American companies moving in very rapidly. General Motors has built a factory there to build cars, Boeing is building airplanes, and McDonald Douglas is also building airplanes. China's new speed trains are being built now, and I guess the new train goes from Hong Kong to Shanghai and from Hong Kong to Beijing, and that's a new bullet train. I also notice the building of a big port, which is expanding the northern end China. And it seems as though China is building their infrastructure and becoming more democratic within, and that is contrary to what I am reading in the papers. 15,000 students come from China to the United States, learning each year, and they return back to China, which means these students carry their own views. Will all that change the government in China eventually?

Mr. Heung: I believe so, because you look back to the late '70s, the early '80s when we were talking about the transition of sovereignty back to China. People were thinking about how Hong Kong is going to be swallowed up by this big brother. Then very soon and very quickly people began to see that it may be the other way around, because as you come down from Beijing you see the influence of Hong Kong, stronger and stronger. So yes, I agree. I think, for instance, we were asked earlier how we survive this change in government, and if we have different leaders in China then will there be a different orientation, a different policy toward Hong Kong? I guess the answer to that is that we don't know what the future holds, but if you look back, we have survived Mao Tse-tung, we have survived Deng Xiaoping, we have survived many, many changes inside China. We have survived the Cultural Revolution and so on and so forth. So that's why people say Hong Kong has a very adaptable population, adaptable in terms of politics and adaptable in terms of business and economics. I think that—back to the question that was asked—with all these people studying in the United States coming back and with all the changes going on—the economic changes—can China say that they can only allow economic change, economic evolution but no political evolution? I don't think I could believe that for one moment.

If you look at China, I think it's one of the greatest fallacies to believe that China has not gone through political changes. They might not advertise it, they might not publicize it, but if you look at China today, if you look at the political content of the common person, ten years ago, fifteen years ago, they may have spent 70 percent of their time going to political meetings, committees, meetings of neighbors, and they were working in factories. Today you probably hear them criticizing the communist government, criticizing their leaders. It's relatively a very much more open society from ten, fifteen years ago. This whole evolution is going on.

And if you look at Taiwan, and look at Korea—if you look at the current leadership of those two places, the majority of them—for instance, in Taiwan, almost a hundred percent of them have some degree from the United States, either a Master's Degree or a Ph.D. from some college or university of the United States. The point is that the evolution will go on, the impact will be there. However, it is very important to understand that China is different than the others. China comes from a very different background. It is a much bigger country, it has a much longer culture, a very different system. That's why it is so important to facilitate communications, because how can you draw the line on democracy? You have or don't have democracy. You're either pregnant or not pregnant. Where do you draw the line? When are you democratic and when are you not democratic? In this whole course of evolution, how do you judge it? If you look at where China was fifteen years ago, from before the Reform Policy forward, you would say that that is the starting point of economic growth, and it is a tremendous growth experience. But if you compare China today with the Western democratic systems, there may be still a distance. So I think it's important for us to keep this balance in mind.

Herschensohn: I want to thank you very much. Before doing that, Dr. Lee, I just want to mention one thing, not in terms of a question, but just as an explanation. You used the term pro-China throughout your presentation—those who are pro-China, those who are not. I want you to know that everyone in this audience and everyone I know in the United States is pro-China; there's no problem with that. The problem is the government of the People's Republic of China. There is an important distinction to be made. So I just want you to know as far as the United States are concerned, we are very pro-China. I thank you so much for expressing your views, they're very important to us. Thank you.

Martin Lee Chu-ming

Conference Speaker
June 29, 1997 - 7:00 p.m.

Larry Arnn: I will introduce very briefly the leader of the Democratic Party, who won 85 percent of the vote...

Martin Lee: 65. (Laughter)

Arnn: With your district, 85.

Lee: With our colleagues, then 85.

Arnn: With his colleagues, he won 85 percent of the most broad-based election ever held in Hong Kong. I have known this man—I shook his hand in his office for the first time in 1984, and there is agreement upon the most profound point between this man and the people who built our country. He believes that there is no force on earth more authoritative than a popular vote by equal souls in a popular government. Among all the powers here in Hong Kong, this is the man, more than anyone else, who represents the people who live here. Martin Lee.

Martin Lee: Hi, folks. Why are there so many Chinese people in Hong Kong? Of course there are some who have been here for generations, but the great majority are here because many years ago they, or their parents, made a conscious decision to leave our Motherland and come into a British colony, knowing that there would be some degree of unfair treatment of the Chinese by the British here. They still chose Hong Kong because that is the nearest place to China which is free. Many swam to Hong Kong through shark infested waters, many not making it the first time. Many, of course, came by land, and again, it's even more difficult because the border was and is guarded. There are barbed wires, and so on.

Why did they come here? Freedom. Freedom is everything. If you look at this pearl of the Orient, freedom is the luster. There is no doubt about that. If we lose the freedom, the pearl loses its luster. It's a simple message, a simple image, but this is what Hong Kong is all about. The prosperity is the effect of that freedom. So when people say we want to be prosperous, but you can take away some of our freedoms, people don't know what they are talking about. They believe that Singapore would be a lovely example. A couple of weeks ago, a lady Parliamentarian came to my office and she sat down and she said, "Mr. Lee, help me. I'm totally confused. Yesterday I had a meeting with a group of journalists from Hong Kong, and they all told me how frightened they were about the future, saying that Hong Kong would be like Singapore." This morning, she said, "I saw a group of business people who told me how very confident they are about Hong Kong because Hong Kong will be like Singapore." So she said, "I'm totally confused." It would normally take me twenty minutes to explain the differences between Hong Kong and Singapore, but now, thanks to the Singapore government, it is easier.

Three weeks ago there was a very important conference in Singapore. Every head of every school was invited to attend, for five days. The theme was how to teach students to think creatively. At the end of the conference the minister of education announced that in Singapore every student will be given a computer, paid for by the state. That must be the first in the world. But does a computer make a student think creatively? If the senior minister, Mr. Lee Kwan Yew, who is in town, would ask for a piece of advice from me, instead of giving me gratuitous advice all the time, I would have told him, "Senior Minister, a computer for every student is a very good idea, but if you really want your students to think creatively, let them be free." Even if the next Singapore government would wake up to this truism, even if it were to bring back freedom to Singapore, I'm afraid it's going to take them more than one generation for the people really to think freely again. But is Hong Kong going down that Singapore route? Is that what the leaders of China want? Is that what our business leaders want, so that their employees will no longer be courageous? If so, Hong Kong will be finished.

Let me tell you a little story: There is a goose which likes to fly in the morning, which likes to squawk in the afternoon, and in the evening when the sun is setting, the goose feels good and the goose lays an egg, a golden egg. Now, a master has taken over, and the master doesn't like the flying about or the terrible noises made by the goose, so the master says to the goose, "You just shut up and sit there." And to assure that the goose would be obedient, the master put a noose around the neck of the goose. The master then says to the goose, "Oh, by the way, let's have that egg in the morning. I don't want to wait." Now how long do you think those eggs would remain golden? How can Hong Kong be as vibrant as before and prosperous as before if the goose is no longer free?

I'm sure you all know some Chinese people in your town, wherever it is. I'm sure you will be impressed by the Chinese students studying in the same schools as your children. Have you ever thought about this, that the Chinese people only attain their maximum potentials after they've left China? Why? There are many, many talented people in China, but they're not free. And if they're not free, how do you expect them to be fully developed? The potential is never fully developed when the person is not free. So we are all concerned about freedom as we are thirty-nine hours away from a changeover of sovereignty. And so everybody—unless they are dishonest—everybody in Hong Kong will tell you that freedom is the most important thing. Of course. They, therefore, will tell you that the rule of law is a very important thing, because without the rule of law, freedoms will not be protected.

Yet somehow they think that democracy is not an important element in that equation because we never had democracy under the British. This is true. But that is to overlook a very important fact, which is the Hong Kong government is merely an extension of the British government, which is democratically elected, eight thousand miles away in Britain. And the British Parliament is likewise democratically elected. So if things are to go wrong in Hong Kong, questions are bound to asked in the British Parliament. For example, what if people were locked up without a trial in Hong Kong? In theory, it might possibly bring down the British government. So our rule of law, our freedoms, are preserved by a democratically constituted British Parliament and government. If a new sovereign, China, also had democracy, and if the Chinese government and the Chinese Parliament were similarly elected, democratically, by the people of China, then I agree, we need not a democracy. So then, Hong Kong would be changed from a free British colony into an equally free Chinese colony.

But we know China is not democratic. So we must make sure that our leaders in Hong Kong, in our legislatures, will find it not only desirable but necessary to defend the people of Hong Kong, to defend the system, in particular our people's freedom. How is it possible? The rule of law requires good laws, laws which protect human rights and not laws which take away human rights. Before Hitler, the German judges did a good job in protecting the freedoms of the people, by and large, but once Hitler took over, because he controlled the Bundestag, he had the laws changed overnight, and suddenly the judges—the same judges—found that they had become instruments of injustice. Some refused to carry out those Draconian laws and they were duly executed. Others followed and applied those laws. I'm not saying that a modern day Chinese Communist is as wicked as a Nazi German during the Second World War, but the point is the same. If the laws are bad, the judges can't help. And what is the guarantee that a legislature would pass good laws to protect our freedoms and not bad laws which take them away? Accountability through a democratic system of government. As simple as that. Yet, why are there so many people in Hong Kong who don't seem to agree with that? There are some who regularly curse me when they are at home, and they are a little more polite when they are in public, still trying to run me down, and yet when they are prosecuted, when they get in trouble with the law, they come to me, willing to pay pretty high fees. Why? Some pretend that, "Yeah, we are only concerned with economic freedom. We're in business. Business is what we know, business is what we care for, nothing else. What does it matter if some people were to be stopped from having public demonstrations? Some of them will lose some of their freedoms, but not me. I'm going to have full economic freedom under the Chinese Communist rule. So why are these people so annoyed about just losing some freedom, the right to a public demonstration? It doesn't hurt me if they lose some of their rights, so long as I keep my economic rights intact."

I remember last year the former British Ambassador to China, Sir Robin McClaren, said in Hong Kong, after his retirement, that Hong Kong people should wake up and be prepared to lose 3 percent of their freedom, in order to preserve the other 97 percent. I asked myself, "Why did he use that logic?" In other words, must you lose something to preserve the rest? Then logically, you have to be prepared to lose 50 percent of your freedom in order to keep the other 50 percent. Or, indeed, to lose 97 percent of your freedom to keep 3 percent. And when I repeated this message at a luncheon meeting the following day, there was this British businessman who said—I would like to censor a little word which I wouldn't normally use but since he said it—he said, "Balls! This guy has balls!" They constitute 3 percent of my body weight and I'm not going to sacrifice them for anything. (Laughter)

It doesn't work out like that with many, because these business people, I think they're just naive. It's wishful thinking when they think that they will be left alone to do business freely. The Hong Kong government has kept twenty files of Hong Kong business people who are in prison in China, who were literally minding their own business. They are business people who were doing business in China, but, of course, something went wrong with the contract, the other party was wrong, and so they would not pay, and the Chinese party of course would pay a bribe, and the Hong Kong parties would be arrested and kept in prison until the amount that's demanded of them was paid. Most people in this sort of predicament would simply tell their wife or friends in Hong Kong to come up with the money and obtain their release, and then they would quietly leave to Hong Kong. But these twenty people could not raise the money. Therefore, the family members reported it to the Hong Kong government. This must be the tip of the iceberg because most people would not bother to report it to the Hong Kong government. So there were these twenty files. Now don't you know the Hong Kong business people who are still doing business here and sometimes in China know about that? Of course they know about that. But they say, "Look, these people go to China to do business, but they don't have clout, that's why. I have clout, so it won't happen to me." Is that true?

Recently Lee Kai-shing, one of the richest men in Hong Kong, one of the richest men in the world, was very angry and he said, "In China there is no rule of law." People wonder what happened to him. He had this big project in Beijing. His partner is a very important man now in Hong Kong, none other than Mr. Tung Chee-hwa. At that time Mr. Tung was just another tycoon. So Mr. Tung and Mr. Lee Kai-shing had a joint venture business in redeveloping a huge site, including one of the very largest McDonald's hamburgers. You might have read about it. McDonald's didn't want to be evicted. Something went wrong, because apparently there were some Chinese leaders who didn't like that scheme, and Mr. Lee Kai-shing was angry about it, and he said, "Well, there's no rule of law in China, and it makes it very difficult to do business there." Lee Kai-shing was in trouble.

There is one guy much more unfortunate than Lee Kai-shing: his name is James Peng. He was also originally from China, and came down to Hong Kong. Then, like so many Hong Kong people, he went to Australia, got himself citizenship there, then came back to Hong Kong, then went back to China to do business, armed with an Australian passport. He found a partner in China, with a lot of clout indeed: Deng Xiaoping's own niece. The company was doing well, flowing with champagne you may say, which happens to be the name of the company. Until one day the champagne turned sour. There was a partnership dispute. It was taken to the courts by his partner, who got judgment against him in a Chinese court. James Peng appealed and he won. In China there is one appeal, only one. So ultimately he won. One day he went to Macau, which is not far away from here—the Portuguese territory. At midnight he was abducted by the Macau police while they were staying in the Mandarin Hotel. He was taken across the border to China, where he was kept in custody upon the complaint of this partner and niece of Deng Xiaoping. The investigating authorities couldn't find any evidence against him, but because of the clout of the accuser, they would not release him. What they did was change the law on Mr. James Peng because of the clout of the niece. So he was convicted of an offense which wasn't even there when he did whatever he did, and he was given eighteen years in prison.

Because he was an Australian citizen, the Australian government took the matter on his behalf more than 130 times to the Chinese government, including the highest level, the prime minister's level. Recently I read that one of the Chinese leaders intervened on his behalf, and at some stage, I was told, he was actually released. But because he refused to sign a confession statement, because he refused to admit in writing that he had been wrong, he's still kept in custody in China.

So businessmen with clout, even less clout, may not be prosecuted. Economic freedom is important, but what good is it to a man or to a woman—if I may quote the Bible—"if you gained a whole world and suffer the loss of your freedom?"

When you look ahead, our future will only be bright like the pearl if the luster of freedom remains. Thank you, I'll take questions now.

Question: Thank you very much. I know you're incredibly busy, and your presence here is a great honor for us. I'm wondering about the legal system. Is it going from the English language, to Chinese? And what will be the impact of that—if that's the case—on the rule of law in Hong Kong?

Lee: The common law will continue in Hong Kong, that's agreed. Of course English is the language of the common law so it doesn't really make much sense to introduce Chinese as a compulsory language of the courts. It just can't be done. When lawyers cite cases to the court there's no point for him to cite it in Chinese, which means opening a book in English and then try to make a quick interpretation of it, when the judge also reads English. The lawyers and the judges here know that there is a limit as to how much Chinese can be used in courts. When it comes to the law, it just cannot be done. Certainly not yet. So I'm not worried about that. But when it comes to the legal system, there are other worries. Under the Joint Declaration and the Basic Law, which is our Constitution, we were promised that the Hong Kong Special Administrative Region shall have the final right of adjudication, which is good news. And both documents provide that our Court of Final Appeal shall be established in Hong Kong and not in Beijing. But when they drafted the Basic Law, our Constitution, it provides in there, in Article 158, that the highest court of the land, the Court of Final Appeal, may not interpret all the key Articles of the Basic Law, or Constitution. For example, both Articles govern the relationship between the central and local governments—these are the most important Articles of course—and the Court of Final Appeals may not interpret them. They must leave that question of interpretation to China, with the standing committee of the National People's Congress. The equivalent is that a U.S. Supreme Court will not be allowed to interpret the U.S. Constitution, but the government will do it instead. That's a great weakness. In other words, on the one hand they gave us final right of adjudication, on the other hand they took back a big chunk of it.

Question: Mr. Lee, thank you sir, it's good to see you again. I was here in October of '95. My question is has your perception of the takeover by China changed in the last year and a half since I was here?

Mr. Lee: In the past I raised my fears about the future of Hong Kong. Today, those fears have actually come true. I couldn't be sure at the time that they would actually replace our elected legislature with an appointed one. I was hoping they would not do such a thing, although they had already said so. The Joint Declaration is very clear about that, it says our legislature shall be constituted by elections. The Basic Law, the Constitution, makes it even plainer: there will be sixty seats, twenty will come from democratic elections, thirty will come from functional constituencies, the doctors will elect a doctor, the lawyers will elect a lawyer, the business people will elect many business people and so on, and the remaining ten seats will come from an election committee. Now what do we find? We have a legislature, called a Provisional Legislature, that's all appointed by Beijing using a body called a Selection Committee consisting of 400 people from Hong Kong with all of them chosen carefully by Beijing. So that—the way this legislature was formed—goes against there own Basic Law. The twenty democratically elected members are not there, the thirty functional seats are not there, the ten, okay, if we accept the Selection Committee of 400 to qualify as an Election Committee, they would only be able to elect ten, but why sixty? So that is the problem.

Beijing, using the same body, selected Mr. Tung, but did they really select him or did China already select him for them? China already controls the Executive through their own man, Tung Chee-hwa. China controls the legislature. China controls the judiciary by controlling the most important rights of interpretation of our Constitution. China will be controlling the education side very easily. We have eight universities, and the heads of seven of them are already appointed by China. The press—there's a lot of self-censorship already, and the most popular television station, the Cantonese channel, has this policy in the news department: "Hong Kong people were given too much bad news," they said, "and we should give them more good news." The things I warned people of one and a half years back have now materialized. You know, I wish my prophecies had not come true.

Question: Obviously you've been an inspiration to the people of Hong Kong, and I think free men and women are deeply grateful. I was wondering, in that connection, your view of the actions taken by the United States and Great Britain in the past several days and weeks with regard to the surrender of Hong Kong. I recall that Emily Lau was quoted by our general consul, Mr. Boucher, as having used the terms "disgusting and contemptible" with regard to the presence of the consul generals of those countries at the swearing in of the Provisional Parliament. I was just curious if you could tell us how you've observed those events unfolding?

Mr. Lee: Of course I'm a very polite person. Madeline Albright made the decision of not giving legitimacy to this Provisional Legislature because its establishment was clearly contrary to the Joint Declaration and the Basic Law. She would not recognize this legislature but, rather, the elected legislature. And soon thereafter the new British prime minister, Tony Blair, made a similar decision with regard to himself and his Foreign Secretary Robin Cook. So these were very, very clear messages that they would not deal with this Provisional Legislature. A few days back there was this news item that the State Department of your country would be sending your consul general in Hong Kong and others to attend that swearing-in ceremony. The British government also made a similar decision. The elected ministers would not come we are told, the prime minister and the foreign secretary, but other members of the British government would come. So what sort of message do we now have? The right hand boycotts this Provisional Legislature, the left hand does not. So what message is this to the Chinese government? They certainly will think there's a change of mind. I've said repeatedly it doesn't matter how low your government sets its bottom line on China, stick to it, otherwise people won't take you seriously.

Question: Is there any prospect that the elections in the spring of '98 can be free and fair?

Mr. Lee: No. Spring would include May I suppose, June would be the starting of summer. We were told that we will be expecting elections in either May or June, within the year from the 3rd of July, this week. I'm sure you have heard, "Oh, don't worry, there will be elections soon, within the year." And you are supposed to rejoice over this. I'm supposed to say, "Bravo!" to that. What would happen, Bruce, if I were to come into your house without your consent and throw you out and lock you out, and you report it to the police, and the police come to interview me, and then they go back to you and say, "Sir, we have wonderful news! We just talked with Mr. Lee and he told me that he would leave the country at the end of the year, and so the house is yours then! Have a glass of champagne!" The people ask why, why on earth do you throw out these elected representatives, chosen by the Hong Kong people during which more than one million people participated to get us there? Why should our places be taken over by people whom we defeated in the last election, or by people who wouldn't dare face us in the last election? Because they were selected by the 400, which we had nothing to do with. And of course they are already today studying options to change the electoral laws. The whole object is planned to make sure that my party, which won 65 percent of the popular vote in September 1995, would, assuming we keep the same percentage, get less than one quarter of the seats. Can you imagine what would happen in your country if one of your parties were to win 65 percent of the popular vote and it, nevertheless, could only secure one quarter of the seats? What you must say is that the electoral laws are unfair. So how can there be free and fair elections when the law making-body has their own interest in mind? And they, of course, don't want to be humiliated again by the likes of us.

Question: There's another freedom that is dear to Americans, and that's freedom of religion. I know that in China in the last several years, the persecution of Christians in particular has been intensified. Christians in Hong Kong have many institutions, colleges, and other kinds of institutions, and I wonder if you think those will be pressed down on here, too?

Mr. Lee: Well, let's pray and hope this will never happen. If you look at the Joint Declaration, if you look at the Basic Law, the freedom of religion is clearly guaranteed. If you look at the Chinese Constitution, on the other hand, you also find religious freedom guaranteed. Tibet was promised religious freedom and full autonomy in 1951. Now here, if you look at the number of articles in the Joint Declaration and the Basic Law, which are already broken by China, how can we derive comfort from these documents? So on paper, fine. In truth, I'm afraid you're going to have to wait and see. Any Christian who worries about the future of religious freedom has my sympathy. In China, they have the Patriotic Church. Now everybody's suppose to be patriotic in Hong Kong, too. Now, will they introduce a Patriotic Church? I certainly hope not, and I don't think they will. Certainly not for the next five years, but thereafter I don't know, because in China they want to control your thought.

Question: Might China crack down on Hong Kong demonstrators and protestors?

Mr. Lee: I certainly would say no, but then how can I be sure? People say, "Look it's in China's interest to keep Hong Kong prosperous and stable; therefore, they would be doing a very stupid thing, indeed, if they do a Tiananmen in Hong Kong. We are supposed to derive comfort from the fact that this is a goose which lays golden eggs, and also from another factor, which is

Taiwan and how they will view China's jurisdiction here. Yes, these are important factors, but the Chinese leaders do not consider them to be the most important factors. The most important factor to the Chinese leaders is their ability to remain in power, and if they see their position jeopardized, they will stop at nothing. Look at 1989, before the massacre, China's economy was doing extremely well. Because the Chinese leaders felt that they were insecure, they brought in the tanks, and the army started to shoot and kill, and ruined China's economy for three years. So I don't think it will happen, but how can I be sure?

At dawn, 12,000 Chinese troops will descend upon us by sea, air and land. Why must they do something like that? It's going to frighten the Chinese people here, and is intended to intimidate the Hong Kong into silence. But it's not going to work on me and my party. You see, we have a very heavy burden on our shoulders. If any one of us were to ask this question, "Now that we are under Chinese rule, what would happen to me if I were to continue to criticize the Chinese government, or even Mr. Tung's government? What would happen to me if I were to write a story which will be sensitive, which will offend some of the Chinese leaders and certainly Mr. Tung?"—If you ask yourself that question, the chances are you won't do it, you won't write it. But if you ask yourself another question, "Since I have been saying these things all along, since I have been writing these articles all along under the British rule, why can't I do the same under Chinese rule? Our freedoms are supposed to remain unchanged." If you ask yourself that question, the chances are that you would do it.

Now, a lot of people are watching us. Supposing the lights suddenly were to turn off, we are left in darkness, and say you have a candle and a box of matches, then you light it. It is only one candle but it brings a lot of brightness into the room. And if the other people around you also have candles and they light up theirs, you have a very bright room. But if you then begin to blow out your candle, and if other people follow your example and blow out their candles, before you know it darkness will descend into this room. So every time those of us who are standing in the front line have to make a decision of that kind, we must remember, other people are watching us. If we make the right decision, I think many people will follow it and will also make the right decision. If we make the wrong decision, even more people will follow it and voluntarily give up freedom. Whatever we do, we're going to start a snowball. Are we starting a snowball of self-restraint or are we starting a snowball of self-confidence?

We will continue to do exactly what we have been doing under British rule until we are stopped, and then we'll shout, "Why, Mr. Tung?" And I hope you will join in the chorus, "Why, Mr. Tung? Why Mr. Jiang Zemin?" I hope Mr. Tung will put a question to President Jiang Zemin, "Why are you doing this?" But if we don't stand firm, we will be giving up our own freedom, we'll be blowing out the candles even though there is no wind.

Question: Are you seeing any limitations on the foreign press at this point?

Mr. Lee: The foreign press, no problem. The local press, we've got to wait and see. The important thing is that as long as there is one person who is brave enough to make a critical speech, and as long as there is one newspaper which is brave enough to publish it, that would exert a lot of pressure on the others to follow, because readers of other newspapers, not finding the stories would ask, "Why is one newspaper reporting it and not my newspaper?" They'll change newspapers. I hope the economic pressure will keep our people in the newspaper business honest.

Arnn: We've heard presentations today from different points of view on the question of the political future of Hong Kong. Judging from the reaction I hear, I think I can say on behalf of all of us that, although we are a citizens of a different country, and it's a powerful country, and it does listen to its citizens, that the ones of us in this room are going to have a lot to say about what should happen to the future of Hong Kong. In our country, we read about the past and we know that certain people fought and they sacrificed and they took risks so that we can have what we have, and it is an honor for us to meet such a man alive today.

The Hong Kong Journalists' Panel

Bill McGurn, Jesse Wong, Frank Ching
Conference Speakers
June 30, 1997 - 10:00 a.m.

Bruce Herschensohn: On this very sad and busy day we have a tremendously impressive and important panel. When you get back home, if you want to keep up with news events, not only in Hong Kong but around the world, I would advise that you cancel your subscription to *Time, Newsweek, U.S. News and World Report* and the *L.A. Times,* and with the money and effort and time that you've saved subscribe to the *Far Eastern Economic Review.* I'd also recommend subscriptions to *The Economist* in London and the *Wall Street Journal,* preferably the *Asian Wall Street Journal,* and you will know a good deal more than most of your fellow Americans. The titles are sometimes deceiving, both in the case of the magazines *The Economist* and the *Far Eastern Economic Review,* and even the *Wall Street Journal,* in that they suggest that you're just going to be reading about economics, which is not true at all. You could be just mildly interested in economics and get more information about foreign policy, defense, and international news, than you'd ever get in the publications that I mentioned that come out at home, in the United States.

Let me give very brief introductions to three very remarkable men.

One is Bill McGurn. He used to be with *National Review.* And Bill is a senior editor of the *Far Eastern Economic Review.* He is a superb writer. Although I don't like the biases of *Time, Newsweek,* and some of the American publications, I can't say that there isn't a bias to the *Far Eastern Economic Review* editorials, but generally I agree with the bias, so it's so much better than the others. (Laughter) And Bill, I also want to thank you for doing so many things for our conference. He helped me very much in the 1995 conference for the Institute, and that made it so much easier for this conference, which is obviously at a much busier time for everybody.

Next is Jesse Wong with the *Asian Wall Street Journal* and, again, an absolutely marvelous writer. His material is in the *Asian Wall Street Journal,* and he's also done a lot of books and any number of publications on Hong Kong, particularly. He also spent a great deal of time in Beijing.

Third is Frank Ching, another senior editor of the *Far Eastern Economic Review,* and he does a column every week in that publication called *Eye On Asia,* which is one of the first things that I read. Sometimes I agree, sometimes I disagree. But when I disagree, I find that I have to read it over again and then argue with myself because his arguments are very convincing. And Frank also does a Sunday night television show called *Newsline*.

Let me just tell you what the format's going to be. Each participant is going to speak for maybe five minutes or so, so that we have plenty of time for questions and answers. We couldn't have done any better on a panel of journalists in Hong Kong at this time, because there isn't any better. So let me start with you, Bill, and then we'll just go down the line to Jesse and Frank, if we may. Obviously the subject is what will happen after midnight tonight in terms of the free press that Hong Kong has enjoyed, the possibilities of self-censorship, and of real censorship in terms of any orders given. Bill?

Bill McGurn: You have to forgive me I have a sore throat today, so I sound crankier than I usually am, but my wife and children probably can't tell the difference. (Laughter)

I'm not sure what Jesse thinks. Frank and I probably have a slightly different view. In terms of press freedom, one of the difficulties I think now is that we don't know the new rules. We know what certain rules are, but when hypothetical cases are brought up the answer is usually, "As long as it is done within the law, there will be no problem." But we don't know the law—more important, what we really don't know is how the law will be interpreted. Remember that the press is a business like other businesses, and it's very vulnerable because it's a business. I think that a lot of people that look for Xinhua vigils, Chinese vigils, authorities to come and look over my shoulder and say, "I don't like what you've written," will not find that to be very likely. There are, however, other forms of pressure.

I can give you a very vivid example of something that I think is very bad for Hong Kong: *Next Magazine* or the Next Group is the popular media group in Hong Kong. It has a Chinese language paper, *Apple*, which is also the most popular paper. The editor of it is a very colorful figure named Jimmy Lai, who some of you may know. And Jimmy got in trouble. He owns a clothing store, Giordono, or did own it. It's sort of like a Gap for Americans. And when Jimmy wrote a column about Li Peng three years ago, Giordono started having a lot of problems; their Beijing shop was closed; they've since had lots and lots of problems in China. Jimmy first agreed that he wouldn't vote his shares, then he finally sold out, and they're still having problems, and I think the stock price is about two-thirds what it was at its peak. I think this is one area where they will attack the business side of an operation if they can. Now the other part is that Jimmy also owns *Next*. Now, *Next* is known for being—I guess it's probably fair to say—anti-Beijing or pro-democracy. It also has a lot in common with the *National Enquirer*. But on the political editorial side it's been very pro-Patten, pro-democracy and so forth, but I wouldn't want to pretend it's the *New York Times*. But they were trying to list on the most popular listing. Their underwriter pulled out, and they claimed the underwriter said he cited pressures, and they couldn't even find a holding bank to take the check for the listing. There's no risk to a bank in this, they make a lot of money just having the cash for a week or so, and in this case hundreds of millions of Hong Kong dollars. Some of the banks told them, and these are very well known Hong Kong banks that dealt with them for years, that they would have to check with Xinhua (the defacto embassy of the P.R.C.) and they didn't get back to him.

Now, I compare this listing with a listing of Beijing Enterprises, which, as you probably know was 1,300 times oversubscribed. It had some decent businesses, but in market terms it did not justify the enthusiasm with which it was greeted. And for me, these are worrying trends. There's a difference in the international press and the local press, because our advertising base is more diffuse and we're stronger and, you know, we're not going to give in to any of the pressures. But if you had a Chinese paper here, all they have to do is have a whispering campaign and tell the advertisers "don't go to this paper," and then the beauty of that to the P.R.C. is that there is no law, there's no fingerprints on anything, and they say "we didn't do anything." And so in some ways I wonder—I'm not for restrictive press laws, but in some ways you could argue that a restrictive press law that everyone knew and was clear would be better than what we have now, which is no one knowing and everyone being afraid.

The editor of the *South China Morning Post*, the largest English language daily, is writing letters, every day it seems, to some other publications that have charged him with self-censorship. I've talked to several editors, and almost everyone has had a letter from him. He hired a consultant from the P.R.C. to sit across the hall.

So anyway, one of the worries is that you can't just look at what is printed and what's not printed, but how they come to be printed and unprinted. When I first got here my second time, five years ago, I interviewed the bishop of Canton, who has been in jail for twenty-four years in China, and one thing that he told me was that they didn't outlaw religion, they didn't say "you can't do this," but rather they raised the taxes on the church and he couldn't come up with the money, and that was how they imprisoned him. So I think that we're always looking at the front door, and it might be a little more practical to look at the back door in these kinds of questions, especially in a place like Hong Kong, which is so business-minded. I'll let you hear from Jesse Wong.

Jesse Wong: I was looking under my desk this morning and found some old socks and also a copy of this very respectable, mainstream Hong Kong newspaper called *Ming Pao*. The date of publication was June 6, 1989. Here it is. This was published two days after what the people in the West know as the Tiananmen Square Massacre, and I'll quote from the editorial, the front page commentary: "We have heard that the order to slaughter the innocent in Beijing was given by Deng Xiaoping after hearing reports from Li Peng, whose now the Premier....It was signed by Mr. Deng after hearing their reports." If that's really the case, this act would be a crime bigger than the sky. This was June 6, 1989.

Here is *Ming Pao* dated February 21, 1997. This was the day after Deng Xiaoping's death, and what does this headline say? "Deng Xiaoping Donates

His Cornea for Medical Research, He Leaves his Love Among the Living." This is the same newspaper, *Ming Pao.*

There are plenty of signs that the press in Hong Kong has changed. Characterize that change whichever way you will; softening, pragmatism, or maybe a more practical view of how things work or how things should be. I think that there is probably some pandering to the incoming authority, but there's also a genuine feeling on the part of the people running the newspapers that, "Hey, we're Chinese and we shouldn't be too harsh on the Chinese government." This really is a reflection, I think, not of the entire community, but, at least to some extent, a big part of the community.

If you look behind the newspapers, Hong Kong itself has changed in the last six or seven years. If you look inside the newspaper, back to the paper after June 4, 1989, this newspaper I'm holding has an advertisement taken out by the Writers Association of Hong Kong condemning the massacre in Beijing: "In painful memory of the dead compatriots in Beijing." There is, here, an ad taken out by a group of employees at Sanwa Bank, which is a P.R.C. bank, and ads taken out by the Professional Teachers Association canceling classes on the 7th of June to protest the massacre, and an ad taken out by vice chancellor of the Chinese University of Hong Kong, accountants, kindergarten teachers, and here is an ad from the Sincere Department Store "in memory of our dead compatriots, we have cancelled the crazy sale." Well, this is basically a special issue which is entirely bordered in black.

Now, back to the paper from February 1997, this year, just after Deng died. It's all taken up by news reports, not much room for ads here, but the same type of advertising from the local organization: "His name will be remembered forever, the Signer-In-Chief of China's reforms and opening to the outside world." And this is happening in Hong Kong. I think if the newspapers in Hong Kong are changing, they are changing to some extent because the community is changing. I'm saying this not in a neutral kind of way. So for someone—I work for an American newspaper and I would think before I criticize—if this is what the community wants, what's wrong with it? It's a question. I don't know the answer, or I'm not sure what the answer is.

Instead of dwelling on this further, I just want to raise a couple of questions. I think in the West, the free press, freedom of speech are taken for granted. It's like truth, you've got to have it, you can't argue against it. I am all for that view. The problem really is, when you come to Asia and you take that view with you, someone could very well ask, "Hey, but look, Singapore is a prosperous society, its people generally seem quite content, proud of their country, it's one of the most successful financial centers in Asia, equally with Hong Kong. And Singapore does not have a lot of what you would call freedom of the press. So it seems that people can live happily without it or with not much of it." How do we argue against that? Another question is, "If in fact the changes we see here are an indirect reaction or response to, let's say, pressure, subtle pressure, as Bill mentioned, how should we look at that reaction?" We should condemn the pressure, yes. I think people who lived under communism in Eastern Europe made lots and lots of compromises under the communist governments. I think only in very rare instances did their journalists, their artists, their writers, stand up. And they will say, "Well, at least we are alive." I think when it actually happens to a particular writer, whatever form of pressure, it's not something you can deal with easily. You can react to it by saying, "Well, this is wrong, I'm for freedom of the press, and I will stand up and refuse to take this." I have in my hands a copy of a story written by a colleague of mine not long ago, "Dateline Beijing," and this is about the Chinese government trying to censor social science research projects, particularly those involving Western researchers— joint projects between Chinese and Western researchers. And my colleague quoted a Miss Hogan from the National Science Foundation headquartered in Virginia, who said the whole idea of the Chinese government restricting an entire area of research is offensive. Right, we agree with that, but let's listen to what Miss Hogan then says. She says that the National Science Foundation is having trouble formulating a response. Why? Because those Western scholars are unwilling to speak out on the issue for fear out of hurting their Chinese counterparts—that's commendable—as well as their own opportunities to travel to China. What do you make of that? You could argue, "Well, that's very selfish, they're more worried about their own projects, their career, than the principle of academic freedom." On the other hand, the academic himself would say, "But if I lose my access to my materials, to my contacts, I will just sit here. I can do nothing. Is it worth it?" Tough questions. I'll leave it for you to ponder. Thank you.

Frank Ching: After those two presentations, I'm not sure what there is left for me to say! I would like you to know that I have a friend who works for *Ming Pao,* the paper that Jesse was showing you. About a month or six weeks ago, the *Asian Wall Street Journal* had a front page story about *Ming Pao*, and how it had been censoring itself in recent weeks and months. I asked my friend about this, and he said, "Well, I think that's a very natural question for people to ask." But he said all the examples that were given in the *Asian Wall Street Journal* article were wrong. Now, I don't know if they were right or wrong but one thing he said to me was particularly interesting: He said that people are comparing *Ming Pao* today with what *Ming Pao* was like in mid-1989, right after Tiananmen Square, and he said that is not a fair measure of comparison because we are not now in the same period we were in right after Tiananmen Square. There have not been tanks on the streets in, what, eight years? And he said we should be comparing the paper with what it was like, say, in 1987, 1988, and he said that is what the paper has gone back to. It's publishing exactly the kinds of things that it did in 1987 and 1988. There is no longer a war atmosphere, and there is no panic in Hong Kong. I think it would be wise to remember that at that time there was, indeed, panic in Hong Kong. People were not rational, there was talk about moving all of Hong Kong to Australia, moving Hong Kong to

Scotland. (Laughter) All these things we now look back on and think how foolish it was, but these were all taken very seriously at that time.

And the newspaper from June 6th that you saw just now—I didn't keep that, but I did look at the headlines, and the headline at the top of the page said Lei Peeing had been shot. Right next to it was a story that said civil war has broken out in China, the 27th Army is battling the 38th Army. None of that was true. Do we want our papers to be like that, to write stories to put them on the front page when they turn out not to be true? Well, I think, as journalists, it's very hard to say that is what ought to be done. So I find it difficult to condemn newspapers because they are not the same as what they were like in June of 1989.

The problem of self-censorship, I think, is a very serious one, and the Chinese University Journalism Department recently did a study on this, and they surveyed journalists in Hong Kong. Currently something like 20 percent of journalists acknowledged that they had been guilty of this—of censoring themselves. And I see that the Hong Kong Journalists Association in their latest annual report says that some of their members are thinking of leaving the profession, because they're not sure that they can continue to practice journalism the way they would want to practice it, which is a rather pessimistic assessment of the future. However, the same person who did the study at the Chinese University Journalism Department said that in his school, the best and brightest students were choosing to go into journalism. The most idealistic ones are not fearful, they do not think that there is no hope for journalism, they're not turning away, they're going into journalism. And I find that very encouraging. I was surprised to find this because some years ago a law professor at Hong Kong University had told me that their best students were going into business administration; they were no longer going in to law because they were afraid that there would be no rule of law, or that the law would change. So I was surprised and very encouraged to hear that at the Chinese University some of the best students were going into journalism.

We've been discussing this issue of the press after July 1, 1997, for many years, and now it's going to be tomorrow! Tomorrow will be July 1, 1997, and I think it's amazing that we're still sort of speculating on what things will be like, but I guess that's because we realize, now at least, that there will not be any dramatic change tomorrow, that if there is change, it will take place over a period of months or years. Now, I think if you look at what Chinese officials have said, there is some reason for concern. The two main Chinese officials have spoken on this, Lei Peeing and Vice Premier Jingo Chunyun. Lei Peeing has said more than once that newspapers will be free to report anything they like, but they will not be allowed to advocate certain things. He drew a distinction between objective news reporting and advocacy, and he said that newspapers would not be allowed to advocate two Chinas, one-China-one Taiwan, or the independence of Taiwan, or the independence of Hong Kong. He didn't mention Tibet, but I'm sure that was just an oversight. (Laughter) So, at one time I thought that that indicated that China would not allow newspapers in Hong Kong to advocate anything that was contrary to China's policies, but after he had said this several times, I realized that he was talking about maintaining the territorial integrity of China. That is, China would not allow any part of the country to break away from it, and Article 22 of the Basic Law calls for legislation against subversion, sedition and treason. So I have now come to the conclusion that the law on secession will probably have some stipulation that nobody is allowed to advocate the breaking up of China and independence for any part of China. I think that is what it means.

Right now newspapers in Hong Kong have the right to advocate the independence of Taiwan or Tibet or Hong Kong, but I don't think anyone does. In fact, certainly not in recent years, and I don't think in previous years either. So this is a right the newspapers have today that they do not exercise and it is a right that they may lose if this law against secession is passed. I think it is not good for any law to be passed that restricts freedom of the press or freedom of expression, but if the only thing to be passed is a law that says you're not allowed to advocate independence for any part of China, I think the newspapers in Hong Kong can probably live with that. Parameters for freedom of the press may shift, and newspapers will lose the right that they theoretically had before, but that they never used.

I think that, by and large, there will continue to be a free press, and there will be a wide spectrum of opinions in the Hong Kong newspapers. I don't think that China wants all the newspapers in Hong Kong to read like the communist papers. I think that China wants Hong Kong to remain an international city, to remain cosmopolitan. In order to do that, it has to have a wide variety of newspapers. They cannot have just one voice in China, otherwise Hong Kong would not be what it is.

Now, as for the other laws provided for under Article 22, the laws against subversion, sedition, treason—I don't know what they will say. I think it's quite possible that they, too, will have an impact on the press. There was a lunch with a member of Mr. Tung Chee-hwa's Executive Council some weeks ago, and the member said that they will not ask the Provisional Legislature to pass these laws, that they will wait for a year until there are elections, until an elected legislature is in place before passing these laws, because, this person said, the existing law in Hong Kong, namely the Crimes Ordinance, already covers these areas of subversion, secession, sedition and treason and that there was, therefore, no need to rush new legislation in. I was surprised to hear that because I thought the Provisional Legislature wanted to pass it, but apparently they decided not to, and so it will be up to the legislature elected next year.

A big question is how those elections will be held. They will not be held in exactly the same way that the 1995 elections were held under Chris Patten. There have been great arguments between China and Britain over exactly how the elections will be held. So I think they will be held according to the Basic

Laws prescription, and according to China's interpretation of those prescriptions.

There will be twenty directly elected legislators and ten elected by an election committee and thirty elected by functional constituencies. Now, Chris Patten had created nine new functional constituencies that gave every working person in Hong Kong a right to vote, and I think that that will be done-away with. So, in that sense, the legislature to be elected next year is said to be less representative than the one elected in 1995. But I think as long as one accepts the Basic Law as the Constitution implemented for Hong Kong, one cannot really argue that what is being done next year is in some way contrary to either the Joint Declaration or the Basic Law.

I'm deviating from freedom of the press somewhat, but I'd like to conclude by saying that I had always wanted to see democracy in Hong Kong and what I had wanted was a time-table. The Basic Law gives you half of a time-table, it gives you a time-table for the times when half of the legislature will be democratically elected, and the other half elected by functional constituencies. I gather that there are now quite a lot of people who feel that the Basic Law should be amended and that direct elections for the entire legislature should take place earlier than is possible under the Basic Law. I find that quite encouraging.

As I've said, I've deviated somewhat from freedom of the press, thank you so much for listening.

Herschensohn: Thanks Frank. May I take the liberty of asking the first question, and ask it of you, Frank, if I may, because I was a little disappointed in what you said regarding the secession issue. In the United States I don't know of one journalist, one writer, who has ever advocated the secession of California from the United States of America. Nevertheless, if there was to be a law suddenly passed by the Congress of the United States and signed by the president that we could not advocate the secession of California, then every newspaper, every magazine, every journalist, every television commentator, everyone who has access to the public, would advocate the secession of California from the United States of America. And the reason would be, not because we would want to secede but we cannot tolerate the idea of one inch of such censorship of ideas. If it goes one inch, soon it will be two, three, and so on, and I would hope that the Hong Kong journalists—you're the brave ones because you're going to be tested after midnight tonight—I would hope that there would not be a giving-in of anything, even regarding the secession of Hong Kong or Tibet or Taiwan. I'd like your response to that, and then we'll go to questions from others.

Frank Ching: Well, I'm not a student of history, I'm not a student of very much, but I know that the United States did fight a civil war, and I don't know if on the eve of that civil war or during the civil war, whether or not the government allowed the newspapers to advocate secession—the South breaking off from the country. It seems to me that if this is not considered to be a very important issue, at least, it's symbolic. If this happens, there will be a restriction in the law on freedom of the press, freedom of expression. But what I'm saying is that even if it happens, it doesn't mean that there will be no freedom of the press. There will be new parameters, but I think that, by and large, there will continue to be freedom of the press.

Question: Last night we heard Martin Lee speak, and he sounded like a person who's on the road to martyrdom, because he's not going to go for a long transition it sounds like. I wonder how long it will be before he's in jail. Do you have any idea?

Herschensohn: Is that directed towards any particular member of the press? Anyone? Why don't you take it, Jesse?

Jesse Wong: I hope that that's not true. I think that there really is no need for Mr. Lee to martyr himself. After midnight he will be free to express his views except, as Frank said, in the case of secession of Tibet and Taiwan and Hong Kong.

To qualify a bit what was said—I have also heard that it would not be legal to say "Down with Lei Peeing, the Premier of China," and then subsequently someone who ought to know better say, "Well, it depends on the intention of the person shouting that slogan." It's all actually very confused right now. I don't think I can answer the question as to whether Mr. Lee would be a martyr. I think the Chinese government and their proxies in Hong Kong understand that it really doesn't do them any good to have Mr. Lee become a martyr. Mr. Lee is too much of a symbol for them to actually try to throw him in jail. I hope that I'm not wrong.

Bill McGurn: I think people here would agree with Jesse that it's not likely that Martin would go to jail, at least right away, because it would be the most incredibly stupid thing China could do right now. I have to confess I'm a good friend of Martin's, but I don't always agree with him on all his policies, but I think he's an honest man and a very, very brave man.

The author of *Life and Death in Shanghai* was in jail for many years during the Cultural Revolution. She said that the advantage of democracy was that a government knows its enemies, and if they don't like you, they speak out and they say "x" and "y," and so you know who opposes you. Bill Clinton knows that the Republicans don't agree with him—actually they don't disagree as much as I would like them to disagree but—(laughter)—but you know who's on the other side, by and large. In a place like China, you always have to suspect that people are just going along, and I think that that's very true here because a lot of these people that are now siding with the new government were all the same people who sided with the old government. If you look at the Provisional Legislature, there's more knights than in the court of St. James. (Laughter)— That's a safety valve. So the important part is that you have this suspicion about someone joining you. Are they really on your side or are they just saying they are? And that's, I think, one of the down sides of 1997. Martin was a big critic of the British for most of his time until recently—he's been criticizing the British for going slow on the Joint Declaration, and so forth, yet Martin is still a member of the Hong Kong Club, which is a British club, and his son goes to a British school. And I think that speaks very well of Britain. I don't think Martin's going to be at the China Club. (Laughter) He's certainly not going to be in the Legislative Council.

One of the things that the British had, was to allow a safety valve: they brought people in. And one of the things that I worry about is that I believe the P.R.C.'s loyalty test is much more severe. With regard to the press, I think I agree with Jesse that, first of all, for us in the international press, it's not being brave—I am pretty sure the rules will stay the same. There's never any pressure on me at the *Far Eastern Economic Review* to write or not to write something, and I write the editorials. There are occasionally those times when they'll say, "When you do it, let's do it in a smart way, let's not get slapped down for no reason. Let's make it count if we're going to do it." But I think that's probably more or less true of most of the international press. It's only because we realize that our credibility is based on being honest. The really brave ones are going to be the local guys that are vulnerable, and I think the emphasis should not be on saying that they've sold out on this or that—I think the emphasis should be on the pressure that's making them feel they have to do that.

The chief secretary, Anne Chan, said that the worst thing for Hong Kong, the worst thing, was the sort of political correctness where people are afraid to say anything—not because people told them they couldn't say it, but they thought, "Well, it's better to just keep my mouth shut," this sort of thing.

I asked her, and I also asked a prominent businessman if it isn't political correctness when the mayor of Beijing is 1,300 times over-subscribed, but the most popular media group can't get a listing, can't get an underwriter—isn't that political correctness? They admitted that there were political considerations, but, they said, this is not unique to Hong Kong—that Singapore probably would be a better example. And, they said, up and down the region you can find all sorts of instances of this kind of pressure. But to me the question is not "Is this unique to Hong Kong?" The question is "Is it new to Hong Kong?" Hong Kong was different, and so we can have all these things and yes, still make money—but is that really consistent with the Joint Declaration about Hong Kong's unique capitalist ethos and lifestyle? I think the goalpost has moved a little bit.

Question: Has there been a different kind of reporting of Martin Lee and his party between the Chinese and English newspapers here in Hong Kong? Is there a difference in comprehensiveness and focus between the two different presses?

Herschensohn: Anyone in particular you want to answer that, or do I just hand it down to the end of the table—to you, Frank? Because you look like you don't want to answer it. (Laughter)

Frank Ching: If I look like I don't want to do it, it's probably because I don't feel I'm qualified to do it. I think to give an answer to this you'd have to be studying all the Chinese papers and all the English papers and making comparisons, and I haven't done this. I'm not aware that there is a difference in treatment. Maybe Jesse?

Jesse Wong: I don't know either, but I'll answer the question. (Laughter) In fact, Martin Lee doesn't get much space in any newspaper in Hong Kong now. He and his party got a lot of space, particularly right after they won a major victory in the 1995 Legislative Council elections, but not now and I don't know if this is political correctness or simply it's a recognition on the part of the press that these guys won't count for much anymore. They won't be in the Legislative Council, so what they say really doesn't matter. So you can hardly see them in either English or Chinese newspapers now.

Question: Frank, you seem to suggest that there are degrees of freedom of the press, and some press is a little more free and some is a little less free, and that it's okay if you're not quite as free as you used to be. In Singapore not too awfully long ago *The Economist* wrote some unflattering comments about Mr. Lee Kwan Yew, and the government there promptly banned *The Economist*, saying it was treasonous, or some other silly nonsense. Do you believe there are degrees of freedom? Or is press freedom something that exists or doesn't exist?

Frank Ching: I think if you look at Hong Kong's history there certainly are degrees of freedom. Several dozen laws have been changed since Chris Patten came, and most of those laws have been changed because they were considered to be inconsistent of the U.N. Conventions on Human Rights. So before they were changed, press freedom was different, and after they were changed, press freedom has been greater. That is, press freedom in 1997 is greater than press freedom was in 1992.

Larry Arnn: I thank you, all three of you. Two of you spoke to our conference here two years ago. Bill was back in Washington at the time. We owe you a debt for the thoughtfulness and candor of your remarks. I notice some differences in the commentary from the journalists this time, from two years ago. I notice an undercurrent of doubt about the standard of freedom of the press: You have given thoughtful, interesting and doubtful comments about it. That issue is very current in the West, too. Lee Kwan Yew and Lei Peng—one in Singapore and one in Beijing—have something in common. They both write in this sense: "We're very smart and we're very wise people, and we can do the job of governing better than the people can do it for themselves, and if we do that in their interest and benevolently, the people themselves will be better able to realize the good things they want in the world, including a large measure of freedom." And I want to remind you about an argument against that. I say this now, because we heard Mr. Martin Lee say a moving thing, which it's not for me to say, because I don't live here and don't face these same perils, but I will repeat to you what he said. He said, certain people are on the front lines. He listed three kinds of those certain people: elected officials, journalists, and civil servants. He said, how they act and what they believe are going to determine the situation. They're going to decide what will happen to the future of Hong Kong. What they think, how they act, how they evaluate the risks, and what's right as they see the right, is important. Now, the argument I'll repeat to you is a very old argument. In the West, we have the argument that the best kind of rule is the rule of the wise. And in the tradition of the scholarship and writing on that, there's a counter-argument which has to do with succession. In the play *King Lear,* for example, one of the three people in all of Shakespeare called a philosopher is trying to give the kingdom to someone to succeed him—one of his children. And the play is a tragedy, it doesn't work right. And that gives rise to the scholarship that underlies religious liberty in America and it's this: What is government but the profoundest of all commentaries on human nature? If men were angels no government would be necessary. If angels were to govern men, neither internal nor external controls on the government would be needed. And the point is this: If someone in power has the power, unchecked, to order people in the army to shoot people in the streets, the fact that they have not done it for eight years does not mean that they will not do it again, or that their successors will not. If a person in power, unchecked, has the power to say that everything except "X" cannot be said in the newspapers, they can add to "X" when it pleases them.

And so, whatever is the degree of freedom of the press that is enjoyed in any place in any time, according to that old standard in the American tradition, which is articulated to apply to all people everywhere—according to that standard—there is a thing apart from what may be done at any given point. That thing is called freedom of the press, and that standard is independent of any of our opinions of it, and that is the standard to which we should be seeking. So unless we think Tung Chee-hwa and Li Peng and Jiang Zemin are angels—it would be worthwhile to remind one's readers out there that these people are not angels, and who are they to have this power?

Bruce Herschensohn: Larry, do you want to direct that to anyone in particular to answer? Okay. Any other questions?

Todd Culbertson: I'll start with a brief editorial comment since that's my job. It's refreshing, as a member of the American press, to be abroad and hear people who are so passionate about defending freedom of the press, because back at home we're held in esteem lower than politicians. Polls tell us that if people wanted to strike out any part of the Bill of Rights, they'd get rid of freedom of the press.

In the United States there is a joke that a conservative is a liberal who's been mugged, and a civil libertarian is a conservative who's been indicted. In that vein, I would ask any of the panelists, or all of them, to comment on what is the standing—and I mean in a cultural sense—of the press in Hong Kong? And what is the standing of the press in China? In the U.S., for better or for worse, we in the press have become a defacto branch of government. Not everyone in America likes the fact that the press has elevated itself into a defacto branch of government, and the fact that reporters and anchors and politicians are on a first name basis. The press, you know, tries to set the agenda, almost refusing to believe what the government says. Although the U.S. public likes to scream about it and condemns the press, deep in their hearts they like it that way. They wouldn't want to live without it. Now, just what role does the press play here to the proverbial man in the street, to the taxicab driver, as it were? What does the taxicab driver think of the press?

Jesse Wong: I think the main difference between cab drivers and the press is that cab drivers are paid better. (Laugher) But, of course, they work harder. I think the press in Hong Kong is somewhat different from the States. I think the press generally in Asia doesn't really have the kind of institutional status that the Western press does. The main difference between the press in Hong Kong and the press in—let's say in the States—is that in Hong Kong the press generally is not highly regarded, it's not a very prestigious job, and the press doesn't have a very high regard for itself. People tend to think they're a failure in life if by the age of twenty-five they're still a reporter. In the States the difference is the public doesn't have a high regard for the press, but the press has a high regard for itself. (Laughter) And that is enough, I think, to keep the press as a kind of institution—it's a job for life. But in Hong Kong it's really just a stepping stone to something else. So the sort of professionalism and the sort of standards you're talking about are different. I mean, who wants to die for freedom of the press if it's a job you're going to keep only until you're twenty-five? These are very practical questions. (Laughter)

Question: There was a poll in the *L.A. Times* a few weeks ago reporting the results of many questions. One of the questions was, twenty years from now do you expect Hong Kong to look more like China, or China to look more like Hong Kong? It was interesting to me—and these questions were asked of Chinese, both living in the United States as well as living here in Hong Kong. The majority felt that China would look more like Hong Kong. As it relates now to the press, what do you think is likely to happen to the press in the PRC? Is it going to tend to look more like Hong Kong's press or is it going to stay the same?

Bill McGurn: We may have slightly different opinions. I don't know what will happen in twenty years. I hope that China looks more like Hong Kong. But I think a lot of these questions on freedom of the press also reflect not just a view of freedom of the press, but of government. I don't think anyone here is for restrictive press laws. I think what Frank says is true—there are degrees of freedom. That's not to say we don't want a totally free press, but the British had a film censorship act for many, many years—and I think Frank broke the story about ten or twelve years ago—where any film that was detrimental to China was not shown. So in practice there are degrees; you can say some things, you can't say other things. I happen to believe in full freedom of the press, and I write editorials out here. But you have to sell that out here. And I think what

Frank and Jesse were saying is when you come out here, you can't say, "if they close down something or say I can't do it, I'll do it anyway, because I believe in freedom of the press and it's a sacrosanct right," because they don't believe in that. Then where are you, especially if they're the government? I think there are several different answers to this.

One is—to get back to Singapore—what we try to argue, for example, is that Singapore wants to participate in the world economy. Okay, it's a very successful financial center. And if you want to attract investors, you need a more open press. And they are fairly open in certain things, and also they've kept it fairly clean and honest, which is why businessmen like going down there. So we argue, just as if you were going to invest in IBM, you wouldn't just go by IBM's prospectives, you'd want independent verification of those things. I think the Asian answer to that is that they will allow freedom to a point on the economic stuff. They try to draw the line saying, "No political talk." I think that's a false line, especially when in China you have the Foreign Ministry owning companies, and so forth. That's what worries me.

As far as your question regarding China, I think China has made extraordinary strides. I think I first went there in 1985 or 1986, and I remember going to church and no one would talk to me. They all scurried away outside. And now it's very friendly, it's very different. I'm not saying it's free, but it's freer than what it was. In practice there are degrees of freedom. Here in Hong Kong, it's legitimate to say, "Well it's not going to be as bad as I thought it was—they're going to let me do this." Now, it's not saying you're happy with it, it's saying you know where to fight, you pick your battles of what you're going to do and try to get. China is much freer and I think one of the problems in the press in the U.S. is that we try to debate this question: Is China a free country or is it a communist country? It's somewhere in between, and you have the unspoken question: compared to what? If you talk about China and you say China is bad—okay, China's bad. But is it bad compared to the Cultural Revolution, you know, when Mao said "jump" and a billion people leapt up in the air? You have to ask compared to what? I don't think that China's going to look like Hong Kong, and I'll tell you why. Because Hong Kong's system is very unique. It's open and it's free. And that is much harder to take than a system of control.

About five years ago there was a debate in the Legislative Council on a fair trade commission. Believe it or not, Hong Kong was debating whether they should have a fair trade council! It was like the College of Cardinals debating people and fallibility. But there you were, they had it. And the financial secretary was asked by Martin Lee, "What's the difference between laissez faire and doing nothing?" And this guy stammered for a while and he said, "Well, I refer you to a six page summary of a 1980 speech to the Federation of Hong Kong Manufacturers by my predecessor, where he called it positive non-interventionism." Not a very persuasive answer.

I would have said every day you have a billion cockamamie proposals on which to spend money—money to do all sorts of absurd things, and we have to mobilize and fight them and shoot them down. It's not true that preserving freedom and keeping hands off is easy. I think it's hard, and we know it's hard by looking around the world. How many people do it? Very, very few. Hong Kong is free on the trading side. So when you ask, will China look more like Hong Kong, I think there will be a lot more big skyscrapers in China. There will be a lot more businesses. I think China will look like the rest of Asia, and what I worry about is that Hong Kong may look like the rest of Asia. It worries me because Hong Kong is different. Hong Kong is unique, and it's free, and the people breathe it.

In terms of degree of freedom, one area I think I would depart from Frank is that there were a lot of British restrictions on freedom of the press on the books, but the fact is no one knew that they were on the books because the British didn't enforce a lot of them. So I think you have to distinguish between what the law says and if the law is enforced. If, de facto, you're able to say things, life is a lot freer. If you're talking about degrees, no one expects that it's going to be freer in three days; people expect quite the opposite.

Think of it this way: there are two Chinese daughters, Singapore and Hong Kong. Singapore is the daughter that sort of gets all the attention, she's very glamorous. Hong Kong's like Cinderella that no one knows and is unappreciated. But Hong Kong has her own virtues and they're extraordinary virtues. The Hong Kong people are not going to to go to Singapore. People came to Hong Kong for freedom. People don't go to Singapore, or at least, not in large numbers.

Frank Ching: I think it's not true that people in Hong Kong did not know that these laws that restricted freedom of the press were not there. In fact, I think the newspaper publishers knew very well, and they were very careful about what they published and did not publish. In fact, I remember the *South China Morning Post* printed an entire Sunday section with a lead story on the superintendent of the Auxiliary Police. He was fired, and he had been fighting to have himself reinstated for many, many years. And the *Morning Post* had already printed this section, and then, I don't know how, some kind of pressure was put on them and they shredded everything, and they had a new section printed, new stories, new pictures, a very much toned down story on all this. So I think that we shouldn't really look back on the British period as a period when people enjoyed great freedoms in Hong Kong. I don't think we should have any illusions about what Hong Kong was like in the past.

Jesse Wong: I also have something to say about that. As an ideal, there should just be either a free press or a press that's not free, not a press that is freer or less free. That's the ideal. In real life, Bill is right, you can have degrees of freedom. In fact, when I go to Singapore people ask me, "What is China like?" And sometimes I like to shock them by saying, "Actually, people in China are a lot freer than people in Singapore." And they're appalled. They say, it couldn't be, because China is a communist country. Well, in fact, in this communist country people can say virtually anything they want. I think there's strict control on what is published on the official media, but people can stand up in a restaurant and say unpleasant things about the Communist Party and nothing will happen to them. But people who stand up in a restaurant and say unpleasant things about Lee Kwan Yew could have unpleasant things happen to them. So is China free? No, it isn't. But is China freer than Singapore? Yes, in some ways. If you listen, if you are able to listen to radio stations in China, you will find an amazing flourishing of opinion on a lot of things. No, they will not say, "Down with the Communist Party," but they will talk about corruption, they will talk about incompetence in government, practical administrative things, not ideological things.

They are moving forward. Now to address the point about whether the British or Chinese is better in terms of freedom of the press in Hong Kong: I think, again, there are degrees of freedom, and sure, the press was not entirely free under the British, but in the period that I know best, Hong Kong was moving forward. The question is, is it now moving backward? I think that's the question that we ought to be asking. I think people are alike, they all want to look forward to a better day tomorrow, which is why one of the pro-China groups calls itself A Better Tomorrow Foundation. Mainly they have the job of selling Hong Kong's image abroad.

Question: How much mainland Chinese money is moving into Hong Kong to buy up radio stations, newspapers, television stations, in order to have an influence on the press here through ownership of the press?

Bill McGurn: I think there have been a lot of significant purchases, but not necessarily of the press. There's a lot more attractive investments in Hong Kong than the press. Also, they don't have to buy the press to get what they want. It's not necessary because the guys that are publishing here want to continue to publish here, and I don't think you see too many of them bucking the line.

Now, on the other side of the ledger, there's a huge influx of Chinese money in almost all the established businesses and, in fact, usually at bargain prices.

Frank Ching: China's former representative in Hong Kong, who now lives in Los Angeles, disclosed in his memoirs that China at one time thought of buying certain newspapers, including the *South China Morning Post*. But Chinese newspapers are coming to Hong Kong. The *China Daily* now has a Hong Kong office, and I think they may have a Hong Kong edition, but I don't think China has bought any television stations or radio stations or newspapers.

Question: This is for Jesse and Bill. Now that Jesse is approaching the age of twenty-five and will probably be going on to better things, (Laughter) I was wondering if the Internet that's coming on board all over the world will affect the publications? Will the Internet change some of the things that are happening in China and in Hong Kong, and will the Internet eliminate newspapers eventually?

Jesse Wong: I think our employers, Dow Jones, would very much like an answer to your final question, which is "would newspapers be eliminated by the internet?" Every newspaper company in the world would like to know the answer to that question. We don't know. There are people that will say that there is nothing like having your own newspaper in front of you, being able to glance at the whole front page and say "I want to read this, I want to read that," and to flip through it. You can't take the Internet into the bathroom with you.

In terms of press freedom and how the Internet affects it, I think theoretically, yes, the Internet should know no borders. In practice, I think that the governments of Asia are trying to put up borders. You can speculate that in time those efforts would fail, but I will give you a vivid example: Rupert Murdoch has a satellite broadcasting operation in Asia called Star TV. When it arrived in Asia, everyone said, "Oh, so now you can't stop the spread of information! They will just beam it down from the sky and everyone who has a dish can receive it." In practice, yes, this can happen, but in many Asians countries people are forbidden to have their own dishes. They have to subscribe to a cable company that receives the broadcast on a dish, and it can be censored at the source. Also, the governments of Asia can put pressure on the broadcaster and say, "We will not permit our companies to advertise on your station if you don't submit yourself to our censorship and control." In fact, Star TV dropped the BBC after a period because the BBC purportedly was deemed offensive by China. So technology holds promise, but it is not easy sailing.

Question: I don't have any authorization to ask this, but I'll do it anyway. Suppose, just suppose, about a year from now The Claremont Institute wanted to have a conference in Hong Kong, and we wanted to have a session called "Tung Chee-hwa, Beijing Puppet." If we were to do that, say a year from now, after the Hong Kong election, and then we had a session evaluating whether or not the election was free and fair, and we invited Martin Lee on one hand, and some other people on the other hand, would people be afraid to participate in those discussions? Would they think, "Gee, if I go to this discussion, could I have bad consequences?" Would people be afraid to talk about those things with an outside group from another country, like us?

Frank Ching: First, I think you would have no trouble at all organizing and holding a conference like that in Hong Kong a year from now. Tung Chee-hwa has already been called a Beijing puppet by lots of people, so I don't think that anyone would stay away from the conference just because you had that as a topic. And the second session would be on the 1998 elections? I fully expect Martin Lee to be a winner in the 1998 elections, so a year from now, if you hold a conference here, he will be back in the Legislative Council. I don't think that there would be any problem holding a conference, and I don't think there would be any problem filling the room. You could probably fill a room even larger than this.

Bruce Herschensohn: What if one of the topics was secession?

Frank Ching: Well, if one topic was secession, I have said—and I don't think very many people have picked up on this—that if there is a law against secession, it would apply not only to the press, it would apply to academics, and it would have an impact on academic freedom. A lot would depend on exactly how these new laws are worded. Now, I think a year from now these new laws would not have been passed yet because the idea is to have the new legislature pass these new laws, and a year from now they wouldn't be on the books. Maybe you should talk about two years from now.

Bruce Herschensohn: I promised Frank, Jesse, and Bill that we'd be done at 11:30, so we're getting close. Let's have one more question, if you will.

Question: We talked a lot about the press and government, but I wonder about some human rights issues. Were the Chinese government's policies of forced abortion and forced sterilization and also the crackdowns that they've had on the unregistered churches within China itself covered in the Hong Kong press? How were those topics covered, and would it be covered today, as those things continue or don't continue in China, and if they should come to Hong Kong?

Bruce Herschensohn: Jesse?

Jesse Wong: I was going to say no thanks. (Laughter)

Bruce Herschensohn: Frank?

Frank Ching: Well, I think all of those things were covered in the Hong Kong press, and I expect all of those things will continue to be covered in the Hong Kong press. I think that it is not possible in Hong Kong to suppress a news story. There are so many newspapers, there is so much competition, that if one paper thinks of suppressing a story, one of its competitors will come out with it. I don't think it's possible in Hong Kong to suppress a news story.

Bill McGurn: I would say that it has been reported, particularly in regard to the churches. In fact, I'm amazed that some of the stuff that they report here has not been reported in the U.S. I remember a case in China two years ago, and I was stunned that it was not picked up: it was the story of a Christian. I don't know whether he was a minister or not. He was taken from his place of work, interrogated, and a cross shaved on his head. It was published here in Hong Kong, but I was stunned that the story was not picked up in the U.S. I don't know if the Chinese press picked it up here, I am not as familiar with the Chinese language press, although I am familiar with some of it, and I know some of these issues do get covered. I would say in the past it's actually been better here in some ways.

Bruce Herschensohn: I want to thank you so much, Bill, Jesse, Frank, for your insight. We'll be reading your material with the greatest of interest in the months ahead. We are appreciative, particularly that you came out on this day, when I know it's tremendously busy for you. This has been one of the most valuable sessions that we've had. On behalf of Larry Arnn and the Institute and all of our delegates, our deepest thanks to you.

The Heritage Foundation

President Edwin J. Feulner, Jr.
Ambassador Frank Shakespeare
Conference Speakers
June 30, 1997 - 2:00 p.m.

Larry Arnn: Nothing like this has ever happened before. It is something historic, not only because of the obvious, but also because of the principles involved. Here we have an argument, a discussion about what are the rights of the people here, and how should they be governed? What are the rights and wrongs of this situation? There isn't any way to talk about these things except in terms that imply a meaning that goes way beyond the details of this situation. It's a fascinating thing. Most of the people who are talking to us in this context are people who live here and who are authoritative in the policy decisions that are being made. But because it has this general nature, because it is a thing that carries implications way beyond circumstances of this island and the peninsula and the New Territories, we've asked two distinguished Americans to come. I am not going to introduce them, but I'm going to say a word of welcome to them for a couple of reasons. One of them runs the United States' biggest institution of the kind of institution that I run in the United States. I admire it a lot, I look up to it for its size. I only run the smartest institution of its kind. (Laughter) And the other man here is also an old friend of mine. In looking around for people from the United States who are available to talk to this group on this occasion, these two people came first to mind. And so on behalf of The Claremont Institute I want to welcome them here, and say thank you to both of them for coming.

Bruce Herschensohn: Whenever I am asked my educational background I say that I attended Shakespeare University in Washington, D.C.—meaning that I have learned so much from Frank Shakespeare. If God ever asks us all for a short list of those things that you appreciated in life, I would surely have on my short list the opportunity to meet, know, befriend and work with—work for— Ambassador Frank Shakespeare. That was at the time when he was director of the United States Information Agency. Prior to that, he was vice president of CBS. After that, president of Westinghouse, president of RKO General; President Reagan appointed him ambassador to Portugal and ambassador to the Vatican. But more impressive than any of those things that would appear on his official biography is just the character of the man. He is a man who has a great sense of values.

And he has a quality that is quite unique for those who have come to Washington to serve. Generally a cabinet ranked official comes to Washington and represents the president to the bureaucracy for a while, and shortly thereafter represents the bureaucracy to the president. That weakness didn't apply to Ambassador Shakespeare. It didn't apply because of his ability to lead rather than follow. The bureaucracy respected him because of his tremendous and skillful knowledge that he brought to the agency.

There is one downside, one negative, to knowing Frank Shakespeare, and that's that I have become terribly depressed with so many of the people who are in Washington, D.C., today. And with that admission, it's a great privilege, it always is, to introduce to you Ambassador Frank Shakespeare.

Ambassador Frank Shakespeare: Well, I don't know how you feel, but I'd like to listen to Bruce a little longer. May I say one thing right at the top? I happen to be a member of the Board of Trustees of the Heritage Foundation, and I'm co-speaking in the presence of the president of the Heritage Foundation, and you might naturally assume that my views might be Heritage's views. They might be or they might not be. I want to indicate that very clearly because I'm going to say things here that are a little bit offbeat and a little bit sensitive. These are purely the views of a private citizen. And secondly, as Larry Arnn pointed out, you've had an array of people, who, I assume, are giving you insights and judgments and perceptions about Hong Kong. What I will share with you are some views about the situation around the world and our own country that might be relevant in your considerations as to where things are going here, in this part of the world.

Let me just enumerate some of the big considerations in the world—and they are very obvious. They would be here in Asia, Europe, Russia, and Japan. And then directly, what about ASEAN, the Association of Southeast Asia Countries? And what about the United States? Those are the big players in the times ahead. I will comment briefly.

What I say now is a personal opinion. Europe is out of the play in the future of Asia. Europe has a terrible demographic situation; the lowest birthrates in the world are in France, Italy and Spain. Europe, because of the tragedy of the twentieth century, and having had great battles ruin its cities in two wars, has lost its will. It cannot do anything in the areas of vital concern in its backyard, Bosnia, et al. It wouldn't have lifted it's finger in the Middle East if it had not been sort of a junior partner to whatever the United States did or did not do in the Gulf War. It's choices for governments can no longer be a model for anyone. They have a hugely high unemployment rate, their economies are stifled, and they're having a tremendous difficulty in working their way out of those problems. And then lastly, simply in terms of their own structure, they're caught up in their own relationships with each other.

So, although I think that while Europe, in terms of the world and non-Asian influence, might have been the dominant external consideration in the nineteenth century, and a very important consideration in the twentieth century, Europe will be not be a player of significance in the twenty-first century. And, in my view, that's hugely important for us to understand.

Secondly, Russia: I mention Russia only because Russia is a huge imponderable for the world, for the Western world and for the Eastern world, if for no other reason than a physical reason, its sheer size—that is to say, Russia in geographic terms, as I'm sure almost all of you know, is the largest territorial state in the world by a huge margin. China could fit in a corner of Russia. The United States could fit in a corner of Russia. We in the United States, if you have a broadcasting background, as I did, think of time zones as the measure of distance. That is, if you're programming something, you must consider that there is three hours of difference in time between New York and Los Angeles. From the eastern most point of Russia to the western most point of Russia, the time difference is eleven hours.

Russia occupies one-sixth of the land mass of the earth, and most of that land mass runs from the Ural Mountains east and hangs right over the top of what is Asia and most of it is empty. The population is from the Urals, west toward Western Europe—that's where the people are. A huge part of Russia is called Siberia and it's under state control. It hangs over all of East Asia and is essentially empty and filled with things: gas, oil, gold, coal.

Russia, of course, has had seventy-five years of the worst tyranny known to man, stifling everything, and they've been out of that six years or seven years. Today Russia is in ferment. And it is probably the case that, at least for the next quarter century, Russia will matter hugely in its potential, but will not matter in its actuality because it simply needs time to get its act together. If it does get its act together, it could be a matter of huge significance here because of the fiber and caliber and strength of the Russian people, and the potential strength of their nation, Russia.

Now, Japan: Twenty years ago almost everyone was saying the great factor of Asia in the twenty-first century will be Japan—that Japan might be the great nation of Asia. They said it might be the idea leader of Asia, it might be the model, either the industrial model or the political or the societal model. Almost no one says that anymore, including the Japanese. If you take polls in Japan, and ask, what will be the nations of dominance—or some word like that—in Asia in the twenty-first century, almost inevitably the Japanese public say first, China, and secondly, the United States. They never say Japan, their own country. So their perception of themselves as the leader appears to be in a significant change. I do not know the Japanese culture, so I do not know the reasons why. But I think it's clear that, at minimum, it's very different than it was twenty years ago. It has nothing to do with their wealth or their technology or that sort of thing. It has to do with a nation's ideas and thrust and considerations and that seems to have gone sideways.

So we have talked about Europe, we have talked about Russia, we have talked about Japan. And I have concluded, rightly or wrongly and shared with you, that two, Europe and Russia, probably will not be significant factors; Europe for the whole of the twenty-first century, and Russia at least until they get their act together if you will, which would perhaps be a quarter century. And Japan is much more problematical. It's not the way it used to be. What does that leave? That leaves, among major factors, China, the United States, and the Southeast Asian nations.

Let me talk first about the Southeast Asian nations. That would be, as you know, depending on how you group it, it would be the great island nations of the Philippines and Indonesia, it would be the nations of Thailand, of Malaysia, of Burma, of Laos, of Cambodia, of Vietnam, of the little island nation of Singapore—that cluster of nations. While you have had the great privilege of being here in this exciting epochal situation for five or six days, Ed Feulner has been keeping us sleepless by hopping us through a significant number of these Southeast Asian nations. In every single case, when you talk to the leadership of those nations, there are two things that they talk about—and in this order: The first thing is the situation in their country, "our trade relations, our economy, our links to the United States, where we're going, investment, how can we improve these things?" And that of course is always and for evident reasons the first thing they talk about. And then the second thing in every case—and this is at the highest level—is "where is China going?" Those nations, in mass, have a large population, if you take them all together and lump them. But individually, nation, by nation, by nation, they're very small. Small not in the objective sense, small in the comparative sense. Individually they have sixty million people, they have forty million people, and they have twenty-three million people. In relation to China, those are large villages or cities. So that is a very important consideration. They're nervous. They have to live here, and where China goes will set the climate and the environment within which they will live, and they know that the United States is six or eight thousand miles away. So those factors of ASEAN mean, of course, that they would like the United States to stay active, because it helps them in trade and marketing and technology and all of those things. And also, we would be a counter weight or an alternate, rather than leaving them be alone. They're very diplomatic as to the way they've expressed this, but it is very clear they hope, they pray, that the United States will stay involved in Asia, because they know in their stomach Europe's not going to play, Russia is out of the picture, they're nervous about Japan for historical reasons, and they just feel that Japan, as the dynamic force, is not there. So it's China and the United States, and that's the way they feel.

Before I leave the ASEAN nations, let's use an analogy about their mind set—now it's a weak analogy, any analogies in sensitive things like this are always weak, but it will give you a general sense: If you were to think about Europe in the twenty-first century, what you think about is where Germany is going. And the small nations, Denmark, Belgium, Holland, Austria, others, are going to be derivative to that. They may do well in their situation, but if Germany goes sour, they're in deep trouble no matter what they've done within their own country. And if Germany stays strong and free and open and all of those things, then they have a very good shot to do their own thing. If we were Danes or we were Belgians or we were Dutch, we would, of course, love our country, and we would want our country to do the right thing, but we would know that where Western Europe goes in the twenty-first century is, bottom line, where Germany goes. And that's the way to think of the Southeast Asian nations. They may sound like big important factors to you, but they're Belgium, and they're Holland, and they're Austria, and that's what they are, and China is Germany. So that may help as sort of a loose analogy of mind-set.

I would like to talk to you just very briefly about China, not in industrial terms or military terms, but in people terms. It is not politically correct, it's indelicate and it's insensitive to talk about the caliber of people. I am going to talk about the caliber of people. The Chinese are a very strong, tough people. There are not so very many strong, tough people in the world. The Russians are strong, tough people. The Germans are strong, tough people. They think the Americans are strong, tough people, but not everyone is. And that's not a good thing or a bad thing, it's just the way God made us. The Chinese are a very, very strong people. Illustratively, wherever expatriate Chinese have been given a fair shot on merit, they've knocked the ball out of the park. Taiwan is Chinese, Hong Kong is Chinese, and Singapore is Chinese. If you go to Malaysia, which is a take-off rocket, 30 percent of the population is Chinese and practically dominates the economy. In Indonesia, I think 10 percent of Indonesians are Chinese, and that's where it's at. The Malaysian's are coming on strong, and the Chinese factor is huge because they work hard, and they're good, and they're tough, and they're strong. So whether you take whether they're a minority, like a little one in Indonesia, or a big one in Malaysia, or they are in places like Singapore or Hong Kong or Taiwan—if they have a shot, it works.

So now you have the billion two hundred million Chinese people in China itself. Napoleon is alleged to have said—it doesn't make any difference whether he really said it or it's apocryphal, because it's true whether he said it or not—Napoleon is alleged to have said, "China is asleep. Let her sleep, for when she awakens, you will wish she were asleep." Now, I point out that the Chinese are a people of an extraordinary caliber. In the twenty-first century the key question is going to be, perhaps even in world terms, Quo Vadis, China?

My time has run out here because we were each to talk fifteen minutes, so I can't develop the Chinese aspect more, but I wanted to just put the thought into your head that when you're thinking about China and the caliber and the fiber of its people, don't think about mainland China as the indicator, because they really haven't had an opportunity, but wherever they have had an opportunity, they have been hugely, hugely successful. And that's the way to measure the potential of the people that constitute the citizenry of China. Thank you.

Bruce Herschensohn: If anyone talks about the Reagan Revolution for longer than one or two minutes and doesn't mention Ed Feulner, it means they don't know anything about the Reagan Revolution. He has served in a myriad of positions for President Reagan, and then, of course, built the Heritage Foundation. And President Reagan gave him the President's Citizen's Medal for what he did for the United States and for the cause of freedom around the world. Of course you know him as the president of the Heritage Foundation, and as Larry Arnn indicated, he's been an inspiration to Larry, to all of us at The Claremont Institute, and he certainly has taken a very large part—and history will, I certainly assume, record it—a very large part in the end of the Cold War. Thanks for spending some time with us while you're here in Hong Kong. I know you have your own very crowded schedule.

Ed Feulner: Thanks very much, Bruce. It's an honor to be able to address a Claremont Institute group. Larry Arnn invited me on a number of occasions, and this is the first time it's worked out—and somehow he managed it without even buying me a meal.

I didn't know quite where Frank was going to go when he started getting politically incorrect there, but, Bruce, I think he toed the line pretty well in terms of his description of what we face in the world.

I commend all of you for being here. Not because there's going to be fireworks, or because all of the sudden the flags are going to flip, and this sort of thing, but because what happens in the world is still important for America. You've heard the statistics: trade with Asia one and a half times greater than American trade with Europe, and within the next couple years it will be twice what it is with Europe. The billions of dollars we have invested out here, the interests we have here—it's more than that.

The world's still a dangerous place. The foreign policy that has been enunciated by this administration is not exactly one with which I fundamentally agree, but beyond that, it's not one I can fundamentally understand, because it zigs and zags and flip flops, and as Frank rightly pointed out is that people in the area want predictable, consistent viewpoints and expression of interest, and expression of leadership from Washington. But before giving a few examples of that, I'd be remiss if I didn't especially recognize—I didn't know if Larry Arnn puts together awards—did somebody get the award for having come the furthest? If anybody gets the award for having assembled the largest internal delegation, it has to be Patti and Jerry Hume. How many are you? You're eight? Okay. Jerry is on our board. Jerry and Patti are very long time dear friends of ours, as are the children, and it's very good to see them. And Pat and Sally Parker, and David and Dolly Keystone. Is Dolly here? Yes, she's here, she's not out buying snuff bottles. Dolly, I just gave away your secret. And Larry Arnn, of course, has been a stalwart fixture of everything we believe, and we are so happy that we are able to collaborate with The Claremont Institute in a whole host of ways, going back to a joint publication we did eight or ten years ago on the Imperial Congress. It had an introduction by a back-bench young congressman at the time by the name of Gingrinch. So, Larry, we must have done some pretty good picking back then. Beverly Danielson, a dear friend of ours from Washington, and other supporters and friends like Jim Martin, it's great to be with you.

What I thought I would do is just talk a little bit about some of my impressions of Asia. Asia's been kind of my love. If you're involved in the think tank business, you have to kind of pick something out that you're particularly interested in. Some of my colleagues pick out things like reforming part "B" of Medicare and, you know, the kind of things that make my eyes just glaze over.

But Asia has been it for me. I first came out here in 1971. I was in Hong Kong at the time. In 1973, I remember being here with Linda when we renewed acquaintances with a Vietnamese family that we were sponsoring to get in to the United States. When I think about the incredible changes that have occurred in the last twenty-five years it's really staggering. A few little vignettes: I was just writing them down last evening. In 1988 I gave a speech in Hong Yang University in Seoul, Korea, and I made the comment that I didn't think was particularly profound, but apparently it was one nobody in Korea had ever thought of before, and that comment was to the effect that the true test of democracy and the presence of a mature democracy is not whether you have elections or not, but, in fact, it's what happens as you have the elections and what happens during the transition, and what happens to the people who lose the election. Unfortunately, it's painful for me to go back to Korea because most of my friends are in jail. It's sad that the last two presidents, one who brought democracy to Korea, the other one who was the first freely elected president of Korea, who was the head of the Seoul Olympics Committee in 1988, are both in jail, and a number of other political leaders, for various reasons, are still in jail. And it's a sign that a lot of places out here still have a lot of growing to do in terms of how the political process comes together with the economic success they've already had.

I'm very close to Taiwan. I get there a couple times a year, and have now gone there for almost thirty years. I know the leadership there well, and yet, right now some of my friends in Taiwan are very concerned because there's a new constitution that's been proposed by the president, a man with whom I'm usually in very close agreement. But in effect, this new constitution would do away with both the governorship of Taiwan Province and also some of the local city councils and local officials. At the same time, across the border in China, my colleagues from Heritage recently were observing municipal elections where, believe it or not, the only names on the ballots were not members of the Communist Party, and, in fact, some Independents and some non-Communists Party members were actually elected to provincial and local city offices. I guess the only thing that those several incidents proved to me is that the line toward democracy, and the opportunity to participate freely in the government, and the people of government that you have, is not going to be a straight line. It's not going to automatically go step by step in a certain direction.

On this trip, as Frank mentioned, we were in Burma—and I was just looking in our index of economic freedom, and Burma ties with North Korea as the least free economy in the world. It's also certainly one of the most politically repressed people. To spend a couple hours with Aung San Suu Kyi and the people there who are putting their necks and their sacred honor on the line day-in and day-out to practice what they preach, to try and uphold the principles that we believe in and we take for granted, is to be re-enforced in terms of what we believe in, and what we're doing. In Burma, the generals with SLORC, State Law and Order Restoration Committee, condescendingly told us that since Aung San Suu Kyi's the opposition, that they assumed at some point they would probably be taking her views into account, and the views of her party into account, as they re-design their constitution. We pointed out—and Frank very eloquently pointed out to them—that in fact she had won two-thirds of the popular vote, an overwhelming voter participation in Burma, and that it was these guys who should be having to ask her for concessions, not the other way around. So again it's not on a straight line.

There are some very hopeful signs out here. In Malaysia, we were hosted by the deputy prime minister, a man by the name of Anwar Abraham, who has written a very interesting book, *Asian Reflections,* talking about the possibility of a multiparty free and open basically Islamic society, in Malaysia—a different kind of Islam from what we're used to when we hear about Iran and Iraq and Sunnis and Shiites and the rest of it. Anwar, incidentally, in his book quotes Hayek. He also quoted John Kenneth Galbraith, so I told him one cancelled the other one out. But he also quotes Alexis de Tocqueville and others. An educated, erudite man.

And that brings me to another point that Frank mentioned when he talked about Chinese accomplishments around the world, and that is the importance out here of something that those of us in this room believe in, but that somehow our younger generation in the United States seems to be losing, and that is the incredible importance of education. And here I'm talking retail not wholesale, of our own kids and grandkids, and making sure that they've got the best opportunities available to them in terms of education. When you go into a place like Malaysia and hear that 14,000 Malaysians are now working on undergraduate degrees in the United States, and in China I believe the number is about 25,000 or 26,000, and in Taiwan it's about the same—you add them all up and have more than a hundred thousand students every year in the United States from this part of the world. Hopefully, they're not just taking back a good professional degree in engineering or economics or chemistry or whatever but also taking back some of the ideas and the ideals that inspire the American system, in the best sense of it.

Last thought, because we really want to get into some Q and A. Our *Index of Economic Freedom* is published every year in December, and last year was the first time we did it jointly with the *Wall Street Journal*, which gave us kind of extra credibility and also extra marketing resources around the world. In the most recent edition, number one, two, four, seven and eleven—five of the top eleven countries with the freest economies, are in Asia. They are Hong Kong, Singapore, New Zealand, Thailand, and Taiwan. The other end, kind of an example in the extremes, from number 140 to 150 you have four, North Korea, Burma, and a couple others that escape me at the moment.

I had the opportunity last December when we launched this publication here in Hong Kong, to present a copy of it to Tung Chee-hwa, the new man in charge of Hong Kong, the new chief executive. He and I had known each other for a number of years. He said, with a twinkle in his eyes, that he'd hoped he would see me back here next December. I thought for a second, I guess it was one of those few times when you come up with the perfect answer on the spot, instead of in the elevator after you've been in the TV studio or something—I said to him, I said, "C. H., that's up to you, it's not up to us." And it is up to them in terms of what they're going to be doing here. We might not see it all in the next six months, but hopefully they're going to keep this place on the right track in terms of trade, taxes, monetary policy, deregulation, an open banking system, and all the other things that make Hong Kong unique.

I argued back in Washington over the last few months, much to the chagrin of some of my conservative friends, when we argued in favor of continued normal trading status or M.F.N. for China, freedom's indivisible. If there's a hundred million people in China right now who are dependent on Western investment, on Western employment, it just doesn't make any sense to me for the U.S. to take that opportunity away from them, because there are other Chinese who don't have religious freedom, don't have freedom of press, and other things. It doesn't mean that we any less despise what the government's doing, but it kind of makes us question those who would cut off our normal trading relationship. Who exactly would we hurt? You wouldn't be hurting thugs in Beijing, you'd be hurting the people who are already making the difference and having a positive impact. But you've probably had that debate over the course of the last couple days. It's been decided now in Washington, at least for the time being that we will continue M.F.N. I think there will be more discussion of it—I hope there will be—in the months ahead. I think there are other things than taking away M.F.N. that can be done in terms of encouraging better policies coming out of Beijing.

Going back to a point Frank made, let me tell a closing story: Over the last twelve years, the last four times I've been in Beijing, I've had the opportunity for a discussion either with my colleagues on the Heritage Board, or in a private meeting, with a foreign minister who's now here in town and is one of the senior P.R.C. officials here for the handover. After the first time, we got the opening ceremonies down to a ritual. He talks for fifteen minutes about how Heritage is wrong in our position on Taiwan, and how Taiwan's an integral part of China, and the future of Taiwan is going to be determined by China, and it's not going to be determined by outside influences. At which point I talk for slightly less time about how Taiwan and the United States are governed by a unique piece of legislation called the Taiwan Relations Act, which supersedes the Shanghai Communique One, and Shanghai Communique Two. It was passed into law, signed by a president, passed by both houses of Congress, and it says that the United States does have special relations and on and on. Okay, we both made our points on Taiwan, now let's talk about something constructive. But he knows where I'm coming from, I know where he's coming from, we get past that first stage, and then we can actually talk about some of the subjects that hopefully unite us, as well as the subjects that divide us. And I think that's what's been missing out here in terms of foreign policy, over the last five years particularly. When you look around, we don't even have an assistant secretary for Asian Affairs and haven't had one for more than a year. The job in Tokyo of ambassador has been vacant now for six months, and on and on. But I'm not here to criticize the current administration's Asia policy, but just to throw some of these ideas and issues out on the table, and to thank you once again, to commend you for realizing that foreign policy is still very important to us.

The fact that the Cold War is over doesn't mean we can go back and retreat into a fortress America. We've got to be engaged, and we've got to be involved in the world, and I commend all of you for being here and for being part of this historic moment. Thanks.

Herschensohn: Thanks very much, Ed. Before we go on to questions, Ambassador Shakespeare just wants to make one quick addendum, one quick point.

Shakespeare: When I was talking, I was highlighting larger situations: Russia, Europe, the United States, China. Every one of those is a state, they are huge material temporal powers. What I say to you now, I never hear discussed ever. It's not discussed in the State Department, it's not discussed at Harvard University, it's not discussed at the Central Intelligence Agency, and it's not discussed at the Heritage Foundation. I never hear this discussed, and it seems to me that it's important—I'm a little beyond my depth in talking about it, but it seems to me that it's something that we ought to have in our minds and it's this:

For two thousand years, more or less, the dominant power, or grouping of powers, in the world has been in the Judeo-Christian tradition. Whether it was Spain or whether it was France or whether it was Italy or whether it was Germany or whether it was England or even whether it was the United States, we were in the Judeo-Christian tradition, and that's been true, more or less, for two thousand years. It's shaped our thinking, it's shaped all of our structures, and out of that tradition came and comes our perception of what is man, what is God, what is the state and, therefore, the structure of the state, the nature of the state, our view of human rights. All of those things stem from that tradition. It didn't save us from making a hash of it many times, the tragedies, the religious wars, the holocaust, all of that sort of thing. I mean we really messed it up a lot, didn't we?

But there always seemed to be something that drew us back, and in my opinion that something was the Judeo-Christian tradition, and that's what is at the heart of Western Civilization. For better or for worse, that has been the dominant philosophical premise of the leading power, or group of powers in the world, for two thousand years. It is now possible, it may not be probable, but it is possible that in the time ahead, not for us in this room, but our grandchildren, Jerry and Patti Hume's grandchildren, they may live in a world where the dominant power or grouping of powers have no real depth association with that tradition. And that's a new phenomenon. If that were to occur we would go into completely uncharted waters. What is it's meaning for civilization and for mankind? I don't address that, I only say that it may be very important, it may be a fundamental consideration. It is never ever discussed. So in your considerations, it might be something that you would care to think about. Thank you.

Question: I was curious about what role India may play in the future.

Shakespeare: Well I'll make a quick answer. You understand that we're blind people in a dark room. In the time fairly quickly ahead, India will have the largest population of the world. But I spoke a while ago about fiber and caliber and toughness of people—I didn't talk about whether it's a good thing or a bad thing. I tried to talk about it as an objective characteristic. God made us all different, and India doesn't seem to be in that posture. As a huge number of people, they can, therefore, effect humanity. They have very, very bright and able students and all of that, but you don't get the sense of India in the twenty-first century moving into a great power situation. And so my fallible human judgment would be, India will matter because of its sheer size, it will matter because of its geography—physically in the middle of Asia—but I would not see India being a huge player in where the world goes in the twenty-first century.

Frank Gaffney: Frank, I want to thank you by your example and by your leadership over the years, and making the point that you've just made here of just how important it is for the United States to be engaged, active, leading, and being powerful in the world. In particular, I commend you for making that point to conservative audiences because we, among all constituencies, seem to lose sight of this in periods when there doesn't seem to be an immediate problem.

If I could digress for one second to say to you, Frank, I think there are indeed those of us who are worrying about precisely the drift that I think you were alluding to a moment ago, among conservatives, among others. The world has dramatically changed following the Cold War; the belief that states are no longer relevant, that we are in one world: one world economy, one world political systems, one world arrangements fashioned by treaties, arms control, environmental agreements, what have you. So I think your raising people's consciousness about that is very well taken. There are some of us, at least, who are worrying about it, and I think we should be.

But to come to the immediate question to both of you if I could, having been on the other side of the M.F.N. debate from you, Ed, one of the things that does strike me as an immediate problem, certainly a near-term problem, indisputably a medium to longer-term problem is what China is doing with the huge revenues it is generating—forty plus billion dollars this year in a trade surplus, more next year in all likelihood, and more beyond that. Those resources are giving rise to capabilities—and I couldn't agree more with your characterization of just how tough, just how ambitious, the Chinese people are—capabilities that are, I'm afraid, over time at least, going to pose real threats to the security interests of the United States. And while I certainly agree, and I think many of us on the other side of this debate agreed, that M.F.N. was a blunt instrument, and that there would be here, people in the States, people in China, who would have been adversely affected by its revocation this year, it seems to me—and I just would invite your response to this, there is no other mechanism at our disposal currently that could as effectively address the problem that this huge windfall is at least exacerbating in China. If we don't come to grips with it as a long, if not nearer-term strategic problem, we're going to be in even greater peril, I'm afraid.

Mr. Feulner: Frank, I agree with you completely. I look forward to the day when we're both back in Washington working side by side as we have been so closely on trying to stop the Chemical Weapons Treaty, promoting the Strategic Defense Initiative, et cetera, the other 99 percent of the times we are working together. And I would say this, that this year's M.F.N. debate has had a very useful impact in terms of forcing all of us to look at some of these other issues. Issues like the crazy, almost privatization of the People's Liberation Army, where we don't even know what businesses they're in, but all of a sudden there's some local unit of the P.L.A. that's out there doing something commercially. Hey! This isn't what we mean by privatization, guys! We want to have somebody in charge of the army and we want to know where they're getting their money from, and what they're spending it on. We want to know what's happening in terms of some of the prison camps over there and, in effect, with slave labor. Because of the really intense re-thinking, there has emerged Spence Abraham's bill SA-10, that I think will give us a good chance to review and re-visit some of the specific targeted questions. I mean there's no difference, I'm sure, between Gaffney and Feulner in terms of wanting to do everything we can to stop China from shipping either high-tech nuclear parts to Pakistan, or missiles to the Middle East, or doing other de-stabilizing things that are outside the range of what civilized nations and proper governments are supposed to do. So let's get on with it, and let's figure out what those are and let's push together through the Congress the right kinds of mechanisms to do that. So Frank, we're going to be back together I'm sure, and we'll be working on that in the months ahead. I admire you always for everything that you and your colleagues do.

Shakespeare: Can I say something on that? If I may add a view, it seems to me, to Frank Gaffney's question there are three factors to be considered, in addition to what Ed mentioned. One is what are the men in Beijing griping about? China will be a rich, industrially successful nation with a very strong people. Two plus two is four. Of course they're going to be a huge power, and, of course, that power will have military applications. It's for sure, that's just the way it will be. The key is the leadership, what will the leaders of the country do with power? Are the men in Beijing primarily Chinese or are they primarily communists or are they primarily human beings who have been corrupted by too much power held too long, or is there some mixture among that? A key question for the United States foreign policy is what the men do in Beijing, and maybe in Hong Kong. That's more important near-term than the fact that they will, of course, be a great power and, therefore, have industrial and military strength.

The second factor relates to China, to mankind, and our policy. How effective really is economic determinism? The great debate in the United States, as I see it relating to China, is the free market. Does it engender decentralization of knowledge and interest and that sort of thing, which act automatically as restraints on central government? Does it engender democracy? That is, in the sense that people participate more and more at different levels and maybe, ultimately, at an open election level? Do free markets lead to that for sure?

The other factor is what is the role of human rights? Because if you put all your chips on the free market, it damn well better work. So, as I see the debate as to how the United States should relate to China, there's an a priori. Each of us, to the extent that we choose to influence or try to influence the critical policy of the greatest temporal power on earth, is, how much emphasis do you want to put on economic determinism as a force, and how much emphasis do you want to put on human rights, and therefore, what should our government do?

Question: When Ambassador Shakespeare got up a second time to make his very important remarks about the spiritual dimension, I poked Todd Culbertson in the side, and I said I hope he mentions the word "Islam." I think that if China is an 800 pound gorilla, then a real understanding of Islam, its prophecies, the way it behaves, might be a 500 pound gorilla that can grow. It's probably the most perfectly conceived warrior-faith we have ever had outside of Marxist-Leninism, and I'd be very interested to know what you think about Islam and it's success. Do we have a Saracen version of it, which was a wonderful culture that rescued Aristotle, or the sleep of Islam? It is very important for human rights, and how we're going to live our lives, and I wonder if you have some comment?

Shakespeare: I just gave the microphone to Ed, and he gave it back to me. (Laughter) Neither of us mentioned Islam. You did, Ed? Did you make a reference to it? Well, Islam's a very difficult question. Any great idea—Islam is a great idea, which has had a staggering impact on the world for 1,300 years. The biggest Islamic society in all the world is Indonesia with a population close to two hundred million people, and they're probably 85 percent Islam. And Malaysia is Islam, 70 percent, but Malaysia is a small country. Burma is 70 percent Islam. I don't think, in the case of China, that Islam is a huge consideration, and therefore, while it would have a relevance to Southeast Asia and, therefore, a certain relevance to overall Asia, it would not have a direct relevance to the evolution of China, which is what we're talking about here. In Malaysia, in Indonesia, even in Burma, they speak of Islam, the government, the people, the leaders, in a very different way than they do in the Mid-East. It's a softer, more moderate, more tolerant version of it. You get a sense when you travel to Southeast Asia that you don't necessarily get when you're traveling in Northern Africa or the Mid-East or even in Pakistan. That's important.

Howard Ahmanson: Christianity is making great progress in Asia and Africa and other places at the time that Europe has almost renounced the Judeo-Christian tradition completely, and large portions of America are turning away from it. What do you see in that?

Feulner: Howard, this time the mike was pushed to me when I'm sitting next to one of the conservative movement's real experts on the interplay of religious principles around the world, and what it means for the future. I think Christianity does have great prospects and is making tremendous inroads here in Asia. I believe, at least from my perspective over the last twenty years, that in the United States, faith-based institutions, churches, are stronger today than they have been in the last generation or generation and a half, at least. At the same time, there's a lot of rot in the secular culture. There is the constant battle that we have to fight over the legitimate role of religion in the secular state, and the crazy interpretation of freedom of religion as handed down by various courts in the United States. But those are kind of passing debates that we will, in the long haul, win. Fundamentally for the middle-term, in the next fifty or seventy-five years, regarding Christianity, I'm pretty optimistic.

As Frank points out, it's the ultimate battle of ideas that we have to engage in, and defend, as best we can for the long-term.

Herschensohn: Thanks so much to both of you. You added a great deal to the conference. Thanks.

If I may ask the delegates, please make sure you have your ID Badge for tonight, and we'll see you at the dock at Victoria Harbor for admittance to the yacht. It will be a long and late night. The handover fireworks display should be at its height at midnight. Tomorrow night will be another late one on the yacht, with fireworks in the harbor again, this time by the People's Republic of China. Since you may want to rest up tomorrow, there won't be any conference speakers until the day after tomorrow, Wednesday morning at nine o'clock.

David Dodwell

Conference Speaker
July 2, 1997 - 9:00 a.m.

Bruce Herschensohn: I know that most of you know of, or read articles by, David Dodwell. He's now with Jardine Fleming as director of Group Corporate Communications. He was a journalist and world trade editor with the *Financial Times*. He's recognized as a true expert on the free market and trade throughout the world, particularly in Asia, and more particularly in China. He's been to hundreds of factories there in most of its provinces and has made a life's study of economics. I'm so glad you saw fit to be here. David?

David Dodwell: I remember a famous line from the book, *Nobel House,* which some of you may have read, in which the Taipan of Jardine Mathison greeted an American businessman at Kai Tak Airport, and the businessman—who was in Hong Kong for the first time—said, "What on earth is that smell? I'm sure you all notice it." And the head of Jardine Mathison said, "That, sir, is the smell of money."

As I watched the fireworks last night and the deep smoke over Kowloon, I suspect a lot of you too, yesterday inhaled the smell of money. A hundred million dollars worth—Hong Kong dollars—of fireworks exploded last night. So the smell of money is often around you in Hong Kong.

Anyway, I'm here today to talk about the transition. I understand that you have had a number of long and interesting sessions already. I'm instructed to try and be brief to allow as many questions as possible. It's testing for me in that some of the presentations that I've had the opportunity to give over the last six months following the completion of the book, have stretched to three and a half hours, so being asked to give you the fifteen minute version is testing.

Anyway, is Hong Kong in trouble? That's the question I suppose you're all here to ask and to have answered. If you were to read a motley scattering of articles in the international media, either currently or over the last six months, the answer you would say is, probably, yes. Now, for many of us in Hong Kong and certainly for myself over the last year and a half, that is a very perplexing position. It's perplexing to try and work out why the international media, and no doubt many people behind them, are so unilaterally or universally negative about the prospects here in Hong Kong.

First of all, I ask myself as a former journalist a great deal of the time, why are journalists so negative? Well, as I was sitting, running the Hong Kong Bureau here through 1984, through the China-British negotiations of the Joint Declaration, I, like every journalist here, was well aware of the fact that you do not endear yourself to an editor back at headquarters if you tell him there is no story here. There is a strong vested interest in telling your editors there's a story. And if you'd heard from the China editor of the *Wall Street Journal* here in Hong Kong, you would have learned that he actually spent a month back in the U.S. early this year, trying to wrestle with his own editorial godheads, who simply refused to accept or publish the more nuanced picture that he was transmitting from here. So it's not just a matter of locally based journalists fretting about their own Pulitzer Prizes, but those back in headquarters that is a long way from the story, bringing forward their own preconceptions.

The reason why preconceptions have had some strong staying power in Hong Kong is largely because Hong Kong's story is an extremely complex story, nor is it very well marketed. You have a very light government here that doesn't actually know a great deal of what is going on in this economy. They're not well equipped. There is not, for example, the Economic Development Board in Singapore that tells you what is going on today or why it's going on, or how it will be going on into the future. There's a sense of what the New Zealanders call, "she'll be alright." You don't really ask any questions about how the economy moved from A to B, it just has, and the fact that it has, by precedent, suggests that it will continue doing the same. And with the light government in Hong Kong, as we have, that's very much the only option open to the government in interpreting what's going on here.

First of all, this economy is astonishingly robust. Not just strong, but robust. More than anything else it's robust because it's immensely flexible. As I've scratched my head over just why it seems trite to say the economy is flexible. Lot's of people say their economies are flexible. But as I scratch my head to work deeper inside this insight, you realize that over the entire post-war life of Hong Kong business, Hong Kong business people have been market-takers rather than market-makers. They take the outside world as a given and work around it. That's been the case as the U.S. has introduced quota after quota after quota and widened the spectrum of quotas over three decades. As we've lived year by year with the annual prospect of the M.F.N. being suspended, as far as China's concerned, this has led local manufacturers here to have to be extraordinarily flexible. As a sidebar, I think this market-taking psychology is important politically as well as economically. Hong Kong people, historically, are not people who plow into problems and try to solve them head on. They're people who historically—through perhaps centuries of learning how useless it is to cajole with officialdom—have spent their energies going around problems and making the best of necessity, rather than hitting problems head-on and wasting a lot of energy in that process. So around this immense flexibility you have, as I've said, an extremely robust economy that is much less weak and worried than many journalists and outsiders imagine. You all know, as well as I, having been here over the last few days, that the stock market is at a record high, property markets are at levels that most of us couldn't afford to buy in, even with good U.S. salaries. As an interesting alternative insight into just how buoyant this economy is, Hong Kong last year, 1996, imported three times more structural steel for construction than the U.K. This is still a busy economy.

Now, why does this reality of immense robustness and immense economic strength not match the international perceptions that I read so extensively in papers of the U.S. and Europe? That essentially is because Hong Kong is what I call a smoke and mirrors economy. Almost nothing that you look at is what it appears to be. Until just a year ago, there was no attempt to measure the G.N.P. in Hong Kong, and still there's a three year time lag in any attempt by the government to offer a G.N.P. number. Hong Kong is the seventh largest trading power in the world if you put the E.U. into a single category. It's actually the fourth largest trading power in the world, but direct trade in Hong Kong almost doesn't matter anymore. Nor do re-exports, which account for a much larger proportion of trade than direct trade. Trans-shipments where cargoes don't touch Hong Kong physically at all are an increasingly important part of Hong Kong's overall trade. What seems to perplex a lot of outsiders is that it doesn't matter. It's the estimation here that in every transshipped transaction, the value added that sticks in Hong Kong is between 12 and 16 percent of the value of the cargo, depending on the particular cargo. This is without the cargo coming anywhere in Hong Kong's territory. The strength is not in the trade numbers, the strength is in capturing value added. Actually as I look at the spats that exist between the U.S. and Japan or the U.S. and China on bilateral trade balances, it simply perplexes me, because bilateral trade balances nowadays, with globalized industry and so on, mean next to nothing, unless you look at the value added that is captured in the process in transacting trade. So the trade figures certainly tell a different story from what the nominal numbers suggest.

Who is a Hong Kong person? We understand that between one and two million out of Hong Kong's six million people have, either directly or through their family, a foreign passport, able to emigrate elsewhere. A Hong Kong Canadian is more often than not a Hong Kong Chinese who migrated to Canada, spent three years suffering hard in the economic adversities of the Canadian economy, and fled back here as quickly as possible to earn money.

Look, too, at foreign investment. Hong Kong is the world's fourth largest source of foreign investment after the U.S., the U.K. and Germany. Hong Kong is the largest single source of foreign investment in the world—26 billion U.S. dollars in foreign investment. This is an economy of 6.3 million people. How on earth does Hong Kong become such an important source of foreign investment—on global terms, not just in local terms? It's a very complex story about why Hong Kong is as important a foreign investor as it is. This is not flight capital, as many in Singapore would suggest it is, because most of it flies into China, and that doesn't make any sense at all if you're worried about flight capital. So the conundrum about foreign investment is a very important one.

The smoke and mirrors is also very important when you look at the debate over Hong Kong's manufacturing. I'm sure while you've been here you've had some people mention the dangers facing Hong Kong manufacturing as it potentially hollows out. In 1980 there were about 900,000 jobs in manufacturing in Hong Kong, today it's about 380,000. On the back of those raw numbers, many in Hong Kong are arguing not only that Hong Kong's manufacturing economy is hollowing out, but also that as a result of that, the government must intervene to support science-based and manufacturing activities. However, Hong Kong's manufacturing economy is not only strong but probably stronger than it's ever been.

Yes, the jobs are down but Hong Kong factories today employ at least six million people on the mainland, they employ many hundreds of thousands across other economies in the Pacific, in the Caribbean, and in Europe, and they have developed over the past couple of decades, immense skills as manufacturers. I see in Hong Kong, an astonishingly large population of what I call many multi-nationals. There was a very interesting survey completed shortly before we finished our own study by consultants here, looking at Hong Kong soft-goods industry, that's garments, footwear, and leather wear—35,000 companies involved. The average size of the company was twenty-four people. Half of those companies have manufacturing capacity in two countries, 29 percent have manufacturing capacities in three countries or more. Now, throughout my career in the *Financial Times*, looking at companies in Europe or the U.S. I never found companies so small that had developed transnational skills. Never. You get companies at 500 maybe, you get companies at 1,000 quite often, but tewnty-four people with transnational skills managing multiple currencies, multi-cultural work forces, et cetera, et cetera, that is very strange and very rare. There are unusual circumstances behind that, but it's enabled Hong Kong to develop what I describe as packaging and integrating capabilities across the region that are very rare. And this goes some way actually to explaining why Hong Kong's manufacturing has not hollowed out. If you develop transnational skills early, if you develop these packaging and integrating skills, then you can actually break down the manufacturing value chain quite easily. If you take from product conception at one end, right through assembly, to the distribution and after sales service at the other end of the value chain, then what these companies have done is broken down the value chain and shifted different parts of the value chain to different areas. Obviously the assembly, which is land and labor-intensive, has gone on to the mainland, has gone into Thailand, has gone to Sri Lanka, but the high value added parts of activity have almost all stayed here.

So what we see is not a dismantling of the manufacturing economy, but when you take the smoke and mirrors away, what you see is a shift from a manual economy to a knowledge intensive economy, from an enclave economy with it's back to China, to a metropolitan economy with roots not only into China but across the region as a whole. You should look at Hong Kong as a metropolitan economy, just as you would look at New York as a metropolitan economy serving a wider part of the U.S. economy, or London as a metropolitan serving the U.K. economy or the European economy, so it's demographics in terms of the amount of the economy dedicated to manufacturing and services and so on, is much less atypical than outsiders would imagine.

But I still hear many people say, surely an economy can't subsist on services; after all 84 percent of the G.D.P. today in Hong Kong is accounted for by services. There is, first of all, a sort of residual chauvinism around manufacturing; real men don't do services. Unfortunately, that's a prejudice that's hard to overcome. But first of all you've got to note in Hong Kong that the growth in services has come not from consumer services, not from the sort of hamburger flipper jobs that are so much a concern in the U.S., but from producer services—legal services, accounting services, civil engineering services, architectural services, trade related services, trade finance and financial services linked with trade and international finance. These are not only quite different from consumer services, but they're also very high value added, and they've generated 14 percent real growth in the services economy per year for the last two decades. The result is in the statistics that you all have seen; almost zero unemployment, 7 1/2 percent annual growth over the last twenty years. Hong Kong is now the sixth or seventh leading trading economy, the fifth most important financial services economy, and now has the fourth highest G.D.P. per capita in the world. It is in effect, if you put the population and per capita G.D.P. together, as big an economy as Switzerland. In fact, if you put Hong Kong's black economy into the raw numbers, then you have an economy that's probably significantly larger than that of Switzerland. Now this has happened very rapidly, very dramatically, and it's crept up on a lot of people without them actually noticing it, which contributes to the smoke and mirrors problem here.

Of course, as I keep warning people, past performance is no guide to future performance. There's absolutely no question out of our own studies that there are uncertainties that do need serious attention. Some of them are linked with 1997 and some of them have nothing to do with 1997. First of all, yes, if anything were to undermine the legal system here, the legal integrity that exists here, then the strengths that we talk about would quickly be eroded, and that has to be something that we watch with great concern as we go forward from today. Secondly, what I call the "three-frees" are critical to defend in Hong Kong: freedom of movement of the people, freedom of movement of capital and freedom of movement of information. Those "three-frees" have been very important in underpinning Hong Kong's competitive advantage in the past, and if they were eroded in the future, they would hurt the competitive advantages that exist here.

There's also a very distinct separation in Hong Kong between government and business. Government doesn't get involved in business. Yes, there are monopolies here and those monopolies are a source of concern. But they are private sector monopolies. The port is run by four private companies with government franchises. The electricity supplied here is supplied by two companies, both of them working on government sanctioned franchises. There are monopolies here, they're a problem, but they are not run by the government. That allows the government to be an honest broker, and that is not common, actually whether you're in large parts of Europe, where the government still runs airlines and telecoms, or whether you're in Japan or Korea or Indonesia or Malaysia or Singapore, where the government is an active player in the economy. And certainly that's true in China. There is a widespread unfamiliarity with an anachronistic British Colonial convention of government staying out of business, and leaving business to do business. If that were eroded, then that would also lead to problems in the future, not least among those problems of course being corruption, which I'm sure a number of you have talked about and thought about over the past few days.

But apart from the 1997 issues there are other issues, which I think are equally, and in some contexts more important. Costs. You don't have to stay in Hong Kong for many days to learn how expensive it is to live and work here. Skills. Skills are in immensely short supply in a knowledge based economy. If you assume that this is an economy that needs not just graduate skills but post-graduate skills in very large numbers, then there is acute pressure on the skills pool, and there is an urgent need to address more attention to the development of Hong Kong's skills base. It's moderately encouraging to note that of 100,000 Hong Kongers currently in tertiary education, 34,000 are studying outside Hong Kong; a full third of Hong Kong's undergraduates study in other countries, many of them in the United States. And it's that internationalness that's actually been a contributory strength in Hong Kong. It's also allowed Hong Kong's economy to draw on skills base much broader than it's own education system could sustain. So that internationalness of education is likely to have to continue into the future if Hong Kong's competitiveness is to continue to be underpinned.

I would say there's a rather interesting or anachronistic challenge facing Hong Kong too, as it becomes middle class and less entrepreneurial. When I was first in Hong Kong in the late '70s, Hong Kong was still very definitely a refugee community. People had fled China, they were going to stay here for as short a time as necessary to put their lives in order, to save money before either things stabilized on the mainland when they might return or before they moved to the U.S. or to Canada or Australia. Hong Kong was a temporary haven. They wanted no interference from the government. They wanted to be left alone, to save and to earn. That is a very important driver, providing edge and energy to the entrepreneurial population here. As China becomes more stable, as it starts to open up slowly, as the region as a whole becomes more prosperous, so Hong Kong has an increasingly large and substantial middle class. But those in the middle class that are an increasingly large part of the population don't have the same entrepreneurial drive that their fathers and mothers had when they arrived with next to nothing from different parts of China. One has to ask where the future population of entrepreneurs in Hong Kong will come from. It's not readily apparent without saying there will be more mainland Chinese coming here intending to go home to China, taking what they've saved here back into their own cities, to build businesses as big wheels back there.

Finally, I think at this point I'd like to raise an issue which I know a lot of people, including Martin Lee, talk about a great deal, and that is the rift in Hong Kong between big business interests and those of ordinary people. There are a number of people among the most politically concerned here in Hong Kong who make a great deal about this issue, and I find it really very puzzling, because if there is any community in the world where a division between business and ordinary people does not exist, it's Hong Kong. Hong Kong has 380,000 businesses in a population of 6.3 million people. Ordinary people are business. My father-in-law—my wife is Hong Kong Chinese here—my father-in-law is a company of one, and he has been all of his life. Her brother is a company of two, and he has been all of his life. These are not big businesses. There are not enterprises where unionized workers are alienated on salary terms from big business who are exploiting them for whatever they can get. Business goes right to the roots of Hong Kong's economy, and to suggest that there is a difference between business and the ordinary people is, frankly, nonsense.

So returning basically to the core thesis, as we were studying Hong Kong's economy, coming to the conclusions of our book, we felt it was important not to ask whether there were challenges in Hong Kong, because, yes, there are. There are challenges actually facing every economy. It wasn't a matter of whether there were challenges, it was a matter of whether there were challenges that were big enough to derail an essentially very strong and robust economy. Actually when you ask that question rather than whether there are challenges, then the answer as we sit here at the moment is a categorical "no."

But what, you say, about the threat from China? Well, first of all the threat from China isn't new. Ever since I've been in Hong Kong in the late '70s, all of Hong Kong's water, the large majority of its water, 70 percent of its food, has come from the mainland. We have been materially dependent on the mainland economy. Secondly, China is the biggest item on both sides of Hong Kong's balance sheet. As an asset over twenty years, China has far outweighed its role as a liability. Driving that has been the fact that the mainland economy has been liberalizing, and liberalizing steadily. Now, as I go back into China and wrestle with officials, whether it's in Beijing or in the provincial cities, I tear my hair out like most businesspeople do. This is an economy that is still very closed. This is an economy where there are not the freedoms that you or I expect. But compare today with when I was living in Beijing in 1982, in the work unit, where even if I was constipated and needed laxatives, I had to go to my work unit leader to get permission to go to a doctor to get the laxatives. If I wanted to go to the cinema, I had to go to the work unit leader, who would apply for cinema tickets on my behalf so that I could go to the cinema. China is not recognizable today by comparison with what was in place even in 1982, and I think as we judge China today and we—all of us—impatiently wait for it to become more liberal than it currently is, and become more an economy with which we can feel any sense of empathy, so we must recognize how far it's come over quite a short period of time and how consistently it's been in one direction.

In addition to that, you have to look at Hong Kong's role on the mainland itself. A lot of people talk about the dangers to Hong Kong: of China influencing Hong Kong, but they make rather little of how Hong Kong has had an absolutely mammoth impact on the mainland economy. There is no province in China in which Hong Kong is not the biggest investor. You go to any province, and Hong Kong is the biggest investor. Fifty percent of the investment from Shanghai today is from Hong Kong. The rebuilding of Shanghai is coming from Hong Kong. There are 120,000 joint ventures across the mainland funded by Hong Kong companies. I've already mentioned that there are at least six million jobs directly attributable to Hong Kong foreign joint ventures. This is not just economically important, this is politically important because China's in the middle of a monstrously difficult task trying to unravel the basically bankrupt state enterprise economy. Since I was first working extensively in China in the middle '80s, the state enterprises have shrunk from something in the region of 70 percent of the industry output, down to something like 45 percent. Foreign joint ventures and what we call township and village enterprises, the market part of China's economy, have grown from the region of 4 percent to 52 percent of the G.D.P. This has been driven by Hong Kong investment and a Hong Kong ethos of doing business. The marketization of China is occurring by virtue of Hong Kong business people going into China and investing and creating jobs. So it is not appropriate simply to say that Hong Kong's role in this context is economic. It is political and profoundly so.

I think it's important also, as I turn finally away from China, to remember that we're focused at the moment almost monolithically on the down-side. There is for Hong Kong an immense potential up-side to which we need to pay attention. China's economy is in the process of liberalizing, opening up, on a very substantial scale, and, as I mentioned already, there are 120,000 ventures across the mainland, a large number of those now serving the domestic economy. As China's domestic economy continues to open, then there is no economy better placed to capitalize on the advantages that exist, than Hong Kong. That is a very important up-side for an economy of 6.3 million people. If you combine that with the fact that the Asia Pacific region at large is today more prosperous, has a larger consuming middle class than at any stage in our living memories, then you also recognize the potential for Hong Kong in serving that economy or those economies.

So let me conclude, quickly. Yes, the concerns for Hong Kong are real, but the vulnerabilities that Hong Kong faces are not new, and actually Hong Kong's track record in managing the problems linked with China over the past has been really quite good. Beyond that, there are benefits that will arise from answering to one landlord, rather than two—those two landlords having spent a large part of the last decade squabbling with each other. The benefit of having one landlord rather than two is no small benefit for the Hong Kong people. As for the question, "What about China taking over Hong Kong?" Actually yesterday is the first day in Hong Kong's history that Hong Kong people have ruled Hong Kong, and that is the future that Hong Kong people are defining for themselves. When the Joint Declaration was signed in 1984, there was not even one Hong Kong person around the table in the negotiations. These were negotiations conducted by diplomats from London and from Beijing. There wasn't a single Hong Kong person at the table. Throughout the subsequent thirteen years to June 30, what happened in Hong Kong was the subject of negotiation between British and Chinese diplomats. As of today, Hong Kong people are negotiating on Hong Kong's behalf and that is the first time in 150 years. That's no small change.

I'd like finally to say, as a journalist having worked here through the '80s, since the Joint Declaration was signed in the autumn of 1984, Hong Kong increasingly has become the victim of what I call 20/20 foresight. There's been an appointed date in the future; everybody has been able to focus on it, rather like a dental appointment or going to a doctor's surgery, knowing there's a problem you need sorted out. You can worry about it, you can scratch away at the problem, and the concern over that problem can be massively exaggerated from the reality. The fact is that as of yesterday Hong Kong rejoined the rest of the world with what I call a normal uncertain future. And given Hong Kong's normal uncertain future; compare that with a normal uncertain future of British people after the Labor Party's election victory or the same in France or in Southeast Asia where Suharto and Lee Kwan Yew are reaching the ends of their political lives with succession problems that are not small. When you look at Korea and Japan facing systemic problems that cannot be underestimated, then I promise you that the great majority of people in Hong Kong would not swap their normal uncertain future for that of other people elsewhere.

Herschensohn: We have a limited time for questions.

Question: There are reports that Tung Chee-hwa and his advisors are interested in imposing an industrial policy on Hong Kong. This is an idea now discredited in Japan and Western Europe, an idea that government can target and support the industries of the future. This is odd timing, because that idea is falling into disfavor around the world. What are the prospects of that happening here in Hong Kong?

Mr. Dodwell: Small. I think there's another important issue which people have lost in the fog here over the past six months, as we focused on Tung Chee-hwa and his Ex-Co. People have forgotten that Hong Kong has been and will continue to be run by civil servants running technocratic departments.

Question: Just very quickly, can you sort out for us the difference between say the "A" and "B" shares listed in Shanghai and the "H" shares listed here, and the so-called red chip stocks that are trading here, and what sort of companies list in these different places, and which of these stock markets you think are going to become preeminent in the future?

Dodwell: That is a very difficult question to answer in any short way. The real distinction between an "A" share and a red chip is very blurred. People use the two terms intermixed very often. Those Chinese companies that are listing in Hong Kong are doing so to raise international capital. They need foreign currency, which they can't get access to inside the domestic economy. Insofar as Chinese companies need international capital, then they will be coming to New York, Hong Kong, Singapore, and London to raise that capital. Hong Kong will, for the foreseeable future, be the principal location for the international fund-raisings of Mainland Chinese companies. This is actually going to grow significantly. I mean Hong Kong's stock market will, ten years from now, be very significantly different from what it is today, on the back of an increasingly large number of mainland companies that list on the Exchange and raise money here. These are going to be large by anybody's criteria. China Telecom is going to list here in autumn, with an initial offering that will involve twenty billion U.S. dollars. This is big money by anybody's criteria, and it's actually as much as the entire red chip list in Hong Kong, in their capitalization. So this is going to, over time, quite rapidly perhaps, change the demographics of Hong Kong's stock market. Now, there is concern over those companies because there is not the transparency that you or I would expect from a company when we invest in them in the U.S. or in Europe. They are coming here asking a lot of people to take risks. They are also coming here to learn the rules of the Hong Kong game, and as a result of that, the firm managers and the investment bankers are essentially saying, "If you want us to raise money for you in the international market then you're sure going to have to give us better information than you have historically." So there is, through Hong Kong, a steady pressure on mainland companies to knock their accounts into shape so that we, as outsiders, can understand what on earth is going on inside them. There's a lot more to say on that subject. It's an interesting one, but hopefully that covers some of the issues you raised.

Question: On that point, one of the things that came out shortly before this group left the States, and I have a copy of it, is a report that's been published by the AFL-CIO about the large and growing number of companies that are doing business under one banner or another, but that are basically operations of the People's Liberation Army. And there's a large number of them in the States, as you know, as well as operating elsewhere. They are involved in everything from ceramics to various metals, to plastic toys. When you speak of transparency or the lack of it, do you see who these people really are in these companies and as they're coming to the marketplace, both for stocks and for bonds? Do you think investors are in a position to adequately understand that their investments may, in fact, be aiding and abetting activities that could quite frankly be very inimical to U.S. interests?

Mr. Dodwell: If you look at the prospectuses as they've been published when companies from the mainland have come here to list, then the short answer is "yes." I mean, those are quite robust prospectuses that would certainly pass muster in the London market. I don't know the U.S. regulation environment clearly enough to know whether they would also pass muster there. I was actually traveling in China as the army was demolished from ten million people down to one million in 1986, and that dismantling of the army occurred as the leaders in the economy realized not only that they couldn't sustain this large military monolith any longer, but, secondly, most of the technologies of any worth in the economy had been the preserve of the military historically. So overnight I was going into factories in which most of the defense industries are based, in the interior for historic security reasons. Those factories had been producing airplane engines and wings for fighter aircraft and God knows what, a year earlier, but when I went in their same physical infrastructure, all of it pretty shoddy, they were making refrigerators and air conditioners, and they were still army factories in terms of central control. So they have civilianized, and that does make the distinction between the military's role in a strict military sense, and it's role in the economy, as a simple player in the civilian economy. Difficult to define. Nevertheless, it is sufficiently transparent for us to give some reasonably clear answers about where the investment is going or where the lines can be drawn between companies. As the township and village enterprise economy grows to account for more and more of the economy, this problem over time will become less. Note that the state-owned enterprises, of whom the military factories are a small part, have shrunk from employing in the region of 140 million people a decade ago to about 102 million at of the end of '96. The township and village enterprises, the small and private enterprises that have been spawned since 1978 have grown from nothing, to account for 120 million jobs today. This is the economy that is attracting international investment, that is offering new jobs to the young as they come out of school in China. It's into those companies that Hong Kong companies are investing, and I would suggest that international investors could and should do the same. That's where the future of China's economy is, not in the over capitalized technologically now wearing out an over-employed state economy.

Question: You mentioned two things that depend on 1997 in a way, that are critical to the Hong Kong economy: First, legal integrity. We've heard some horror stories about that in the past few days, about people jailed, people who got on the wrong side of somebody in China and who have lost their businesses and their physical freedom, let alone other freedoms, the freedom of movement, and people and capital and information. We've also heard and read horror stories of the abuses of human rights going on in China, increased persecution of

Christians, and also of people's choices about how many children they can have. As you were talking about the army and the army businesses, I couldn't help but wonder about the geopolitical aims of the people who are, indeed, in charge of the political and legal future of China itself. So what's your read on the prospects for the future on those critical things?

Mr. Dodwell: I think the core answer is really that the world's media and most of the world's embassies are based in Beijing. There are at the heart of official China. Their contact is with official China. When I've been to Beijing and Shanghai I was hassled more by officialdom than anywhere else in China. The thing that has happened in China, that journalists, and diplomats for that matter don't track properly because they don't have the time to travel away from Beijing, is just how the wider economy, the wider country has been liberalized. If you go to the far north, then you find populations that no longer live in fear of a police state. Now, you have a central authority that is still, by our standards, immensely regressive, but I ask you to compare what exists now with what existed just fifteen years ago, and track the amount of change. Yes, there are horror stories. I can tell you horror stories from 1982 when I was living in China that would make most people's hair curl. But I also know most of those Chinese people that I came to know then, who risked their lives talking to me in 1982, can talk freely today. They can call radio phone-ins and complain about the government. Things have changed. They haven't changed as much as we want them to change. They're going to have to change a long way before we're happy with the circumstances that exist on the mainland. Of course the central authorities are going to tell you they are in control of what's happening across the country at large. That isn't, however, what is happening. Even back in 1987, '88, when I was visiting factories across different provinces in China, I'd arrive with cuttings galore from radio monitorings of bulletins from the leadership in Beijing saying that this reform had been introduced at the factory level, and these reforms had been introduced in terms of workers, and workers' terms of employment, and where they could recruit from and so on. I would arrive and I would say, "I understand that there have been all these changes. What's been the effect here? Do you have more powers here?" They didn't know what I was talking about. Secondly, when I went into the next factory, I got a wholly different set of answers from what I got in the first factory. The fact is that what happens on the ground across China today bears almost no reflection on what Beijing says is occurring.

In certain respects, my anxiety is less over the heavy hand of the state agencies, even though they are worrisome. My concern is over the anarchic state that exits in an economy that has been growing in excess of 10 percent a year for the last two decades and which has grown basically out of control of the central authorities. This is the environment where corruption can be fostered and where the principal cause is actually the pace of change, not the regulatory control or the grip from the center. Anarchy is a much bigger problem in China today than the admitted and serious problem of central regulatory control.

Mr. Herschensohn: I promised you that you'd be out by 10:00, and we made it. Thanks so much for sharing your insight with us.

Hugh Davies

Conference Speaker
July 2, 1996 - 10:30 a.m.

Bruce Herschensohn: We've all been witness to a lot of history on this trip. We have more history today. This is the first public address—the first public session—of Hugh Davies, who is the senior representative of the Joint Liaison Group between Great Britain and the People's Republic of China. He will be holding that position through the year 2000, unless he's posted elsewhere in the interim. But that group will go on through the year 2000. I know at the last meeting of the Joint Liaison Group, which was May 30, there was a number of disagreements, and Hugh Davies was more than courageous in stressing them in regard to the right of abode of Hong Kong people, and regarding the transfer of government files from Great Britain to the People's Republic of China. He was born in India and he served in Beijing. We're privileged to have him with us. This is one of those sessions that I hoped like the devil would come off. We're grateful to you, Hugh, for being with us at this particular time.

Hugh Davies: Well, thank you very much. I was delighted to receive your invitation, and as you say, it's the first day after the first day of Britain's relinquishing its colonial responsibilities. Frankly, I couldn't have managed any earlier date, because two days ago I was still negotiating until the last minute on the choreography of the arrangements. And yesterday I was doing my diplomatic duty by attending all the first functions of the new S.A.R. and of the Central People's Government. So today, in this what one might term British weather, I can begin to think about what happens next.

As I understand it, you've asked an important question, which is what Britain's future responsibilities should be in Hong Kong, and how we will carry out those responsibilities. Well I hope that I'm entitled in addressing this question to step back in time and say something about how we got to where we are now. I take that as a good way to proceed, because I noticed that Lee Kwan Yew the other day at a similar sort of conference here was asked to predict the future and spent all his time talking about the past. So who am I to deny that sort of way forward?

Looking back, Hong Kong's links with Britain were always destined to be redesigned. The Chinese made clear that Hong Kong would never follow other colonies to independence. The ninety-nine-year lease on the New Territories was to run out, as we know, in 1997. Following Mrs. Thatcher's visit to Peking in 1982, Britain and China began discussing the future of Hong Kong. The Chinese made clear that they would reassume sovereignty this year. Discussions were protracted and difficult, but by December of 1984, we had reached agreement on the terms of the Joint Declaration. We agreed that Hong Kong would continue to exist for at least fifty years from 1997, as a Special Administrative Region of China, which would enjoy a high degree of autonomy. It's way of life would be preserved under the concept of "One country—two systems," whereby socialism would be practiced on the mainland, if that's what you call it these days, and capitalism in Hong Kong. The Joint Liaison Group was established to act as the channel of consultation between China and Britain on matters affecting the transition. There were twelve and a half years between the signatures of the Joint Declaration and the transfer of sovereignty on the 30th of June.

The transition couldn't be easy. Most of Hong Kong's population preferred the status quo, and the process was immeasurably complicated by the event of Tiananmen in June 1989. Almost all the major difficulties which have arisen during the transitional period can be laid at the door of Tiananmen. It had a devastating effect on Hong Kong where over a million people came out on the streets to demonstrate. In China the leaders decided that Hong Kong had supported the democracy movement, and that they would never tolerate Hong Kong being used as what they saw as a base for subversion in the future. The result? First, the people of Hong Kong demanded greater guarantees of human rights and accountability of the government beyond 1997. And secondly, the leadership in China demanded a greater degree of government control to ensure that Hong Kong could never play a subversive role. Inevitably, these conflicting attitudes have led to great difficulties in areas such as preservation of the legal system and, in particular, the constitutional arrangements.

In the immediate aftermath of Tiananmen, the Hong Kong government, with the full backing of the British government, pursued three confidence-building measures: construction of a major new airport, a Bill of Rights introduced to incorporate the provisions of the two U.N. Human Rights Covenants, and special arrangements for 50,000 selected heads of Hong Kong families to be given full British passports with right to abode in the U.K. While these measures were widely welcome in Hong Kong, they were each seen by the Chinese government as a challenge and a provocation. The period of reasonably constructive relations, which had followed the signing of the Joint Declaration, was replaced by a period of·stand-off and obstruction. The arrival of the new governor, Chris Patten, in the summer of '92, provided a change of style. Unfortunately, the Chinese chose to make this a pretext for increased confrontation and reduced cooperation. Attempts to seek consensus on the way forward for Hong Kong's constitutional development were rejected by Peking. Eventually, after many rounds of negotiation, the Hong Kong government introduced legislation on constitutional development, which was passed into law in the summer of 1994. The Chinese government denounced the arrangements and announced that the Legislative Council elected in 1995, under these arrangements, would be disbanded at the moment of handover and that a new so-called Provisional Legislative Council would take its place until elections under amended electoral legislation had taken place.

So much for history and background. I'll come to future prospects in a moment. Let me first remind you of Hong Kong's importance and economic dynamism, although I have no doubt you've heard about this from others. This is why Hong Kong matters to you, and to us in Britain, and to the world—and to China. Hong Kong is the freest economy in the world and the third most competitive. It has the second largest stock market in Asia. It's the world's fifth largest banking center and the fifth largest foreign exchange market in terms of turnover. Its average annual growth rate in real terms over the past ten years has been 6.5 percent. Hong Kong is the seventh largest trading entity in the world, or the fourth if the European Union is counted as a single entity, and has the busiest container port in terms of through-port. It has the third busiest airport in the world in terms of international passengers, and the second busiest in terms of volume of cargo handled. Hong Kong is building, as you know, a new airport to open next year, with the capacity to be the world's busiest. The G.D.P. is now among the highest in Asia following Japan and slightly below Singapore. It surpasses the levels of several industrialized economies, including Canada, Australia, and my own country, the United Kingdom. So Hong Kong's shape right now is pretty robust. It's growing now at around 5 percent per annum. It's fiscal reserves, which the S.A.R. has inherited, will total some forty-seven billion U.S. dollars. The currency is strong. Foreign exchange reserves are around sixty-four million, the seventh in the world and six times those equivalent figures in 1986. Investment is strong, and in April we opened here, in Hong Kong, the world's longest road and rail suspension bridge. Hong Kong's position as the business harbor of the Asian Pacific Region is stronger than ever. Over 2,000 multinationals now have regional quarters or offices in Hong Kong, and more continue to arrive. Some move away, usually citing reasons of cost, but arrivals comfortably outnumber departures. The numbers of expatriates coming to Hong Kong continue to mount.

Let me now say something about the Joint Liaison Group, of which I've been the British side's leader for the last four and a bit years. First its origins: During the negotiations culminating in the Joint Declaration in 1984, the Chinese pressed hard for some form of joint commission to oversee the final years of transition. We resisted this. One of the final compromises during the very heavy negotiations was, instead, to establish a Joint Liaison Group, which began its work in 1985. Its terms of reference are to conduct consultations on the implementation of the Joint Declaration, to discuss matters relating to the smooth transfer of government in '97, and to exchange information and conduct consultations on such subjects as may be agreed by the two sides. The Joint Declaration specifies that the J.L.G. shall be an organ for liaison and not of power and that it will play no part in the administration of Hong Kong, nor have any supervisory role over that administration. For our part, we have seen the J.L.G.'s main function to educate and persuade the Chinese of the value of the systems which make Hong Kong successful. We have, therefore, concentrated on working to preserve continuity in the legal system and continuity in Hong Kong's international relationships. For example, we have, through the J.L.G., reached agreement on localizing the Hong Kong statute book: British laws which were previously applied there because Hong Kong was a U.K. dependent territory. We also worked to amend all the 630-plus local laws to remove colonial law inappropriate connotations. Particularly important was the agreement in 1995 on the establishment of a local Court of Final Appeal to replace the previously used Privy Council in London. We've worked to ensure that Hong Kong's participation will continue in over 200 international treaties governing questions like civil aviation, maritime transport, telecommunications, labor relationships, and so on. We've more or less completed this exercise, as we had planned, so that all other parties to the various treaties can indicate their acquiescence in these arrangements. We have, unfortunately, been unable to overcome one particular obstacle relating to the U.N. Covenants on Human Rights, and I'll answer questions on that later.

In addition, the J.L.G. has dealt with more sensitive issues. For example, the Chinese proposal to garrison Hong Kong with units of the P.L.A. We had to agree on the precise locations of those units. We had to reassure people about the relationship between the garrison and local laws. Negotiations on the advance stationing and arrival of small parties continued until last week.

We had long negotiations about finance arrangements for the new airport, since lenders need reassurance that loans would be honored beyond 1997. As a result of these long negotiations, the commissioning of the airport was delayed, but, as I've said, it will now be opening next year.

We also had long negotiations over the award of a contract for the building and managing of one of the container terminals. Other franchises and contracts and major infrastructure projects became ensnared in Chinese suspicions, land reclamation, sewage disposal projects, and even licenses for mobile phones. The problem here was that China was suspicious about franchises which would straddle the handover and wanted to make certain there wasn't an uneven playing field being developed by the British side.

There have been a few language difficulties we've gone through, and misunderstandings do occur. A recent example, when the Chinese sent us back their translation of a recent contractual document, we found that act of God had become "religious activities." Unfortunately, the J.L.G.'s work has not always been smooth sailing. The Chinese side has often delayed progress when, for unrelated political reasons, they wished to indicate displeasure. Our main aim, as indicated, was to emphasize continuity, theirs was to preserve their position on sovereignty. They've consistently worried away at our proposals of Hong Kong government policies to safeguard their concept of the restoration of Hong Kong to Chinese sovereignty, to avoid any smidgen of doubt about Hong Kong's future status. To put it bluntly, they emphasize one country, and we have been emphasizing two systems. Another strand has been their unremitting suspicion that the British would leave Hong Kong with the family silver. Their attitude calls to mind the comment by one observer in an earlier epoch, "I know why the sun never sets on the British Empire, God wouldn't trust an Englishman in the dark." As a Welshman I feel I can pass on that comment without a blush.

In the past, Hong Kong benefited from the U.K.'s bilateral ties and membership of the commonwealth to ensure that, for example, air services agreements were in place. From the first of July, new arrangements are required. In the Joint Liaison Group we've worked hard to build up autonomous networks with third countries with Chinese agreement. In the case of the U.S.A. this includes surrender of fugitive offenders, a transfer of sentence persons, a mutual legal assistance agreement, and an investment promotion and protection agreement.

So Hong Kong enters the brave new world of the S.A.R. in remarkable economic health. Not only all the fundamentals are robust as earlier indicated, but also many of the other signals are flashing encouragingly; the stock index bumping along at record highs, and property prices once again touching record levels. I'd like to pause there for one second. Think about it, twelve and a half years ago, when the Joint Declaration was initialed after two years of often nail-biting negotiations, I doubt whether anyone could have imagined in their wildest dreams how much Hong Kong would thrive in the period of transition. Who could have imagined the same extraordinary resilience and dynamism continuing right up to the moment of handover? Surely this is an achievement worth celebrating. And it goes to prove, yet again, that no one has yet won by betting against Hong Kong. None of us can be particularly happy that a population of 6.3 million souls has been delivered into the care of a government of a country with such very different values and such very different regard for civil and human rights. But for heaven's sake, at least we in Hong Kong have reached the moment of destiny in good heart and good shape. It has not been easy politically, practically, morally, or emotionally. It is nevertheless an astonishing truth that Hong Kong has just gone through its transition, and no panic, no mass exodus, no major flight of capital is taking place; rather the opposite. Everything has been managed in a mature and cautiously weary way. Even crime is at an all-time low.

Look around the globe; how many other places or people facing such a fundamental shake-up in their way of life could have survived the immediate prospect with such calm and such pragmatism as has Hong Kong? The tragedy of the situation is that everything could have been set for a more or less seamless transition were it not for the unnecessary, politically motivated actions of the Central People's Government in tearing down the democratically elected legislature, and in repealing or amending laws bearing on law and order, and civil and human rights. In the last sensitive months, Peking chose to flex its muscles, both to demonstrate that its will is not to be flouted and to emphasize that the most important elements for China are control and sovereignty. Since the very beginning, since the negotiations of the Joint Declaration, indeed before then, with the amendments of the P.R.C. Constitution to permit the establishment of Special Administrative Regions, China's whole engagement in this enterprise has been designed to recapture sovereignty over Hong Kong. And while "One country—two systems" was seen as a more expedient method of recapturing this troublesome, non-socialist enclave than the harsh invasion meeted out to Shanghai in 1949, let no one suppose that it was more than expedience. It was a means to an end. And the end was the restoration of sovereignty over Hong Kong in the first place and Taiwan in the second. And while "One country—two systems" would allow a continuation of certain aspects of the so-called capitalist way of life in Hong Kong, this could only go so far. Control was still at the heart of Peking's concern. It would be hard enough to explain to other people in China why the people of Hong Kong had such special privileges and treatment, but if, in addition, the freedoms in Hong Kong were allowed to expand uncontrollably, then this would threaten contagion into the rest of China, and control there would be compromised.

So, as I said earlier, Tiananmen was the turning point. Hong Kongers suddenly saw the reality of what control meant in China, and Peking perceived in Hong Kong's earlier support for the democracy movement and it's later widespread revulsion of the crackdown, all the proof required that the Central People's Government was right to fear Hong Kong's influence on the disaffected in China. It could serve, in their eyes, as a base for subversion, and as a role model for those who might be tempted to harness popular emotions against the center. The reaction was incorporated in Article 23 inserted into the draft Basic Law, which was then being worked out as the Constitution for the future S.A.R. Article 23 was a post-Tiananmen addition and it reads as follows, "The Hong Kong S.A.R. shall enact laws on its own to prohibit any act of treason, secession, subversion, against the central government or theft of state secrets, to prohibit foreign political organizations from conducting political activities in the region, and to prohibit political organizations or bodies in the region from establishing ties with foreign political organizations or bodies." This was an all-embracing constitutional control mechanism, one which was extremely badly received in Hong Kong, and it has become a symbol of what those such as Martin Lee and Emily Lau have been protesting against and drawing attention to ever since. It is partly the popular reaction to the introduction of this article into the Basic Law at the final stage that obliged the Hong Kong government and Legco to introduce the Bill of Rights Ordinance, against which China immediately and loudly railed. This argument has continued ever since.

So much for the background. The clash between two cultures, between one set on maintaining maximum control and one, which paradoxically was the colonial power, set on establishing the maximum degree of democratic accountability for the executive. It came to a head in the disagreement over constitutional development. Put simply, the British wanted to move faster toward more directly elected seats, and the Chinese wanted to go slow. The results of the first properly constituted elections in 1991 alarmed Peking by bringing in a landslide of democrats perceived in China as anti-China. With Chris Patten's arrival, the confrontation became acute, the Chinese refused his attempts to seek compromise, and they set their minds firmly against any move which could, in their eyes, have allowed the likes of Martin Lee to ride the so-called through-train of the legislature through the transition. Constitutional arrangements were set up for the 1995 Legco elections, which the Chinese denounced as a "three violations political reform package," violating—so they claimed—the Joint Declaration, the principle of convergence with the Basic Law, and a series of letters exchanged between the two foreign ministers. The Chinese have never been able to justify or explain precisely where these were violated, but they've convinced themselves by repetition that they were right. So they decided that the 1995 Legco would have to be disbanded simply out of principle and out of peak. They also decided a whole series of other actions and sought to justify them by reference to our purported breaches of the Joint Declaration. They refused to allow us to carry through so-called "midnight legislation" to ensure compatibility of Hong Kong's laws with the Basic Law from the first of July. This would mean, they said, allowing our Legco to pass laws for their S.A.R., and this would be particularly unacceptable if done by the 1995 Legco, elected under "the triple violation" political package. They denounced the Bill of Rights Ordinance and the amendments made by the Hong Kong government to certain laws in recent years to ensure the compatibility of these laws between the Bill of Rights Ordinance and the two U.N. Covenants. The two principle laws to which they objected were the Society's Ordinance and the Public Order Ordinance, but above all, they announced the formation of a "second stove," which was a phrase originally coined by Deng Xiaoping and which eventually became the Provisional Legislature, which was to replace the duly elected Legco, as we have seen from the first of July. Meanwhile, of course the level of rhetoric against Chris Patten himself was constantly stoked up, and the propensity to do business with us in the Joint Liaison Group was sporadically reduced to indicate displeasure or worse.

So none of what has happened in this last six months is in any way surprising, but it does not make it any more excusable, nor is it in any way helpful to achieve the mantra constantly recited by the Chinese of a smooth transition.

So we've now come to the point of transition, and I would just like to go forward a little bit and consider what Britain's responsibilities will be for the future. We don't yet have the text. But put simply, the Joint Declaration is an international treaty, registered at the United Nations, and it provides for a continuation of the ways of life, the freedoms established in Hong Kong under the Joint Declaration for a period of fifty years and for a high degree of autonomy for Hong Kong. Now this, as I say, is an international treaty and as a result, two sides have committed themselves to certain undertakings in that treaty. For our part, the British side undertook in 1984 to deliver Hong Kong to China in good condition on the first of July. I think that we've fulfilled our obligation. Now it is for China to deliver its promises, and those promises are enshrined in the Joint Declaration to preserve Hong Kong's way of life for fifty years. Now it is, therefore, in a legal sense incumbent upon them, as co-signatories of a bilateral international treaty, to deliver those things, not simply to Hong Kong but also to the United Kingdom. We have a right to expect them to deliver what they have promised us. So it is our responsibility to keep reminding them of our right to expect that. And the Joint Liaison Group has a—what one might call—something of an afterlife. We continue to exist for another two and one half years after the transition, and during that time our role will continue to be what it was described in terms of reference in the Joint Declaration, and that is to consult on the implementation of the Joint Declaration and to ensure a smooth transition.

Now, the smooth transition has more or less taken place, but one could argue that we shall require the Chinese to continue to observe the Joint Declaration provisions to ensure that there is no sudden move away from the smoothness of that transition in the future. We've had an argument with the Chinese about precisely what the Joint Liaison Group's role will be in the immediate future. We have maintained, and I think perfectly legitimately, that the British side will be monitoring the Chinese side's performance under the Joint Declaration. And the Chinese side has said publicly that the word "monitoring" does not appear in the terms of reference of the Joint Liaison Group, which is absolutely true. There is something of a misunderstanding, I think, on the Chinese side about what the word "monitor" means, because in the Chinese language monitoring and supervision are similar concepts, and as I said earlier, it is not the role of the Joint Liaison Group to supervise in any way either the Hong Kong government or the S.A.R. government. But monitoring is a perfectly legitimate activity, which we shall certainly be undertaking. In what form that monitoring will be carried out remains to be seen. We will certainly be keeping closely in touch with people such as the democrats and those who have an interest in themselves monitoring the Chinese position on the Joint Declaration. We will be regularly in touch with our Chinese colleagues in the Joint Liaison Group, and so on and so on.

John Major, the outgoing prime minister of the U.K., came here in March and at that point made a very strong public statement about the British commitment to Hong Kong for the next fifty years, in which he used the phrase, "you will never walk alone." That has become the sort of—as it were—a mantra on our side, which we repeat from time to time. And I noticed yesterday at his press conference here that my new foreign secretary, Mr. Robin Cook, again repeated that. So it will continue to be our role to walk beside Hong Kong over the next fifty years, and certainly it will be the role of the Joint Liaison Group to do that in the immediate future.

But we have, of course, other diplomatic channels of expressing our views to the Chinese. We have established in Hong Kong now, a consul general. Of course there was no such thing before, because it was a British territory. The Consulate General Building is up and running. It was constructed last year, and we've been occupying it, my own office as well as the consulate general office, since last autumn. It was formally opened on the first of July and it will be, in fact, one of the biggest consulate generals that we hold anywhere in the world, largely I may say because of the massive responsibilities we have for the three and a quarter million people in Hong Kong who will continue to travel on British passports. There's an enormous amount of immigration work that is required to be done. But it will fulfill its other roles of trade promotion, and then, within the Joint Liaison Group Office, of course we will be particularly involved in the political reporting, the political monitoring and so on.

I'm asked, from time to time, how Britain will actually react if there are breaches of the Joint Declaration. The fact is that in this day and age, we don't pursue the old gunboat diplomacy. We do not have that sort of means at our disposal. So it is all diplomatic channels and the mobilization as necessary of international support. And I know that the United States administration has been extremely supportive of everything that we have been trying to do in Hong Kong over recent years. We have varied successes in mobilizing other government support. In the past we've found it very helpful to discuss our policies with other Asian and Pacific countries, such as Canada, Australia and New Zealand. We do have a number of friends in the European Union who take similar views as ourselves about the importance of maintaining Hong Kong as it now is, not only in terms of their individual interests in Hong Kong, which are of course largely commercial and investment driven, but also in terms of the wider picture, about what sort of China we can hope to see developing over the next fifty years. Hong Kong has an enormous amount to contribute to China, not simply on a commercial front but also in terms of lessons about the effectiveness of a level playing field and the rule of law. So far Hong Kong has not been able to do as much as one might have hoped in, as it were, entering into the spirit of the Chinese system on that front. Although, already in Shenzhen, just across the border, Shenzhen has a certain degree more autonomy in these matters than other parts of China. They have adopted quite a number of commercial laws from Hong Kong in order to regulate that commercial framework. It would be nice to think that gradually other laws bearing on civil liberties, and so on, would gradually spread from Hong Kong into the rest of China, and of course that would have been very difficult for the Chinese to accept while Britain remained the administering power here. But one might hope that when it is, as it is now, a part of China, and has systems which are quite clearly superior to the systems being applied in China, in terms of not only commercial propriety, but also civil liberties and so on—one might hope that in the future some of that will wash back into China, provided they don't see that as subversion.

When Chris Patten gave his last Legislative Council speech last October, he sent out a number of what he called benchmarks about how Hong Kong was likely to develop in the future, where he pointed out that we would be watching. The world, and Hong Kong itself, would be watching whether or not there would be, for example, a continued independent civil service, a monetary authority that was free to make its own decisions, and so on and so on.

I would like to just end by pointing out some of the questions that I will be particularly interested in. For example, how independent from Peking will the chief executive turn out to be? What role will the new China News Agency play after the first of July? What role will the head of the large Ministry of Foreign Affairs office play now that he's established his office from the first of July? Will there be some sort of shadow figure behind Mr. Tung Chee-hwa, a political advisor from the north? What will be the position of the Communist Party in the S.A.R.? Will that Communist Party, as it were, come out and participate like other parties in political life? How much real freedom will the chief executive have in making his decisions and in upholding the promise of Hong Kong's autonomy, and what will happen to press freedom and freedom of assembly? And these are all questions, which I think we are entitled to ask, and which Hong Kong itself is anxious to ask. They're probably the most significant issues relating to Hong Kong's future. But since we cannot, at this point, satisfactorily answer them, we must cling on to what we know, and this includes all the positive points about Hong Kong's current well-being, which I've already set out. It includes the extraordinarily broad spread of Hong Kong's autonomy existing in international economic relations. It includes the rule of law, a professional and highly motivated civil service, an excellent police force, an independent commission against corruption, and the resilience and determination of the people of Hong Kong. And can one really believe that China will deliberately kill the golden goose? They have too much at stake: the benefits that Hong Kong brings them, the precedent of a good transition which would set for Taiwan, the international prestige which a successful S.A.R. would bring for China. There's also the important point that Mr. Jiang Zemin, himself, has much riding on the outcome, personally. So I'd like to leave it at that and say that I am personally pretty optimistic, but we will be wary and hope that things turn out as well as they currently look as though they should. Thank you.

Question: One might speculate that the P.R.C. wants Hong Kong to become a Singapore with a vibrant economy but without political freedoms. What would happen if Hong Kong transitioned into a Singapore-like situation, and do you think that's likely to occur?

Davies: Well, I have to say that when I first came here I had a lunch with Emily Lau. Since I had served in Singapore in the past, I said to her that I felt realistically that if Hong Kong ended up in a few years' time in the situation that Singapore is in, it will be doing pretty well. Although there are clear limits on freedom of expression in Singapore, and there are people there who are very upset about those limits, nevertheless, it's not a bad place to live. The people's livelihood is looked after extremely well, it is extremely paternalistic, and is not to the taste of most of us, but considering that Hong Kong is attached umbilically to a system and a regime which is so totally contrary to our fundamental beliefs—considering that Hong Kong is in that position, I think that it would be surprising if there were not some erosion of the sort of liberties that the Hong Kong people have become used to. And it is certainly the case that Mr. Tung Chee-wah has seen Lee Kwan Yew and Singapore as something of a model. Now, Hong Kong people and Singapore people tend to see each other as different people. Singaporians do tend to have accepted, on the whole, that a very controlled environment suits them. Hong Kongers tend to see that as unacceptable, because they've gotten used to a much broader range of freedoms. I think that inevitably—and I say this without wanting to approve of it—I think inevitably the press, as it has already demonstrated, will be becoming less outspoken—there will be elements of self-censorship here. The law, on the other hand, at present, is very accommodating, and it will be up to the people of Hong Kong to ensure that there are no further erosions of their civil liberties through the law. That is one of the things we in the Joint Liaison Group will be watching over the next two and one-half years, and no doubt successors of mine will be watching through various other channels in the future. But ultimately, we must let Hong Kong find its own destiny, and so our own position in relation to how we monitor, and how we try to encourage developments in certain directions, is a very delicate one. One could argue, if one was on the Chinese side of the equation, that any continued British attempt to monitor—to discuss—is in fact an interference in internal affairs, or indeed could be seen as near-colonialism. So we have a delicate position, and it will remain delicate, and I'm not certain at the moment that I can really speculate how we will deal with these things.

Question: I have a question about public opinion in Britain, since obviously in a parliamentary system, how the British electorate feels about how their country's practicing their foreign policy will be of prime importance. I use an example from the United States: When we have arms control agreements with the Soviet Union, there would occasionally be debates on whether those agreements were violated, and one of the debates would be denying that a violation occurred, and Congress would get caught up in whether the Soviet Union violated the agreement or not, et cetera. Sometimes it would be admitted, "Well, maybe a violation has occurred, but it's not worth pursuing because the overall process of communication is so important that we really shouldn't try to enforce the letter of the law." What do you suppose the attitude in Britain will be? Will there be pressures like, "Well, maybe the agreement is being frayed around the edges here, but we must continue to engage and not press forward a claim?"

Davies: Well, it's difficult to judge, I'm afraid. Clearly the Hong Kong issue has become extremely central to British foreign policy over recent years, and I think the level of interest in Hong Kong will continue for some while, but I think it would be unrealistic to assume that say five years down the line there would be tremendous public interest in Hong Kong. We are a long way away. Those of us who are involved in this endeavor here, those of us who have experience in the Far East will obviously take continuing interest in the future of Hong Kong, and there are a lot of people scattered around Parliament who have that sort of experience, but they don't, by any means, make up more than a very small number. Of course if there were any major breach—if God pray, let us pray it doesn't happen—if the Chinese were to take some awful action against Hong Kong of a sort of Tiananmen in the future, then I suppose there would inevitably be a massive response in terms of public outcry in the U.K. But if it is, as it were, fraying around the edges, I fear that although we will certainly be seeing Parliamentary opposition to that sort of fraying in the few years, certainly up to the millennium let us say, I wonder whether in the longer term that will be the case. It's very difficult to judge this. But we will—those of us who are involved in this now and those of us, like Chris Patten, who have been here throughout; I am sure they will be continuing to draw attention to what is happening in Hong Kong. But I'm afraid that I can't be too optimistic that our Parliament in the longer term will be following the developments here with that sort of detailed interest that perhaps they should have.

Question: I think we would all be shocked if, in fact, the Chinese did kill the economic golden goose, and it would be incremental if they did. But what would be immediately visible to the world? How do you think the Hong Kong police force, the people on the police force, would respond to orders given of the nature that were given in Tiananmen Square? You said it is an excellent police force. Could they carry out orders such as that?

Davies: Well, the police here are well equipped to deal with public disorder. They tend to use a philosophy of massive use of numbers of personnel to keep things under control without allowing things to get out of control. I think it's inconceivable that the Hong Kong police would use the sort of force that you are talking about in terms of dealing with demonstrations here. The problem is that we don't know what the People's Liberation Army might feel that they should do. The Joint Declaration and the Basic Law make it clear that internal security is a matter for the Hong Kong police and not for the People's Liberation Army, whose presence here is related to a sovereignty issue and also to external defense. But we've had a question mark over this in the last week or so because we were somewhat surprised about six weeks ago when the Chinese suddenly announced that they wished to bring in their People's Liberation Army garrison before the handover. What particularly upset us was the Chinese announcement that they would be bringing in armored personnel carriers, and that they wished to station them in Hong Kong before midnight on the 30th of June. We told them that was absolutely out of the question and that there was, in our view, no call to have armored personnel carriers in Hong Kong at all. But sadly, they ignored that advice. Of course we were able to insist on it as far as before midnight was concerned, but as soon as the midnight hours passed they came over the border. Fortunately, it was raining very hard, and not many people noticed. Frankly speaking, had there been more light on the scene at the time and so on, I would imagine that the international press would have made very much more of that issue than they appear to have done so far. It is true that the British garrison did have some armored personnel carriers here for many years, but they were never ever deployed on the streets. I don't know actually the background to that, but we did have here in 1967 very severe riots provoked by the communists at the time, and although the police were in fact the people who controlled, all that time there was in the background the possibility, if things really got out of control, of deploying military units which otherwise were kept in their barracks. So the armored personnel carriers were there, and the Chinese have drawn that to our attention, but most of us were totally unaware they were there. The problem with Chinese A.P.C.'s is that we saw them trundling down the street, down the Avenue of Eternal Peace in Peking not so long ago, and the image they create is bad. But I'm a great supporter of the Hong Kong police. They have really done a magnificent job. Perhaps a little bit too magnificent since recently they prevented me crossing a particular line when I was trying to get to the Royal Yacht, Britannia.

Question: I would like to know what pressures you think that the Western powers—I won't hold the United Kingdom fully responsible, and I say Western powers—can bring upon Peking in case Peking gets unruly?

Mr. Davies: Well, we've been through the question of M.F.N. and all that. What depresses me as an observer of these events in recent years is the inability of the international community, of the democratic countries of the industrialized world, to work together to help to bring the Chinese to understand that, if they are going to be a member of the international community, they have to behave in a way that is more acceptable to the rest of us. I find it profoundly depressing, for example, that we had that breakdown in March about the U.N. Human Rights Committee's Resolution. Most of those had in the past supported that resolution, but the European countries decided that they had commercial reasons why they should be less supportive—that they wouldn't line up with the rest of us. So I don't know I think it is a question of a combination of political persuasion and making the Chinese understand that we're not all rushing to the great bonanza of the Chinese market without any principles. We really must maintain our principles and make the Chinese understand that it is not a gold rush syndrome where we fall over each other to pursue what it has so far turned out to be an almost totally imaginary bonanza. There are very few companies that have made very much money in China, but they all believe they're about to, and so they all chase after it and they persuade their politicians that they can't afford to offend the Chinese. But if we all hung together on this, I'm sure that the Chinese would understand that if they are to be accepted, for example, in the World Trade Organization, they really have to behave in a way which the rest of us find acceptable.

Larry Arnn: I'd like to ask you a question about Taiwan. China looks toward Taiwan as the next opportunity to ultimately reunify China. Could you describe what is the legitimacy of China's claim to Taiwan in comparison to the legitimacy of China's claim of Hong Kong?

Davies: It's a very complicated historical question. It was part of China for a number of centuries before the Sino-Japanese War in 1895, under which the Japanese took Taiwan. And then it was part of the Japanese Empire until the end of the Second World War. There was an international conference, I think it was the San Francisco Peace Conference, under which it was agreed that, as part of the settlement of the Second World War, Taiwan would be restored to China. However, that was all overtaken by the final stages of the civil war within China itself, which resulted in Chiang Kai-shek and his K.M.T. withdrawing to that island. In point of fact, the island was taken over before that, at the end of the Second World War, by the Chinese military administration under the K.M.T., which was then the government of China. And when the final settlement came, nobody could quite decide whether or not it had been restored to China. In fact the British coined a phrase which then became adopted by a number of the other Western countries which were interested in these matters: we said that the status of Taiwan was undetermined. This became extremely problematic in our relations with China. They said that we had deliberately created a legal status for Taiwan which meant that people did not understand. And I have to say that when we negotiated with the Chinese in 1971 or '72 or thereabouts to establish full ambassadorial relations with China, as part of the deal we undertook not to say ever again in public that the status of Taiwan was undetermined. So we invented some awful gobbledygook to describe our view of the status of Taiwan—I'm afraid I can't remember what it is now.

Question: With the I.S.O. being so present now in China, do you think that will help change some of the government views, since they are becoming very active in I.S.O.?

Davies: Golly, I'm not very familiar with the I.S.O., I'm sorry. Could you explain a little bit more what you're —

Herschensohn: I have no idea.

Davies: Oh, you haven't any idea either.

Question: It's an international standard which, in order to manufacture goods and deal with the international market place, you have the international standards that encompass everything that they do.

Davies: Well, I think you ought to be able to tell me a little bit about this because I cannot claim any —

Question: Well, for instance, in the aircraft business, if you're making a bolt or a nut or any kind of equipment, it has to go by I.S.O. standards. England is, of course, one of the big representatives in that field, but also France and other countries. The meeting takes place either in China or England or other countries. Just like you had the S.A.E. standards, each industry has their own standards, including environmental issues, and these issues are very strong in China. And these influence the thinking of the governments in the way that they have to conduct themselves, because without that they won't be able to do any business. So I'm wondering how that could influence China into changing to a more democratic society.

Davies: I think that all the various standards that the Chinese gradually adhere to, are bound to have a steady influence in moving the Chinese in the direction we would like to see. That is why the World Trade Organization is an important sort of benchmark for that. I've been posted twice in China, the first time was in the Cultural Revolution in '69 through '71, the second time was in the mid-'80s just after the introduction of the Reform Movement, and it was very interesting to see how keen the Chinese leadership and its various officials were to steadily improve its understanding of internal norms, because they recognized that these would help them in their own economic development. In some cases we found the international norms that they adopted, for example, on the certification of electrical products or something, were of a lower standard than we in the U.K. thought were appropriate. I am certainly not familiar with the I.S.O., I'm afraid, but I'm sure that if those things are being adopted more widely by the Chinese, this must have a beneficial effect. But I come back to the W.T.O. The Chinese have been agitating for a very long time to join the GATT and now the W.T.O., but they don't seem to understand that this is not just a question of rights but of substantial obligations. And at the moment coming back to the point I was making about the way everybody chases the Chinese market—the Chinese use political privileges, commercial privileges, to bribe various countries to take certain political positions. Now, they could certainly not, in theory at any rate, pursue that sort of line once they'd signed up to the W.T.O. So, similarly, presumably the greater spread of adherence to I.S.O. standards and so on must be beneficial. But I don't feel very capable of really exploring this subject.

Question: May I just say at the outset that the candor of such a diplomatic representative is particularly welcome. I think you've been very forthright on a number of points. I'd like to follow up to a question you addressed a moment ago. We've had the privilege to meet several of the leading democrats and we've seen others at close quarters in the past few days. I believe I saw in the paper yesterday, a report that the United Kingdom was going to confer upon outgoing members of the Legislative Council some sort of continuing special status. I wish you would clarify, if you would, if that's in fact true, or how you intend to proceed with respect to these displaced persons. And more to the point, are there other steps like that, that our own government or other governments concerned about not only civil liberty in the abstract—but even the personal safety of those who epitomize these liberties—can take to try to help protect them and advance their cause?

Davies: I think what you're referring to is some statements made by my foreign secretary yesterday at a press conference. I wasn't at the whole of that press conference. I'm not entirely clear what he did say. But it is undoubtedly the case that the foreign secretary is very anxious to ensure that nobody gets the feeling that we are abandoning those members of the previously legitimately elected legislature, just because they have ceased to be members of the new Provisional Legislature from yesterday. As a sign of that, for example, I had Martin Lee to lunch yesterday, and he had lunch with one of my ministers who's in town. We are certainly going to maintain very close personal contact with these people, and we do regard them as the people who were elected with the largest majority in Hong Kong and, therefore, representative of the aspirations of many ordinary people in Hong Kong. We are also going to be taking a very close interest in the development of the new electoral arrangements, which will be worked out by the S.A.R. government over the coming weeks and months. I think that none of us should be under any illusion about what those might turn out to be, because their whole objective is to ensure that the Democratic Party has a much smaller representation in the Legislative Council. So we will be watching all of that very carefully. And I am absolutely convinced that the United States consul general and the consul generals of other like-minded countries will also be watching that. Now, at the moment we have no reason to believe that the personal safety of these individuals is in question. Of course that will depend, perhaps, on their own personal behavior. If they were to take what one might call rash action in terms of public protests and so on, and actually break the law—and the laws are fairly clear on these matters—then they might, of course, find themselves brought before the courts and be subject to whatever penalties those laws require. But I think that Tung Chee-hwa is, himself, very committed, however much he may be a supporter of Lee Kwan Yew, to the rule of law, and he will not allow P.R.C. type procedures to creep in here.

Question: Is China's one-child policy and the enforcement or non-enforcement of that specifically addressed in the Joint Declaration? And should China decide to enforce that policy, what would be the position of the U.K.?

Davies: In Hong Kong?

Question: Yes.

Davies: No, I'm afraid it's not addressed in the Joint Declaration. The Joint Declaration doesn't get into that sort of social issue. I haven't got a copy of the Joint Declaration with me, I'm afraid, but the freedoms of the individual, which would incorporate their freedom to decide the size of their family and so on, are set out in the Joint Declaration. There are, in Hong Kong, some fairly large families, but there are other people now, because of the way in which they live, in very small accommodations, who choose for themselves that they may only have one child. And we've noticed in any advanced society that as people become wealthier, they tend to reduce the size of their families automatically. But I don't think that there is much likelihood of that being introduced in Hong Kong, at least in the immediate future. It's just not a question that anybody has raised. There is, however, a serious problem in Hong Kong in that we've already seen a massive increase in population in rather a small area. When I lived here in the '60s, the population was only 4 million. We've now got a population of about 6.3 million, and the projections for the next ten to fifteen years are up to 8 million, 8.5 million by 2010, and then they're talking about 10 million within ten years after that. So you can see that there is going to be very serious pressure on resources in Hong Kong. Tung Chee-hwa, in his address yesterday, did say that the housing problem was a major issue that would have to be addressed, and that he believed that there was sufficient land in Hong Kong to take account of what was necessary over the next years. But I'm afraid that whatever happens, this place is going to become increasingly crowded. Now, I don't know whether in the future, say ten years down the line or something, someone will say, "Let's try and encourage people in some way or other to reduce the size of their families." That may turn out to be a decision that is taken here. I just don't know, but at present I think it's extremely unlikely, and I don't think that the Hong Kong people would react at all well to that sort of direction.

Arnn: I have a short comment and a question and a word of thanks. The comment is, there is a loss of straight talk, I perceive, here in recent days, and one of the costs of that, if you read the press for example, is the distinction between free government and the other kind, and it gets blurry. We talk about the Lee Kwan Yew model, and that might be a decent thing. My comment is that your remarks are extremely refreshing and good, and I see you have a text there, and if you would let us publish that text, we would be proud to do it. That's my question, could we do that? And my word of thanks is this, I'm married to an English lady, still a British subject, and this morning I've been especially proud of that fact, listening to you.

Davies: Well, I have a sort of mashed up text here; it would certainly need some work on it. But I'd be happy to pass over a copy of it when it's been edited a bit.

Herschensohn: Hugh, thanks so much. I just want to say that no government, including our own, could have done better with the jurisdiction of Hong Kong. And no government, including our own, could have done better and had more dignity than your government had and Governor Chris Patten had at transition. We admire you very much.

Frank Martin

Conference Speaker
July 2, 1997 - 11:45 a.m.

Bruce Herschensohn: Frank Martin is the president of the American Chamber of Commerce. He's held that position for almost seven years now and prior to that for twenty-five years with the Security Pacific National Bank and fourteen of those years the Security Pacific Asian Bank—I believe that I'm right on that—and certainly the leading expert on the United States economic interest in Hong Kong. Thanks Frank for being here.

Frank Martin: Thank you. Well I am indeed delighted to have this opportunity to address the delegation here from The Claremont Institute. I am going to keep my comments brief so that we'll have plenty of time for Q and A. I'm sure that you've heard a wide range of views and opinions since you've been here, and, of course, that is not unusual considering the fact that Hong Kong is a free and pluralistic society. I can assure you even within the American Chamber of Commerce there's a wide body of opinion ranging from maximum bullish to being fairly skeptical about the future here. Most of my comments will mirror the chamber's view, but I'll also weigh in with a few personal opinions based on the some twenty-seven years that I have spent in this region. A lot of the speeches recently and media reports—and I'm not going to bang the media too badly today—have been quite negative and pessimistic, and at the same time many of the articles and speeches and presentations have portrayed an overly optimistic view of the future—sometimes self-serving I would add. I'm going to try to give you the American perspective, which I would hope would be a bit balanced. I will say right at the beginning there are indeed compelling reasons for optimism about the future of Hong Kong, but I don't think that you can ignore the challenges we will be facing, and there certainly is a downside. I will talk about some of the threats to Hong Kong's stability and prosperity.

I'd like first to talk a little bit about the American Chamber of Commerce. I mean, we're somewhat of a unique organization, I think. As an American Chamber, you will not be surprised to know that we advocate free trade, open markets, and private enterprise. But what sets us, I think, apart from many of our colleagues and other business organizations is our dedication to the free flow of information—freedom of the press. We have, in the past two years, embarked on a free speech forum, where we have had thirty or forty individuals; editors, academic, business executives talk on the importance of the free flow of information, in order to ensure Hong Kong remains this vibrant center for international business and finance.

Another thing that I think sets us apart is our commitment to ethical business practices. I am not suggesting for a minute that other organizations don't practice ethical business. What I'm saying is that we emphasize it. This has been part of an education program that we've had here in Hong Kong for some time.

I sit on the governor's—I guess I won't be able to call it this in the future— Governor Patten's Ethics Development Council here in Hong Kong, as an advisor. We have, over the years, convinced thousands of Hong Kong companies, and even mainland China companies, to embrace ethical business practices and to issue their own codes of conduct generally based on American models. We've met with some frustration because the focus in Hong Kong tends to be on corruption rather than on the whole broad spectrum of business ethics. In fact, our chamber will be conducting, in October, a conference on business ethics. The new commissioner of the Independent Commission Against Corruption and the new chief justice have both agreed to speak at this, and we will also be looking forward to bringing some executives in from the U.S. to talk about their own company and corporate experiences.

I heard the tail end of Hugh Davies's comments, and I want to say right now that I am a fan of Governor Patten. I give him high marks. The local business community does not necessarily share this view. At one point, after he took a particularly difficult bashing by the Hong Kong General Chamber of Commerce here, I was asked to call the Chamber and suggest that they ought to lay off, because it was not doing any good whatsoever for business confidence. After that, Governor Patten mentioned that the only friends he had were the Americans. So I felt pretty good about that. He spoke at the Chamber just two weeks ago. It was his farewell speech to the business community. I thought it was quite sad that it had to be the American Chamber of Commerce that invited the governor of Hong Kong to give his farewell speech.

It was sold out. In fact, this was the first time ever we had the American Chamber, the American Women's Association, the Democrats Abroad, the Republicans Abroad, the League of Women Voters, the Hong Kong International School, the American Club, the Boy Scouts, name it. Everything having to do with America sponsored this particular event. We had to pay off the debts that we had from our Election Central last November, to be perfectly candid about it. One of the comments that he made that I don't mind making to you, he said, and I quote, "I'm an unabashed Americaphile and I'm an unabashed fan of the American Chamber of Commerce," and he went on to then talk about some of the work that we have done here in Hong Kong. We've had an extraordinarily good relationship with him and we contrast this with some of his predecessors, quite candidly.

The Chamber was founded in the aftermath of the 1967 riots here in Hong Kong by a group of like-minded business executives who felt that we ought to have a say in the reconstruction of Hong Kong and also provide a forum to exchange views and concerns about the future here. It took us from the late '60s until 1982 before the first Hong Kong governor would even agree to a meeting with us, and that was a Thanksgiving lunch, which has become a tradition. Governor Patten, on the other hand, has met with me almost every month during the five years that he has been here. Americans serve on the various committees now, on the International Business Council, which is chaired by the chief secretary, Anson Chan—I guess I have to find out what her new title is—and the governor's own business councils and various sundry advisory committees. I, myself, served for five years on the Inland Revenue Review Board—I don't know how I got that distinction.

I will tell you right now that we have already met on six separate occasions with the new chief executive, Tung Chee-wah, who was himself a member of the American Chamber of Commerce from 1970 until January of this year. He is a strong supporter of our activities here. We have very good access to him, and our meetings with him have been extremely candid. We have, for example, advised that the 1998 elections should be modeled after the 1995 elections—of course that's not going to happen, we knew that when we took that position—and we said if that can't happen, then they have to be as open and free and transparent, and no one should be prevented from participating. As an American, by the way, as of tomorrow, I become a permanent resident of Hong Kong. I've lived here for so long, and anyone who's been here for seven consecutive years actually will have that status. At the present time I don't require a visa to enter Hong Kong or to work in Hong Kong, nor do my son and daughter and wife. The change will be that I will also enjoy the right of a vote, which I have not had up until June 30th, and they could have decided to get rid of me at any particular time they wanted.

We also weighed in on the proposed changes to the Society's Ordinance and the Public Order Ordinance, which I assume you may have heard about: the so-called rollback in civil liberties here in Hong Kong. I have to tell you the business community is not losing any sleep about this, but we nevertheless decided it was important to weigh in and to express our views that no changes should be made whatsoever. Tung Chee-hwa respects that, he knows where we stand, and he does listen to us, and I do think we had an impact in at least affecting the final outcome. The rollbacks won't be quite as severe or as serious as first contemplated.

The U.S. has significant economic and strategic interests, not only in Hong Kong and China, but in the entire Asian Pacific region. Americans are the largest foreign business community in Hong Kong. We have some thirty-six to forty thousand passport holders residing here. The number may even be larger because many returning ethnic Chinese with American passports use their I.D. card to enter Hong Kong rather than their passports. We have over 1,100

American companies in Hong Kong, and over 400 American regional headquarters. The Department of Commerce estimates American investment in Hong Kong to be about fourteen billion U.S. dollars. That's based on historic costs, and we estimate that it is significantly higher because that number only includes the investments reported by the parent companies of offices and subsidiaries here in Hong Kong. It does not include property owned by American citizens here. It does not include stock market investments. It does not even include the investments of the dozens of American fund managers here in Hong Kong. So it is very, very significant. We think that the U.S.-Hong Kong Policy Act is very important, and, in fact, we testified before the Senate Foreign Relations Committee in favor of that particular act. We think it serves our interests very well. This requires the State Department, initially, to report every other year on every aspect of our interests here, including human rights and many, many other factors.

U.S. banks here have around fifty to sixty billion dollars at risk on their books here in Hong Kong. We have twenty-one insurance companies here. So the numbers themselves are very, very important. And of course the trade between Hong Kong and the United States is about twenty-five billion dollars. This is one of the few places in the world that the U.S. enjoys a surplus. We actually have a surplus of about 4.1 billion dollars with Hong Kong, which sort of distorts the trade deficit with China.

Our Chamber conducts an annual confidence survey here in Hong Kong. The last one was conducted in November. We regularly recheck with our corporate executives with the Hong Kong International School to see how enrollment is, with the moving companies to see whether more people are leaving than arriving; we check with the property agents and other sources to make sure that our current perspective is still accurate. We ask a question, "What is your outlook for the business environment in Hong Kong for the next five years?" 95 percent of the respondents indicated very favorable or favorable, only 5 percent indicted that they were unfavorable, and this is up from 80 percent two years ago. We think that that's probably the situation today. They're not looking at Hong Kong through rose colored glasses—and I must emphasize this is a survey of corporate attitudes. You might get a slightly different response from grassroots surveys. Now, the fact of the matter is, again, for what surveys are worth—sometimes I really question their value, but grassroots surveys also indicate a fairly high degree of confidence. The Worthlen Group conducted a survey—you may have heard about this in the U.S.—about perspectives. A very small percentage of Americans were even aware of the fact that Hong Kong was subject to a foreign sovereign in the first place, but of those who were, 4 percent thought that the people of Hong Kong would look forward to a change of sovereignty, to sovereignty under the Chinese. In fact, local surveys here indicate that it's somewhere between 60 and 70 percent. How do you explain that paradox? I think that as Americans we tend to underestimate the degree of emotion that was involved with the Chinese losing the Opium Wars, 156 years of humiliation. We also tend to underestimate the patriotism of a lot of Chinese individuals, particularly those in Hong Kong. The majority of the population here, as you're well aware, fled China in the first place, but they were largely economic immigrants, illegal immigrants. In the old days they had a touch-base policy; as long as they could make it to Boundary Street they were home free. They changed that about five years ago. I think that a lot of folks here, and certainly by no means a majority, but a lot of folks here, do characterize the past 156 years of British administration as a period of humiliation and degradation at the hands of a foreign power. That's one school of thought. There are certainly a lot of others, who would vehemently disagree with this, but it is a paradox, and it's one that's not fully understood.

Here we are now on the second day of Chinese rule. A lot of questions, not very many answers. In a transition of this magnitude I suppose that's not surprising. I think one concern that we have is that the Basic Law, which in itself is a good document—a few warts, but it's subject to final interpretation by the National People's Congress. The question foremost in my mind is that when there is a conflict between Hong Kong's interest and China's interest, which is bound to occur, what's the interpretation going to be? There's concern about whether the new S.A.R. government will maintain a level playing field, whether or not mainland China interests will be favored, say, on government procurement or contract awards. I don't lose a whole lot of sleep on that issue. The field was slightly tilted in favor of British firms in the first place, and certainly there's always been a lot of potholes. We'll be able to compete is basically what I'm saying.

Will the new government become bureaucratic? The best decision that Tung Chee-wah has made to date is the appointment of the twenty-one policy secretaries who will continue in their office in the post-1997 period, and I truly hope they stay for years, not just a few months. I think that Tung Chee-wah had to play a chip when he demanded that they continue. This gives me some comfort that he will stand up when it is important and when it is in Hong Kong's interest. Because it was very clear to me, based on discussions that I personally have had with Chinese leaders, that they did not favor a few of those Hong Kong secretaries continuing in office, because they were viewed to be too strongly pro-democracy or too strongly pro-Governor Patten, and they had been vocal and open in their criticism of some of the Chinese decisions. So Tung Chee-hwa had to play that chip because he knew that it was extremely important for Hong Kong.

Corruption ranks as the number one concern, both in the grassroots and in business surveys that have been taken, and it is endemic across the border. Corruption was a major problem in Hong Kong in the '60s and even in the mid-'70s when I arrived. The Independent Commission Against Corruption has done a marvelous job of eradicating it to a large extent, but there is a concern that because it is endemic in China it will spill across the border, and there are even signs that cross-border corruption is already on an increase. This is something that we will be watching very, very carefully.

Free press, free flow of information, self-censorship; I'm sure you've been hearing about these concerns, and they are valid concerns. Some of the local business communities have been known to comment, "Well, look at Singapore. They don't really have a free press there." But my response to that is what gives Hong Kong a competitive advantage over Singapore. I mean, Singapore is a fine place. I mean you get fined for chewing gum, you get fined for spitting. (Laughter) I actually like Singapore.

I think one other point that I'd like to make is this: why does the community, why does business, both local and American, why do we believe that China will respect the Joint Declaration and Basic Law? There are no guarantees. I'll tell you right now if China sees Hong Kong being used as a base for subversive activity—and I'm concerned about how that term is defined or if the people here start demonstrating in favor of Taiwan independence or Tibetan independence—all bets are off. The Chinese leadership are obsessed with these issues, and this is a non-negotiable point, just as the return of Hong Kong was non-negotiable. But in a word, maybe a hyphenated word, the reason that most folks believe that China will adhere to these obligations is self-interest. I'll try to give you—again this is not a Chamber view, it's a personal view—what has been happening in China since 1979, when economic reform was introduced. There has been an incredible transformation, although it is still a totalitarian society. Nevertheless, people today enjoy a higher standard of living, a higher quality of life, more mobility and freedom to make choices, fundamental choices, like "where do I want to work?" It's still tricky and it's still a major problem, but that has been a result of economic reform. Now with that, you have also had the unintended consequences of economic reform: corruption, nepotism, high inflation, income disparity between the coastal provinces and the hinterlands, seventy million people below the poverty line that is defined, and growing unemployment. Fifty percent of state-owned enterprises are viewed to be inefficient, insolvent, and unable to meet their payroll. You couple this with rising expectations on the part of millions of people who have had a taste of a better life and want it to continue, and you have a recipe for massive social instability, and, of course, that's the worst thing in the world for Hong Kong. People here tend to get a little paranoid when they hear about problems in China. Of course the reason why we feel that China is likely to take steps to ensure that Hong Kong remains stable and prosperous is because Hong Kong is the conduit for China's capital. I mean Hong Kong companies have over one hundred billion dollars invested in China and employ over six million people. China's companies are listing on the Hong Kong Stock Market. That's where they're getting their capital for their future infrastructure development needs.

The Chinese leadership recognize that they have to keep the economic wheels turning, or they are going to have revolution on their hands. They have to keep that economy primed and running. Hong Kong is the source of that capital and the source of the entrepreneurial and the management skills. The conventional wisdom is that China is not going to kill the goose.

Just to conclude, our outlook for Hong Kong is a Chris Patten quote, "a Chinese society with British characteristics," and I would add to that, with a whole lot of American influence. Thank you.

Herschensohn: Frank, if I could just ask the first question—you said you believed that China would adhere to the Joint Declaration and the Basic Law because it would be in their self-interest. Just before the Tiananmen Square massacre, so many foreign policy experts and business interests were saying that the government wouldn't clamp down, there were a million people out there, Gorbachev was there, Dan Rather was there, and they simply wouldn't allow anything to happen. And it happened. Then twelve days after that, Deng Xiaoping said that the West would be back knocking the door down as soon as China gets its economic house in order. Westerners were back long before the economic house got back in order. What would the American Chamber do if there were to be something similar to those things that we've seen in the past like the Democracy Wall Crisis and Tiananmen Square?

Martin: That is a very good question, Bruce. Let me just mention that a week before or two weeks before Tiananmen Square, I called our embassy in Beijing because I had to give a speech to the Security Pacific International Board, who chose that time to visit Hong Kong. The response that I got from the embassy was, "Well, look. You don't have to worry. All they need is a little bit of hard music and some pot and it would be another Woodstock." Somehow our intelligence agencies got it wrong. It was a tragedy. One would hope the Chinese leaders have learned something from the worldwide condemnation that followed. And you're quite right that it didn't take long for the business community, probably led by the Japanese and the Europeans, to get right back into China and get things turning ahead. We have extraordinarily candid comments with the Chinese leadership. We have very good access. I suppose it's because of the fact that we have, as free traders, been strong supporters of most favored nation status for China that we continue to enjoy this access. We get a lot of this finger wagging at us, you know, "you tell your government—." The fact is, we don't hesitate to tell the Chinese what we think, and we discuss everything, believe it or not, from human rights to weapons proliferation and our concerns about these. Because they see us as important players in the Hong Kong economy, we have received lots of reassurances. But no one has a crystal ball. I suspect at the time of Tiananmen I was in the bank, not in the Chamber, although I was still an active member of the Chamber, and I can assure you some companies did close shop and pulled out, and I suspect that would happen again. Those taking a long-term perspective would probably hunker down and say, "My God, how do we stop this insanity, and is there anything we can do about it?" I'm not sure exactly—I'm predicting it's not going to happen.

Mr. Herschensohn: Did the chamber have an official reaction?

Mr. Martin: Oh, we condemned it the last time, absolutely.

Question: I'm interested in your comments about how this changeover will impact Shanghai. Certainly Shanghai is one of the few cities in mainland China that would have a competitive relationship with Hong Kong. Is the change going to result in Shanghai becoming more competitive? Are the rules going to change for Shanghai?

Mr. Martin: Another very good question, and a topic of a lot of discussion and debate. You know, you'll hear individuals who believe that Shanghai will actually take over Hong Kong's role as the financial capital for the region. It's an important city. It will be, I think, the most important city on mainland China, and to some extent the roles will be complementary. We haven't even seen the tip of the iceberg yet. One of the reasons that Shanghai cannot compete with Hong Kong is the rule of law. We have a transparent open legal system, an independent judiciary, and that, I honestly believe, will continue. The people who are sitting on the Final Court of Appeal here in Hong Kong are respected jurists, they are experts on constitutional law and the English Common Law system, and Shanghai, of course, does not have that. They're making up the rules as they go along. Now, the legal system in China itself is evolving, and, unfortunately, most of the judges currently have no legal training. They tend to be former military officers. Now that is changing. Where are they getting their training? They're getting their training in the U.K. and in the United States. It's a matter of time. We have a philosophy, and that is, development begets democracy. I think China is not going to be a Jeffersonian democracy—well, not in my lifetime. But I also said that the Berlin Wall would not come down in my lifetime. Unfortunately, they have this propensity for shooting themselves in the foot, two steps forward, one step back, one step forward, three steps back, but it is occurring. The change in China will come from within, and what will change China will be McDonald's and Kentucky Fried Chicken and Coca Cola and karaoke and Sony VCRs, and a lot of American students studying Chinese, and a lot of Chinese studying in American universities. That's what will change China.

Question: A couple things: One of my favorite British authors, whose name is C. S. Lewis, said that the economic and the erotic motives don't account for everything; that the desire for the inner ring, which is the desire for power, accounts for a whole lot more, and when Bruce was speaking I couldn't help but think of C .S. Lewis's writings, and when I watch Deng Xiaoping on television I can't help but think remember the big order Li Peng gave in 1989. I can't help but think about that fact. My question to you is, given the horrific human rights abuses in China—the one-child policy, the forced abortions, the forced sterilization, the abridgement of freedom of religion, the pressure on the unregistered churches and others within China—things that in our American founding, are dear to us, how do you, as an American Chamber of Commerce, promote M.F.N.? At the same time, we give China a lot of subsidies, as well as free trade, and it's not just free trade, there's a lot of other things that go on. How do you at the same time do more than condemn their horrible actions but put real pressure on them to behave in a different way?

Martin: A lot of questions there, all tough questions. First of all, again, withdrawal of most favored nation status is not going to do anything to resolve any of our concerns. We find any form of repression anywhere in the world to be reprehensible, whether it's religious, human rights, or the one-child policy, and we're vocal in our condemnation. We don't hesitate to express our views and our concerns. We also firmly believe that if you look at China fifteen years ago and China today, it's night and day. And we believe that it's been economic reform that has transformed China, and that will transform China in the future, and that American investors and traders have played an important role as a catalyst for positive change in China to the extent that it's changed. We are not apologists for China, and I reject that notion. We do hear frequently, especially when we go back to Washington, that business is only concerned about making money, and I reject that completely. If that were the case, I suppose I would be working for a bank instead of the American Chamber of Commerce. It's a personal view, but it's also a philosophy, which our business organization has adopted, and it's going to take time. It thinks we're on the right road.

I'm surprised there hasn't been a question about the book, *The Coming Conflict with China,* because I'd like to comment about that. You know, I read the book, and you know, I didn't sleep well that night and wondered if all these notions that we've had here are indeed correct. Then it occurred to me, what do the authors, Bernstein and Monro, know about military issues? So I decided, "Well, we're having a breakfast meeting with the commander in chief of the Pacific Fleet. Why don't we ask him what he thinks about the book?" And I did. That next night I slept a whole lot better because the technology gap is so enormous. Now, I'm not suggesting that China has no military ambitions. I worry about that, and I think that we ought to be watching that very, very carefully. But Henry Kissinger, Dr. Kissinger, just the other evening said, if you take China's growth rate—economic growth rate, 10 percent—and our economic growth of 2 and one-half percent, and just straight line them, and then you take our military technology and China's technology, the gap isn't becoming narrow, it's widening, and so I think the solution is a strong military presence in the Asia Pacific region, a continuing military presence, and a continuing investment in our military technology. That's a personal view.

Herschensohn: If I may just interject, I hope you realize that Dr. Kissinger called Deng Xiaoping a great man. I think you have to take that into consideration when he makes a statement. Further, the skepticism comes from the fact that we don't know where many businesspeople draw the line. When is it that the Chamber would say, "Enough is enough." We're going to do this, not because of business interests, we're going to do this because morally we feel we are harming free people, including our own"?

Martin: Well, Bruce, that's a good question. I suppose I would resign as head of the Chamber if, in fact, things got to be so incredibly difficult that we were faced with that decision. The fact of the matter is the Sinologists, including our own academics who spend most of their lives in this field, honestly are convinced that anything other than what we are currently doing in terms of—I hate to use this word, engagement, but I can't think of a better one—dialogue perhaps—is not going to solve any of the problems that we're faced with. It's not a question of objectives, it is a question of tactics. I felt that this policy we had out here of strategic ambiguity was silly. I mean, what kind of a foreign policy is strategic ambiguity? I think our policy ought to be absolutely crystal clear, and, frankly, it hasn't been. I think we should be tough. I think Speaker Gingrich, when he was here in Hong Kong, and when he went up to China, laid it on the line, and I think we should continue to lay it on the line. The Chamber, like any organization, is responding to member views. Sometimes we don't always know what those views are, so we have what we call a common sense test, and we apply this to every issue, and if we don't know what the views of the membership are, we try to find out. But we don't have the means of taking a referendum. We're bound to have very diverse views when it comes to what the Chamber should do, other than continuing to slog away day in and day out, making our views crystal clear, and confronting the Chinese leaders when we have that opportunity. The problem is, when the relationship is on the skids, we don't have that opportunity because they won't meet with us. It's only when the relationship is as it is today that they're willing to listen to what we have to say.

Frank Gaffney: At the risk of giving you another sleepless night, I wanted to give you an alternative view on the military situation. May I just say that I thought where Bruce was going to go with the comment about Henry Kissinger is that the people who are on retainer with the communist government of China are not necessarily to be relied upon in exactly calibrating where China is going or how much of a problem it will represent. I don't want to suggest that the commander of the U.S. Forces in the Pacific is on retainer with China, but I will tell you that he's dealing with a world that is defined by certain political realities. I believe that one of those political realities is that he's not going to get anything like the resources that he knows he needs to have to project the kind of power that you say—and I certainly agree—this country has to have in this part of the world. And the real rub is, as I see it, it doesn't take nearly as much power to threaten our presence as it does for us to have it. The danger, specifically, that I would suggest to you about the policy of engagement, on basically, Beijing's terms, is the transfer of technology that is taking place, specifically militarily related technology. It is very rapidly closing the gap between what China is able to bring to bear to threaten our interests and what we are actually bringing to bear to defend those interests. That's a function partly of the build-up they're engaged in—it's partly, and not inconsequentially, a function of how little we're doing to modernize and improve our own military capabilities. Those two things, I would suggest to you, sir, are causing the narrowing. That's not necessarily to say that China is going to have any time soon a power equal to ours, let alone more than ours, but ample to prevent us from having the capability on our terms with the coming conflict with China.

Martin: I agree with you. I'll sleep.

Question: I'm fascinated with the fact that you've had dealings with the new governor, Tung Chee-hwa, in a business context. In an American business context, there are examples of extremely wealthy businessmen who have gotten involved in politics. One would be Ross Perot, but there are others, and if such a person were to get in political power—to give one example—they would put all of their assets in a blind trust. That would be one thing that they would do, so that there would be no hint that they would be using their office for personal gain. I don't suppose Tung Chee-hwa has done that, but—

Martin: He has.

Question (continuing): what I do wonder is, based on your knowledge and your experience and your insight with him in a different kind of context, do you think that he can be an able politician, recognizing that his life has not been one of a politician? It's been one of a businessman. Can he bridge that gap? Can he do well in a totally different context?

Mr. Martin: Let me just comment briefly about my perception in both positive and negative terms regarding Mr. Tung. He is an individual of very high integrity. Sometimes that's a rare quality for businesspeople in Asia. He's a man of principle, a Confucian patriarch who believes strongly in Asian values. Now that, in itself, is a very controversial and hotly debated point, because often the principle of placing collective responsibility—giving priority to collective responsibility over the rights of individuals—is just an excuse for authoritarianism. I don't think that is the case with Tung Chee-hwa, but I do believe that he believes very strongly in at least some aspects of Asian values. He has indeed, according to my understanding, placed his family assets in a blind trust. In fact, he declared everything that he currently, presently owns. One of my biggest concerns, and I have expressed this to him, is that we have in Hong Kong what I describe as a lot of born-again Chinese patriots. I don't mean to be disrespectful, but these are some very good friends of mine who have become more Chinese than the mainland. They've dropped their Christian names in some cases, and they are tugging in one direction—typically they're from the business community—they're tugging in one direction, and then you have other people tugging in another direction.

I wonder if today Tung Chee-hwa is really having second thoughts about his decision to be chief executive. In fact, he has joked several times about how difficult this job really is, and how difficult it's going to be. I think he cares deeply about the people of Hong Kong and has taken steps to ensure that they realize that he's concerned about education, he's concerned about housing, and he is going to try to do something about those things. I don't have a formula for solving these problems, but I hope he does. I think the bottom line is that we have to give him a chance, and he is going to require a whole lot of guidance and advice, and, frankly, we will continue—whether he wants it or not—we will continue to express our views on things which we feel are important to us.

Question: Back to the issue of the M.F.N., most favored nation status, which I know has been sensitive for you as the head of the U.S. Chamber. Watching C-SPAN the other day with a debate on this subject, I thought it was ironic to see someone like Richard Gebhardt speaking out passionately against it, because of the human rights issues and so on. Well, Phil Crane gets up as the next speaker, and he favors it, and one can ask what has happened to the issues where the Republicans were traditionally the protectionists and the Democrats such as Kennedy were the free traders? An article in the *Wall Street Journal* recently told about Mattel Toys laying off 3,000 workers in Los Angeles and setting up factories in China, where the shift of the rural to the urban areas for jobs is not resulting in an increase in the standard of living of the average Chinese worker. So is it really in the best interest of the United States to maintain the trade deficit and policies that seem to be heading in that direction?

Martin: It's a complicated issue. The reported deficit is 38.5 billion and growing. This is neither economically nor politically sustainable, and we say that every time we visit China, and to anyone who will listen to us. We have the tools to address that if they are used effectively. But it is a complicated issue. I mentioned we have a 4.1 billion surplus with Hong Kong. If you look at the sum of the trade balances between Hong Kong—add together Hong Kong, Taiwan, South Korea—both Taiwan and South Korea have shifted production of low-tech goods to China, and as a consequence, that has impacted there because those were goods that they were previously exporting to the United States. Footwear, for example: Nike previously did all of their manufacturing in Taiwan. They now do a lot of it in China. But if you add the trade deficits, the deficit overall, the sum of the deficits has not significantly increased. So effectively, what has happened is other countries have shifted production to China, including the U.S. That has impacted the deficit. We have market asset agreements with China, and we should obviously enforce them. We have intellectual property rights agreements with China. Our most important asset, frankly, is our technology. We don't manufacture much underwear anymore, but we do a very good job of producing high-tech goods. The problem there, and a paradox we're struggling with, is you don't want to be selling dual-use technology in something that's going to come back on the end of a warhead. At the same time, that's what we do now. So that issue has to be reconciled.

I'm on the board of a company that manufactures glasses in China. It's a factory, and I will tell you right off hand they have no one under the age of eighteen employed in the factory, I wouldn't be on the board if they did. But this part here is manufactured in Japan, the plastic is manufactured in the U.S. from U.S. cotton, the tiny machine screws come from Germany, the glasses are designed in France, the owner of the company is from Hong Kong, and all of the capital to finance this and the management comes from Hong Kong. About 10 percent of the value of these glasses is actually from China, and yet 100 percent of the landed value in the United States goes into the trade deficit. We need to find a new way of calculating that. A lot of studies have been done, and no one has come up with a solution yet.

But I think we need to continue to be tough on these countries that run huge deficits with the United States, and they should be required to open their markets for our goods and our products. Certainly the American farmer has a vested interest, and that's why most of the farm states consistently supported most favored nation for China. One thing that I believe would help is if we can get China into the World Trade Organization—on an acceptable commercial, viable acceptable basis. In other words, on our terms, not on their terms. I think that would be helpful. Unfortunately we're going to see that deficit grow before it becomes smaller. I suspect that will happen next year. As somebody said—I believe it was a congresswoman from the Seattle area— "Well, we don't like the way you're behaving, China, so we're going to put twenty thousand people in Seattle out of work to punish you." Of course that's obviously Boeing. So that's the other side of the coin.

Question: If we could go back to the point that you made about the book, *The Coming Conflict with China.* There was one point that I thought was an implied clandestine position: that there was military technology that was not being presented. Do you have a view on that?

Martin: I don't. I'll tell you right up front that I am certainly not an expert in this area. I have read a couple of book, I read the *Rand Report*—which I would commend to your reading—I've read excerpts of it, and I've read the book, and there was in *Foreign Affairs Magazine* a brief rebuttal to that. Frankly I'm no expert. I was a combat Marine squad leader, so I know everything about an M-14, but I can't tell you whole lot about F-16s or SU-27s.

Question: I was hoping you would comment on an opinion I have. In the United States we have states rights versus federal rights. The State of California can sue the federal government. In effect, Governor Wilson can sue President Clinton, and he has. Regarding the current governor here and any future governors appointed by Beijing—on large issues, I can't see them as being anything other than puppets. I envision the current governor in a private one-on-one meeting, which I'm sure he has had, and will have in the future, with Jiang Zemin, and offering to the Chinese leader an opinion, and saying, "Hey, I think we should do this!" And I can see the Chinese leader raising his finger and saying, "No!" And I see the current governor bowing and acquiescing to whatever he says. I don't see any comparison to our governors with real autonomy.

Martin: Well, that remains to be seen, I guess. We won't know until we have the acid test, and even then we may not know. I believe that it has happened twice already: the appointment of the twenty-one policy secretaries, including the former Chief Secretary Anson Chan, who, by the way, would have been my first choice for the chief executive. The other issue was on their acquiescence on some of the changes that they're planning to make, which we're still not happy with, but nevertheless it's better than it could have been. But we don't know. I will tell you, of the other candidates who were considered, I would not have been happy with any of them. One in particular would have really caused me a lot of heartburn. But at the end of the day, China's going to have the final word, and there's no question that it would be naive to assume differently. So I guess we'll just have to see and to continue to try to encourage him to have backbone and stand up for what is important to Hong Kong.

Herschensohn: Got time for another one?

Mr. Martin: Sure, I'm fine, this is fun. You have to appreciate, I'm probably very close to your own philosophical views.

Question: We certainly appreciate you coming here and sharing your views with us. I have a question concerning the relationship between the business community and the Democratic Party here from a couple of standpoints. We heard Mr. Szeto Wah say, when we first got here, that the Democratic Party was going to have some funding problems as a result of losing the funding they're currently getting as members of Legco. We heard Mr. Martin Lee express concerns about them becoming less visible, both in the press and publicly here. And I see they have put through some last minute legislation, creating collective bargaining rights and sort of a National Labor Relations Board, which might not be viewed favorably by the business community. Now I see that they're calling on Mr. Tung to take some action against the land development community to bring down some real estate prices. My question is, to what extent will the business community support Martin Lee and the Democratic Party, and is the community is going to have more in common with the powers of China, or can you folks be counted on to help the Democrats here?

Mr. Martin: I want to make one comment before I forget and then I will answer your question. We would be very, very strongly opposed to any interference with free market principles and I don't care who it is, Democrats or Liberals or anyone else, who call for any form of rent controls or artificial means of controlling this market. That would be Hong Kong's death. This goes against everything we believe in. So if somebody now says, well he doesn't agree with Martin Lee, you're right, I don't, if that is indeed his view. Martin Lee spoke at our Chamber on June 20. We were the only business organization that would give Martin Lee a platform. He even made a comment to the effect that "I wonder if you're now going to be branded a subversive organization for allowing me to speak?" In fact, he has been a frequent speaker at our Chamber, as has other more conservative politicians. I'm really getting terribly confused now with these terms. The Liberals are not really liberals, in fact that's the pro-business, pro-China party. Anyway, we're a non-partisan organization so we would decline to assist pro-business candidates as other business organizations, in fact, did.

You know, Hong Kong has this unique thing you may have heard about, functional constituencies, and as a banker I could vote for the one candidate, whoever ran for that particular banking functional constituency. But we were invited to actually have a seat on the Legislative Council as either the American Chamber of Commerce or a Group of International Chamber of Commerces, and, of course, all the other chambers said, "Oh yeah, we have to have our voice." But we declined. We declined because we did not feel that it was appropriate for us as a business organization to have a seat in Legco and, besides, it wasn't very democratic anyway, so how could we support functional constituencies?

I hope Martin Lee is re-elected. I think it would be good for Hong Kong to have somebody out there who espouses democratic values and principles. I think I would agree that they're going to have difficulty raising funds. I don't imagine they're going to get much support from the local business community. Their other source of funds, which would be Americans, has effectively been cut off. That's going to be a problem for him. I suspect, however, that—you know, it's perfectly legal for Hong Kong residents who may be American passport holders but who, in fact, carry Hong Kong identification cards—to contribute to political parties here in Hong Kong. I suspect that will be a major source of his funds. He'll have the kind of problems that we've just had in the U.S., I suspect. The question will be determining who is a real Hong Kong resident who is legally allowed to contribute, and who is somebody else?

Question: I certainly hope that you're right in your assessment of Tung Chee-hwa's ability to say, "No" to Jiang Zemin, and for his business integrity, and so on. If I'm not mistaken, however, before he placed his assets into a blind trust, which is commendable, his shipping firm was in some financial trouble, and if I'm not mistaken, it was Beijing that came to his rescue. Would that not then make him somewhat indebted to Beijing?

Martin: I truly wish that I had the actual facts of the matter. I was here in the 1980s when his shipping company got into trouble. We were very fortunate not to have any exposure to his company, and one of the persons who was hired as an investment banker to help him sort out the mess was Jeffrey Garten. He was previously number two in the Department of Commerce. I'm not suggesting anything at all. That's a fact. We know that Henry Fauk, who has had very strong pro-China connections, a local Hong Kong business entrepreneur, and wealthy, we know that Henry Fauk arranged the bailout. I don't know the source of the funds. We don't know exactly where they came from. I would like to get the answer to that. Certainly that will cause a lot of folks to wonder about his loyalty, but the fact of the matter is, he is the chief executive. We think he was a far better choice than some of the alternatives, some of the other names that we were hearing at the time, and I do believe, as I've said, that he is committed to doing what is best for Hong

Kong. Now, he will not take a confrontational approach to dealing with China. Frankly, that doesn't work. We know that from our own experience, but we'll just have to see at the end of the day.

Herschensohn: Frank, we're indebted to you. This has been a very important session. Thanks so much.

Joe Zhang

Conference Speaker
July 2, 1997 - 3:00 p.m.

Bruce Herschensohn: I asked Brent Christensen at our Consulate, for a suggestion of who could speak to the conference as an articulate and good spokesperson, giving the view of the P.R.C. Without any hesitation, he mentioned the name of Joe Zhang. And then he asked Joe for us, and I'm really delighted that Joe agreed to be here. I never met him before today. He has a very impressive biography. He's a Chinese national, he was born in China, May 5, 1963, the second anniversary of Alan Shepard's flight, and he's a senior economist at Credit Lyonnais Securities. He was at the People's Bank of China in Beijing between '83 and '89, and for six years he was in Australia, but frequently traveled back and forth to Beijing. Joe, I appreciate the fact that you're with us to give us the views of the People's Republic of China. Thanks.

Joe Zhang: Good afternoon, ladies and gentlemen. I'm delighted to share with you my thoughts on some important issues for China and Hong Kong today. As a Chinese national, I have spent twenty-five years in China and ten years outside of China. I am asked to offer you a Chinese perspective of events, and I hope I will manage to do that. Naturally, I speak for myself, not the government, nor my employer or previous employers. Never one to shy away from contentious issues, I would like to say a few words at the outset about the Hong Kong Provisional Legislature. I think the Provisional Legislature is the result of the British government's miscalculation and the refusal to honor its agreement with Beijing. As we all know by now, there was an agreement between Beijing and the British government before 1990 regarding the legislature's "through-train," meaning that the legislature created in 1995 under the old electoral system would not have only been seated two years before the handover, but two years after, and then a free election would be held for a new legislature in 1999. However, as a result of British unilateral action, the so-called electoral reform in 1995 was less democracy for Hong Kong, not more democracy. Western countries and the media have only criticized China, but not Britain. Of course one may say Britain has successfully achieved its objective of appearing on a moral high ground. But regrettably, the British unilateral action and Beijing's subsequent reaction to it have set basic parameters for all transitional arrangements since then. They have only served to activate Beijing's bitter memory of the Opium Wars and how Hong Kong was taken by Britain by military force in the 1840s. The end result of all that is Beijing's heightened suspicion and the mistrust of Britain. When China was a lot weaker it might have been forced to succumb to the intense diplomatic pressure from the West regarding the Provisional Legislature, but not today. One may also argue that the sooner democracy is achieved in Hong Kong, the better. I personally fully agree, but Beijing asks, "What was Britain doing during the first 154 years of its 156 years of colonial rule? Why did it suddenly occur to Britain that there should be a democracy in Hong Kong in 1995, two years before the handover?" Clearly the colonial system of government, not democracy, suited Britain.

We hear a lot about corruption in China. It's a very serious concern. But I also believe the scale of corruption in China is definitely on the decline. Not because of the government's efforts in prosecuting a large number of high ranking officials. I happen to believe these type of efforts generally fail. The reason why corruption is falling in China is due to the country's economic liberalization. Let me give you an example. Until a few years ago, most of the industrial and the many consumer products were under price controls in China. This has resulted in a two-tier price system. The market price was much higher than officially controlled prices. Well connected individuals usually got the products with product coupons at officially controlled prices and then sold at market prices. The two-tier price system was responsible for a large proportion of corruption in China. In recent years, however, most price controls have been lifted. The dual foreign exchange regime has also been abandoned. Many loopholes have been plugged. Of course new loopholes are being created, and corruption is rising in other areas, such as the government's granting of business franchises. But on balance, I believe that corruption is falling.

Now the question is, will corruption in China invade Hong Kong and eventually kill business here? I'm an optimist. The economies of Hong Kong and China have been integrating over the past twenty years. There is a large number of Hong Kong businesses in China and vice versa. Corruption from China has already invaded Hong Kong, but Hong Kong businesses have survived and prospered against the odds. This speaks volumes about the resilience of Hong Kong institutions, and this will continue in my view.

I'm as concerned as other people about privileges Beijing gives to large state-owned enterprises and the unleveled playing field in China business. But let us not forget, the British government was equally guilty during its 156 years of controlling Hong Kong. When at the handover ceremony on the 30th of June, Governor Chris Patten spoke of the ending of British responsibility in Hong Kong, some people in Beijing would say that this was the end of British profiteering in Hong Kong. We all know that the communist propaganda machines in China are guilty of many things, but in my view the Western media are as guilty as the Chinese propaganda machines in at least one important respect: applying double standards. On political donations, for example, it is okay for the U.S. to ban donations from foreign citizens, but when the incoming

Hong Kong government proposed a few months ago to ban foreign donations for political activities, what did we witness? All foreign media and the politicians that have responded have criticized the move as a restraint and a limit on democracy. Were people applying double standards?

On the selection of the Hong Kong S.A.R. chief executive—Hong Kong government's chief executive—many foreign governments and the media have spared no efforts in criticizing the selection process as undemocratic because only a few hundred people in Hong Kong were involved. But let me ask, how many of the democracy crusaders in Hong Kong and elsewhere have ever uttered a single word of complaint about the appointment of the twenty-eight British governors to Hong Kong? Who elected Chris Patten and his twenty-seven predecessors? How many Hong Kong residents have ever had a say in their appointment?

Many in the West are dismissive about the euphoria in China about the handover in recent days. Personally, I'm very concerned about many things to come. But if we want to understand Beijing's sentiment at all, let's think about these things: In the 1830s and '40s the British sold opium—this is the argument Beijing frequently puts forward—by force, the Opium War was fought on China's territory, not British territory. Therefore, it is not difficult to know who were the invaders. Britain taking Hong Kong as a colony was a victory for the pirate. This is the view of at least 25 percent of the world's population. The handover of Hong Kong to China on the 1st of July gives a sense of justice.

On imposing one's own views and values on others, I think we should consider the following issues: Is the U.S. system of government the most superior? Should other countries adopt the same U.S. style of democracy? The U.S. and its allies have intensified their imposition of values on other countries. I personally support a high level of democracy in Hong Kong, as much as everybody else. But I am opposed to intervening in other countries' affairs. I also think democratization is a long process. Impatience can only backfire. Let's face the reality; many things will be easier to accomplish in Hong Kong and China without Beijing's opposition, but Hong Kong's democracy crusaders forget that we are entitled, all entitled, to defending our own interests. In front of their constituencies, U.S. officials take tremendous pride in defending the U.S. interests by being tough on foreign countries. Has it ever occurred to the same officials that their counterparts in other countries have the same right to defend—the same duty to defend—their country's interests?

Coming back to double standards, when there is a dispute between the U.S. and Britain, or between Britain and Canada, commentators in the West appear generally capable of thinking for a moment before arriving at a judgment. But that's not the case when there is a dispute between the U.S. and China, or between Britain and China. In fact, between any country and China, and that's Beijing's frustration. Beijing feels it is a lone traveler. When there is a dispute between China and any other party, some media in the Western governments immediately take sides and say it must be the Chinese that are wrong. Doesn't

China have the same duty, the same right, to defend its own interests? How many commentators have had a sufficient knowledge about China before making their sometimes emotion-charged comments?

The U.S. has some allies, this is a legacy of the Cold War. The Cold War now is over, but these allies have not changed their mentality. They still take joint actions to force smaller countries to conform. China is one of the countries that refuse to conform in some cases, but not in all cases. Western countries are, in my view, hostile to China. If China is treated as an enemy, then China will be one. We should criticize the Chinese government for many things it does when it shouldn't, and it doesn't do when it should. The Western media and the foreign governments have done a lot of that. Personally, I often agree. What I am trying to do here is to ask, have people considered those issues from a different perspective?

Thank you very much for tolerating some different views. Thank you.

Herschensohn: Well, I asked for an articulate spokesman stating the P.R.C. view, and we sure have one. Thank you. Some questions?

Question: I think it's wonderful for you to come here, and I want to thank you very much. It really is wonderful. You indicated that you, personally, were for a high degree of democracy here in Hong Kong. Would you explain to us what is it about democracy that you like? What are the good points of democracy?

Zhang: I think democracy is equitable. Everybody has the same say. My understanding of democracy, I must admit, is shallow. But having spent 10 years outside of China, I have started to learn a little about democracy, and I'm fully supportive of that. I think Hong Kong needs a high level of democracy. What I'm saying here is that a lot of other people have got it wrong in Hong Kong. If they had been slightly more patient, they would have achieved much better results. Today, what's the result? The result is Beijing has turned very suspicious, and very attentive to this thing, and it may scrutinize everything regarding election and politics in Hong Kong. Because I am a former manager of the Central Bank and I've traveled through China frequently, I got to know what they think. Regarding elections, I believe if the British government had been more patient and waited, according to the older schedule, Beijing would be far more relaxed about this thing, as long as Hong Kong's system of election and democracy doesn't invade China, which is what Beijing fears.

Question: Taiwan has said it wants to once again become a part of China, but with certain conditions. And the conditions, as I understand them, are that China will have universal suffrage and a multi-party system. Do you see, based on your previous comments, universal suffrage and a multi-party system coming to China?

Zhang: At the moment there are fifty-one political parties in China, of course, de facto. In my personal view other parties are irrelevant, there is only one party. Gauging from the political sentiment in China at the moment, I don't see a multi-party system in ten years, to be honest. We may have to wait for ten years, at the least.

Question: I'm curious, what would you have preferred?

Zhang: Between Taiwan and China?

Question: No, between Hong Kong and China.

Zhang: Between Hong Kong and China, I think reunification gives me a sense of justice. It should happen. I indicated a little earlier, Hong Kong's institutions are very robust and very resilient, but to Beijing, this is such a delicate thing. I'm concerned about several things: freedom of speech, a level playing field for business, individualism, and other things. Beijing is certainly not used to the Hong Kong system. I'm very concerned. They do sometimes take a step back when they make a mistake. They say, "Oh, I'm sorry I didn't know this is so sensitive." One example would be the trading of China's Treasury Bonds in Hong Kong. A year ago, a deputy finance minister said we should support Hong Kong's market, therefore China's treasury bonds should be traded actively in Hong Kong to boost the activity in Hong Kong. But then it was taken very badly by the Hong Kong market. This is such a sensitive issue. Is Beijing trying to impose some sort of tax or surcharge on Hong Kong? Then most officials have not had the experience of travelling to other countries, hearing different opposing views, therefore, they think in a straight line, "this is what I want to do, and I think this is good for you as well, so let's do it." That's the danger, and I'm concerned.

Question: You made the point that under British rule for the last 150 years, the Hong Kong people weren't able to choose their own government; they didn't have any say in who ruled them, and you said that was a bad thing. Yet the P.R.C. has replaced Legco with the Provisional Council when Legco was chosen by the people of Hong Kong. Would you comment on that?

Zhang: What I did was to explain why Beijing instituted a Provisional Legislature, which will be abolished in May of next year, to be replaced by an elected one.

Question: You rightly criticize the British for exercising some authoritarianism over the history of Hong Kong. Is it your view that if Hong Kong had been ruled by China during this last hundred years or so, that it's liberties would be further advanced or not so far advanced?

Zhang: I don't think on that point our views are different. I think our views are the same. Had Hong Kong been ruled by China, it would be like China, another Chinese city. What I'm saying is that doesn't justify Hong Kong's current state of democracy. British people in Britain have enjoyed a democracy for hundreds of years, why not here? That is the point. I think they should have instituted and developed democracy here much earlier.

Question: There will be a Party Congress this fall in Beijing. In the last few years there has been a greater degree of local democratic elections at the municipal level, but it's subject to limitations, but there have been some elections locally. Also we read that the Party Congress has a little more—it seems from what I read in the press—a little more power. Can you give us some insight as to what will happen at the next Party Congress? Will Chinese nationalists, who are more authoritarian, solidify? Or do you think there are prospects for greater reform, greater liberalization?

Zhang: Liberalization is occurring very gradually, but it's fair to say today that government officials can criticize the government policies but not the Communist Party single-party rule. Apart from that—you can criticize very freely the economic policies, trade policies, other things. When I was the manager of the Central Bank—in I think '87—I even published an article in the *People's Daily* criticizing the government's policy on banking. That was just after the law was enacted on the management of cash control. So there is a certain degree of freedom, but within a cage. As Beijing frequently says, a bird can fly but within a cage. That's a problem. Of course, after I left China, I published articles in the *International Herald Tribune*, the *Wall Street Journal*, and other outlets, frequently very harshly criticizing the Chinese government policy. And I don't have a green card of any country, and I hold a Chinese passport. For business reasons I have to travel to China on a weekly or monthly basis. I left China ten years ago. So far I have had no harassment from the officials. I'm, in a way, encouraged by this. In a way, I am always conscious of this.

Just a very little story, if I may: I published an article in the *Wall Street Journal* in '95, criticizing the government policy on economic management. It was probably the harshest criticism of economic policy. I was very, very concerned for quite some time with all my traveling to China. Of course, since then I have traveled backward, forward many times. It seems okay.

Herschensohn: Anything else? Any other questions?

Question: You've said that the British move to elect the legislature, in effect, set things back. Had that not happened, what would be the situation today in terms of an elected legislature?

Zhang: Today the legislature would be the legislature created in 1995 under the old electoral system. A few would be appointed, a few would be elected by a functional constituency. So although that would be, of course, not a full democracy, the thing is, Beijing would be slightly more relaxed—probably far more relaxed. Then two years after the handover there would be a new electoral system and then an election would be held. So during the past two years there would have been far fewer disputes, far fewer, between the British government and the Chinese government regarding the transitional arrangements. Because there are so many issues to be resolved, many parts of the body of law, the whole parameter would be different, the whole atmosphere of cooperation and discussion would be very different.

Question: Thank you. It's very enlightening to hear what you have to say, and I appreciate it, and I want to thank you. I notice that you criticize the West very strongly for criticizing the internal affairs of other nations, and you basically accused the West of a double standard. As an American, we're a nation of people from all over the world, united under a constitution that tries to set some standards that are universal about what it means to be human, and about where government ends and where individual choices begin, so we criticize ourselves all the time. We fought a bloody civil war over such an issue and that's a part of who we are. And I wondered, and I personally am concerned and many Americans are concerned about various human rights issues within China. I personally am a Christian and I'm concerned about the treatment of Christians that don't register with the state churches in China. And I see that as a universal human right that's above all governments. If my government did it, I'd be the first to scream, too. So I really want to understand how the Chinese mind looks at individual human beings, and of what the higher value is.

Zhang: There are many standpoints in the West and in Beijing. I'm probably in the middle. I share the concerns. But should the West do what they are doing in the way they are doing it? That's the main thing. I'm opposed, in many cases, to the U.S. government's debate on things in other countries, mainly lecturing other countries. This is my personal view.

Question: You made a comment about the U.S. I think you were talking about the U.S. government. I think most of the people in the United States wish nothing but the best for the people in China. I think that as long as we see Chinese leadership progressing in the direction of doing things for it's citizens and not for itself, I think we'll probably relax. Otherwise, we'll probably not relax.

Zhang: On many things Western governments are not tactful enough, they are too aggressive, and on other things they are not aggressive enough. This is another hypocrisy. Regarding the Chinese government policy, I think repression is certainly there, but it's everywhere.

Herschensohn: On behalf of The Claremont Institute, all of us want to thank you. You're a heck of a guy—that's an American expression. We received much more than we expected, and we have a great deal of respect for your candor in front of a group where you know there is disagreement. Thank you, Joe.

Larry Arnn

President of The Claremont Institute
Conference Speaker
July 2, 1997 - 8:45 p.m.

Mike Warder: This is a great learning opportunity. It is one thing to sit in Claremont, California, or wherever you sit, and think abstractly about the idea of freedom and its importance, but it's another to come here and see what is at issue. We've had ample opportunity to do that. I would like to ask all of you for your support. Some of you here in this room are supporters of The Claremont Institute, and I appreciate you for helping us. We're a small organization, and we'd like to do more. We'd like to do additional international conferences. There are actually a whole variety of things that we could do, and we will do, with support. If those of you who are here are current supporters, I want to express appreciation. For those of you who aren't, if you'd like to know more about The Claremont Institute, we can help out in that regard and we'd like to invite you to become members. There's no great mystic ceremony, and for those of who do become members you also, in a way, are shareholders. We're a non-profit organization but we pay attention to the people who support us. Your ideas, your experiences, your suggestions, are welcome, and I look forward to them.

Let me also mention to you that on July 16, at the Biltmore Hotel in Los Angeles, we are going to be having a debriefing. We're going to go over these experiences, and we're going to debrief for those who were unable to make the trip. I expect there will be a good crowd, and you're all welcome to come to that, and if you can come, it would be appreciated.

Also, I'd like to mention we're giving serious consideration to having another tour. We haven't made the final commitment, but it looks like we will be making a decision shortly about going to Israel in late August of '98. We decided that since we all got soaked in the humidity of the South China Sea, we will dry out in Israel. In any case, we're going to see if we can do that. And there will be other opportunities for similar kinds of conferences in the future. If you have suggestions about that, do let us know.

In any case, I want to express my appreciation to you, and also I'd like to thank Mike Finch, who works very closely with me. He's a great help and I know all of you have had a chance to meet him. I rely on him greatly, and Mike, I want to express that to you. Thank you.

This point in the program falls to the president of The Claremont Institute, Larry Arnn, to share his final thoughts. Larry is going to be leaving tomorrow morning, so he will be unavailable for the wrap-up session. He is going to share his views on what we've experienced here right now. Larry?

Larry Arnn: I want to begin by introducing Patti Hume, who has something to say.

Patti Hume: Briefly, I mentioned to Larry that in these affairs the unsung heroes are the ones that are never toasted, and I thought that tonight we could all lift our glass of wine to Michael Warder, Michael Finch, and Chuck Caramelli. That's it. Thank you, Larry.

Larry Arnn: That was gracious and just, and I thank you.

I think Howard Ahmanson may have said his first prayer on communist soil, and he's asked me to say that tonight he's going to smoke his first communist cigar on communist soil, and I'm a follower of his on most things, and I'm going to smoke with him, and I hope many of you will come and join us.

There are two reasons why we have witnessed monumental events, and I want simply to mention what they are. What is happening here is important because it has implications for the world. My friend Patrick Parker, who's sick in his bed tonight I gather, will tell you that there are war games conducted at the Naval War College every year, and they assume that the Chinese economy will grow at the rate at which it is growing, and the Chinese defense budget will grow at the rate at which it is growing, and that, if those two things happen together, that they will wipe the floor with us in about twenty-five or thirty years.

Frank Gaffney will tell you that the Chinese are building a missile system capable of attacking not only the mainland of the United States, but probably more immediately important, but not necessarily, denying access of our navy to the coastline of Asia where so many of the world's people lives. If that were to happen our status would be compromised.

Jerry Hume will tell you—I've heard him say it on this trip—that the power that China exercises in the minds of business all across America—serious, important, powerful business people—is very great. So power is being assembled right here. Potentially, if it goes on as it's going, it is power on an unprecedented scale. The questions are two: Will they continue to assemble this power, and if they do, how will they use it?

China, we know, has always had trouble remaining united. The two famous capital cities in China, Peking and Nanking—Peking means northern capital, Nanking means southern capital—have often warred with each other through Chinese history. In the fullness of time, probably China cannot be united and strong except on some principle of justice that reaches very broadly. It might be possible that these people over here in China are very different from people in the West. It might be possible that they will follow in massive numbers, in some slavish way, someone who just happens to be their same color. But they have not done that in the past, and they probably wouldn't do that in the future. So one possibility for the future is that they will have some system of real justice. If that is the development that happens in China, then I think we need not worry too much, but it is not necessarily the development that will happen in China.

Mr. Hugh Davies deserves knighthood if he hasn't been given it yet. He said that he is impressed with the fact that what they care about there in Peking—I like that British habit of sticking to the English name—what they care about is control. They love control. Mr. Dodwell from Jardine said that the private economy is growing much faster than the central authorities can track or manage. So they like control and they are losing control. That is the making of a crisis; the kind of crisis that produced the events in Tiananmen Square, the kind of crisis that produced the onslaughts in Austria in 1936, or the German attack upon Poland in 1939.

So the first prospect for the future is that there will be justice. The second prospect for the future is that there will be control. We have in history examples of the sort of human beings who really care about control. We have Hitler, we have Stalin, more than either of them, we have Mao. Today in the world we have the Internet, and we have instant communications, and we have world trade, and we have the press, and the flows of information, and the power of economic competition. These are very powerful forces; they are more powerful than they have ever been. In different forms, all of those have been depended upon in the past. All of those were depended upon by the Western powers in advance of both world wars. And both world wars demonstrated that force matters very much. The Internet is powerful, so is a gun. If a man is willing to shoot a lot of people—six million, thirty million or sixty million, to give the numbers associated with three men in modern times—then a lot can be done. It would be foolish to think that such a thing could not happen again here in the modern world where we have the Internet, the free press, instant communication, and so on. Ponder that. We're going to put on the Internet a copy of the speech by Mr. Davies. Read that speech again. Read how they have conducted themselves in these negotiations and ponder that. If you do, you will have begun to learn one of the lessons that is to be learned here. So much for the meaning of all this for the world.

The second point is also about the meaning of all of this for the world, but as a microcosm. Hong Kong itself is a microcosm of the entire world. You've seen the beauty of this city. It's harbor is magnificent, it has these imposing views which are a combination of nature putting something really beautiful here, and then these fabulous achievements of human engineering, and ingenuity, and production. It has to be said that it constitutes one of the great achievements in modern history; human beings working together to build a life for themselves. In the course of about fifty years, Hong Kong has gone from a backward place to one of the richest places in the world. Richer per capita, we learned this morning from Mr. Davies, than Canada or Great Britain. Now, in the last few days, if anyone reads the press or hears the speakers who come here, we've heard a lot of criticism of the British and their colonial rule. I myself share in one of the criticisms. I believe that they might more quickly have begun to build democratic institutions in this place. But mark this fact and remember it's import: they did it from neglect and not from malice, and this judgment can be rendered here on this day at the end of that long rule. When they were finished, the people they had ruled were richer than the rulers. That is an amazing thing to think about.

We in the West have lately fallen to the use of the word "culture," and the use of the word "values." Culture means that each people may decide for itself what is right. Values means that each individual may decide for himself what is right. Today, by Mr. Zhang, we heard the use of the word "culture." He criticized the West for its aggressive assertion of its own values upon the people of the East, that we are so talky, after all, and do we think we know it all? But did anyone watching him doubt that he was a supporter of the freedom of the press? It is a value that reaches across a culture. Here, from the mouth of a man who denies it, is testimony in action that he agrees with it.

There's a powerful argument now about the future of Hong Kong. It is the strongest argument that supports the regime of Mr. Tung Chee-hwa, which regime is the colleague and the agent in Hong Kong of Mr. Jiang Zemin and Mr. Li Peng. And that argument is that Mr. Martin Lee is no friend of a free economy, that we Americans who believe in the market and the prosperity that a modern economy can bring, should separate ourselves from Mr. Martin Lee because he wants more welfare spending, and would regulate the economy for the environment more tightly. Now, I do not know everything there is to know about Martin Lee's position on these subjects, but if they are as they are said to be, then I for one disagree with them. I think they are in error. I believe the miracle of Hong Kong has been worked by people taking care of themselves and not by taxes upon others so that they might be cared for. But this argument is put forward, this argument is calculated, by people who care about control. It is advanced for us to hear. It is meant for us, and to persuade us, and unless we are fools, we should look deeper.

Mr. Martin Lee makes a response—although I think not explicitly enough yet—he tells a story of the man who was a partner in a firm, and his partner was a niece of Deng Xiaoping, and the man made a lot of money. Now understand that Mr. Dodwell did not mention this point, but if you go into partnership with the government, there's a conflict of interest involved because the government has the power to say what is done, and if it has a money interest in the transaction, then it becomes a judge in its own cause. That's why the government should not compete with business in any country anywhere. So the man who had an Australian passport had a dispute with China and he won a legal case—which is a miracle if you know how the courts work in China—and he got away, and then he went to Macau, and he was abducted, and he's serving eighteen years, and he lost his property. He lost what James Madison would have called his property in his own body and his own rights of freedom of action and movement.

You can read the story of the American Revolution for years and search in vain for a mention of free markets leading inevitably to prosperity. That is not what they talk about. They talk about the right to property. The right—every human being, understand, this is the argument—every human being is born to reap the fruit of his own labor. Abraham Lincoln said, "Every man is born with one head and one mouth and two hands." The plain implication being the head is to direct the hands in the feeding of the mouth. "It is strange," he said in the Second Inaugural, "that men should pray to a just God to eat their bread from the sweat of other men's faces." That was his condemnation of slavery. It's a property rights argument. It runs everywhere. It is a commentary on what kind of creatures we are by nature. Property rights means contracts that are freely made and then enforced equally in the courts, regardless whom you know— regardless of whether you are the niece or the brother or the son. Property rights means you make for others what they will freely buy, and you keep the benefits of your own labor for yourself and your family and those you choose to give it to. It means an equal entitlement to that. If James Madison were alive today— this is always a difficult thing to say, but here is a clear case—he would say the continent of North America has been converted from a wilderness to the greatest economic power on the face of the earth by the power of understanding, not of markets, but of the right of every individual to labor for himself. And he would go on to say, that's what happened here. And that is what Mr. Martin Lee says too.

If a person with the power to say to another, without that other's agreement, that "I will govern you in the way that I please," then that man stands in relation to the other as a human being stands to a horse. In the last letter we have from the pen of Thomas Jefferson shortly before he died on the 4th of July, fifty years to the day after the passage of the Declaration of Independence, he wrote that some men are not born with saddles on their backs, nor others booted and spurred to ride them. He did not say some North Americans, some children of British descent. He said men. He meant human beings, everywhere, all the time.

There is an argument going on here right now with enormous consequences for the whole world. Think about the first point, the power of China, and the amazing number of the Asian people. There is this argument going on, and in its roots and elements are essentially the same as the argument that was made on the east coast of North America in the late 18th century.

Oddly enough, our nation is the only nation that can have any serious influence on how that argument goes. So we've come here to learn, and we go away with a responsibility. We are citizens of the last best hope of mankind on earth. We shall soon see if we are up to the job that comes to such people.

This is a very serious thing that we have watched here, and I cannot think of a better company of people with whom to watch it. Thank you.

Roy Huang

Conference Speaker
July 3, 1997 - 4:15 p.m.

Bruce Herschensohn: Roy Huang is our guest. He lived for a long time in the Bay area of California, which is a shame, but he did. Roy has a great background, he's a lawyer, he came to Hong Kong for three years in the late 1980s, then he went back to San Francisco, then came back to Hong Kong. His official title is assistant director of listing of the Hong Kong Stock Exchange, and he is an expert in the stock market. Thanks, Roy, for being with us, I appreciate it. He went to the wrong Hyatt.

Roy Huang: Thanks very much. I did go to the wrong Hyatt, and I apologize for being late. I was there at the right time, but it was just the wrong place. So that addresses my fourth point, which is post-handover efficiency! (Laughter)

I must correct the introduction. I'm not an expert in the stock market. I'm not allowed to be. Working for the stock market, I'm not allowed to invest in it. But I do know a little bit about the securities industry in Hong Kong and how it's regulated, and specifically where the stock exchange fits into the scheme of things. After I do an overview of the regulatory scheme, I will discuss, very briefly, the work of the stock exchange itself, and specifically what I do. Then we can talk a little bit about the post-handover type of questions that you probably have.

So let me start right off with the regulatory framework. Prior to this meeting we received a note from The Claremont Institute suggesting the kinds of areas that you might be interested in, and one of the sentences in this note was that the United States has an S.E.C. Well Hong Kong has an S.F.C., the Securities and Futures Commission. It is our securities commission, and it functions much like the S.E.C. in the United States. The chairman and the directors of the S.F.C. are appointed by the governor, now the chief executive of the S.A.R., and that will not change. Under the S.F.C. come the two stock exchanges and the clearing house. The two stock exchanges are the Stock Exchange of Hong Kong and the Hong Kong Futures Exchange, and then the Hong Kong Securities Clearing and Settlement Corporation.

I want to share with you a couple things about the S.F.C., although I'm not from that particular body. The S.F.C. is a member of the International Organization of Securities Commission, of which the S.E.C. is a member.

Recently, last year, the S.F.C. was appointed as the chair of the Technical Committee. Now you have to understand that the I.O.S.C.O. is the principal international forum for developing international standards governing securities markets, and the Hong Kong S.F.C. was recently appointed as the chair of the Technical Committee, which is where all the work developing these standards is done. So this is quite a comment on the maturity of the Hong Kong Securities Market and the view of the international community with respect to the Hong Kong Securities Market. As I mentioned earlier, directly under the S.F.C. is the Stock Exchange of Hong Kong. The S.F.C. and the Stock Exchange have a relationship that is governed by statute and by a memorandum of understanding that has been entered in between the two of them. By statute, the S.F.C. is the official supervisor of the Stock Exchange of Hong Kong. The memorandum of understanding entered into between the organizations provides that the listing function—that is the function concerning listing of companies on the stock exchange—will be delegated to the stock exchange.

The stock exchange has about six operating divisions; everything from options, trading, I.T., and then listing. Now, listing is where the bulk of the work is done; it's where the bulk of the employees are. Listing is where companies seeking a listing on the stock exchange submit their application, where the application is vetted, where the back and forth take place between the issuer, the company, and the Securities Authority. You have to understand that, with respect to trading in equities, the Stock Exchange of Hong Kong is a statutory monopoly. There isn't another board, there isn't another stock exchange in Hong Kong, unlike in the United States where you have New York, you have American, you have Pacific, you have Philadelphia, and so forth. Just as an aside, one of the interesting projects that we're looking at right now is to develop a second board, and there's a question whether we will develop an entirely new stock exchange or develop a second board under the current stock exchange management. This second board would be directed at growth companies, sort of a NASDAQ for Hong Kong. This is something that we're looking at now.

I mentioned the NASDAQ is a member of I.O.S.C.O., an international organization of high standing and reputation. The stock exchange, in turn, is a member of about six international organizations, and probably the most prestigious is the F.I.B.V., which is French for the Federation of International Stock Exchanges. That, again, is an international forum for stock exchanges around the world, including the New York Stock Exchange and NASDAQ, in which they have working meetings and set standards. Another credit to the Stock Exchange of Hong Kong was we hosted the last annual general meeting of the F.I.B.V. last year in Hong Kong.

The stock exchange is organized by statute. There are about thirty-one members on the council, and they're elected by the broker members. The broker members number about 600, and they are divided into three different classes, depending on the size of the turnover they have, in terms of the size of the turnover in the market. The first class elects the first ten, the second class elects the next ten, the third class elects the third ten. Now, the first ten are represented by your top brokerage companies, such as Morgan Stanley, Merrill Lynch, J.P. Morgan. They're all members of the stock exchange, and they all have representation on the council of the stock exchange. Under the council is the Chief Executive, who is the operations person, who has the day-to-day hands-on activity, with control over the stock exchange, and, again, under him are the six operating divisions, which includes listing.

Now, let me get to listing. Within listing we are divided into five units. My position in listing is fourfold. One, I'm head of the Listed Companies Compliance Unit, which is that unit that oversees all the issuers listed on the stock exchange, and now we have about 620 companies listed on the stock exchange. Its function is to ensure that the issuers comply with our continuing obligations regarding disclosure, regarding corporate governments, regarding notifiable transactions. We have a special set of rules concerning large transactions in which the key is notification to the public on a timely basis. We have a whole set of rules governing those kinds of things. One of the busiest areas for the Listed Companies Compliance Unit is to ensure compliance with those rules. We also have within the Listing Division an Accountancy Unit, and its function is essentially to review the interim and annual reports of companies as they come out. In Hong Kong companies are required to issue financials every six months. The first six months report is called an interim, and then comes the annual report. This is in contrast to the United States where you usually receive financial reports on a quarterly basis.

Let me just tell you a little bit about trading here in Hong Kong. Trading costs are fairly expensive. This is one of the things that we're looking at right now. We have a brokerage fee, which is a minimum of .25 percent of the value of the trade. We have a transaction levy, this is how the S.F.C. and the stock exchange are financed essentially. The transaction levy is made every time there's a trade, a buy or a sell in shares. .013 percent of the value of the transaction is payable. We have an advalorcm stamp duty, which is Hong Kong 1.5 dollars for every one thousand dollars trade. Then we have a transfer deed stamp duty. All of these things require a document, and we have a stamp duty, and then we have a transfer fee. This makes Hong Kong one of the more expensive places to trade shares.

There are a couple of things that are now on the agenda at the Financial Secretary's level. There are discussions about reducing or eliminating the stamp duty, but that's in quid pro quo for reduction of the transaction levy. Of course the stock exchange in the S.F.C. would like to see reduction in the stamp duty. However, if it also means a reduction in the transaction levy, which is where they get their revenues, so there's some tension. That discussion is going on right now. Trading happens on a T plus two basis, which means that after the transaction is entered, the matter must be settled, and an exchange of shares and cash happens, two days after the transaction. That's unlike the United States where it's T plus three.

That's just a very quick thumbnail sketch. Now I'll just open it up to your questions.

Question: I've heard of red shares being traded and blue shares, and somebody mentioned purple last night. Is there such a thing as a purple transaction?

Huang: There's no such thing. We have companies incorporated in China, which have listed here in Hong Kong. Then we have red chips, which are companies not incorporated in China but are either controlled through share holdings by Chinese entities, or have a substantial amount of their assets in business in China. We have about fifty-eight red chips listed on the stock exchange and this is out of a total of about 620 total companies listed on the stock exchange.

Question: If General Electric wanted to register itself on this exchange, could it be done?

Huang: We have rules that cover primary listing and secondary listings. Primary listings are your straight-forward typical listings. That is listings of companies that do not have listings anywhere else. Secondary listings usually involve those companies who have a listing, typically in their home market. These secondary listing rules are directed at foreign companies, companies listed elsewhere who want a listing in Hong Kong. Now, the reason why a foreign enterprise might want to come to Hong Kong for listing is because they usually have some sort of a China angle, they're looking for that kind of profile within the region.

Question: Do you welcome the secondary listings coming in from a good company showing good profits?

Huang: We welcome secondary listings, but frankly we only have a handful. If you look at the secondary market activity, that is trading after they're listed, you'll find that there's very little trading here in these companies. But that doesn't involve too much constancy of the Hong Kong Stock Exchange, because with the secondary listing we're not too concerned about regulation of those companies. We rely on the home market, the domestic market for regulation of those companies.

Question: A lot of these companies that are listed on your exchange are doing business in China, manufacturing in China, but the ownership is primarily here. I understand that the P.R.C. does not allow their citizens to invest in this market or at least they control it. Is that correct?

Huang: P.R.C. citizens are not allowed to purchase shares on the Hong Kong Stock Exchange. That's correct.

Question: But I also understand that there's a great underground amount of money that finds its way over here to invest in the market, and other things.

Huang: Other than anecdotal type of evidence, I don't think anyone's really done a study to find out the size.

Question: Sounds like a lawyer. (Laughter)

Huang: It does sound like a lawyer, but I think it's perfectly true. I don't think anyone's really done a study to see, and I don't know if such a study would be possible to find out how much of that money is coming over.

Question: Two questions, quick ones. A company is based in China, and it provides financial information. Could you comment on its disclosure? The second thing is, could you comment in terms of the Hong Kong market and its competition for raising capital versus the emerging Shanghai market?

Mr. Huang: Taking up the first question. We have very specific guidelines and rules on what needs to go into financial disclosures, interim's, and annual reports. Those are met because we ensure that those are met. I think the real problem that investors have with Chinese companies—not only Chinese companies but Hong Kong companies—is investor relations. By the time the annual and interim's come out, they're maybe three to six months old. Even though the information they provide is complete insofar as our listing rules are concerned, the information is old. And there's just no follow-up, there's just complete silence between the interim's and the annuals, between the different financial reports. That's where the problem is—investor relations. But that's not a problem confined just to Chinese companies; that also is a problem that we encounter with what we call the second and third liners listed on the Hong Kong Stock Exchange, the Hong Kong companies.

There was a previous question about blue chips. When we talk about blue chips, we're talking about the Hang Seng constituency of thirty-three stocks, plus maybe another fifty companies, at most 100 companies out of 600, where they do pay a lot of attention to investor relations, and there is that additional disclosure. But as far as minimal disclosure as required by the listing rules—that's happening.

The question about Shanghai was—I think the question was how do we see ourselves in terms of competition with the Shanghai Stock Exchange and Shan Zin Stock Exchange? As you all clearly know now, we do have two systems, and we think that what makes the Hong Kong Stock Exchange so attractive to international investors and local investors is the system we have here, the rule of law and so forth. They have a different system in China, and I think unless they become more like Hong Kong, in terms of transparency, accountability, in terms of regulation, you're probably not going to see Shanghai or Shenzhen out-pace Hong Kong in the near future, at least. This is where the two systems are going to differentiate the two markets.

Mr. Herschensohn: Roy, thanks so much. We all appreciate it a lot, and I'm sorry for your inconvenience in running through the island and then all the way to Kowloon again. Thanks Roy, very much.

Open Forum

Final Conference Event
July 3, 1997 - 4:30 p.m.

Bruce Herschensohn: Let me just start off with my deep thanks to all of you. It's always tempting in Hong Kong to get outside the hotel doors, and you've been here for all these sessions. And particular thanks to the people that I've been working with on the conference; they have been absolutely marvelous. A lot of people have said, "Gee, this must have been tough to put together!" Not at all. I had the break of working with Mike Warder and Mike Finch and Chuck Caramelli. I've worked with a lot of people who are good but are no fun, and I've worked with a lot of people who are fun but no good. In this case, I had the advantage of working with those who are both good and fun.

I want to give all of you an opportunity to state whatever it is that may be on your mind. I'm just going to say one quick thing about one guest. I heard from so many people in the delegation, what a great guy Szeto Wah is. They were taken with him. He is a great guy. But it's so strange to me that an aura of a person can do what it does. He's certainly not articulate to our ears because he can't speak English, and the translation process seemed to be difficult. But there's something about him. He is a magnificent man, and as I mentioned at the time, very humble, and somehow that aura of Szeto Wah spread to the entire audience. Everyone felt it. It was just his presence. If you passed him on the street, he could be carrying a load of bricks or driving a taxi or something, there's nothing that special about his physical presence, but something very special about his aura. And in a sense, I've got to tell you that that's what's predominant about Hong Kong. Something about it—like there's something about Szeto Wah—that is hard to define. When landing at Kai Tak, there was always a thrill that came with the aura of independence that took hold, and I'm not sure it will be here anymore. When I landed here this time, because of what's happening, there was something that hurt that I can't explain, I can't put my finger on it. And it's not that before, on past trips, that when landing I thought of the British or government at all, I thought of Hong Kong. It just had such a separate and individual identity—an aura—and I hope it isn't lost.

With that, I'd like to hear your comments.

David Keystone: David Keystone from California. Yesterday I was given a copy of the *Far Eastern Economic Review*, special 1997 edition, done by Bill

McGurn and Frank Ching, who spoke to us. However, the lead article was by Paul Johnson, arguably the greatest historian around today. It brought out several points that I had not read previously and I just thought I'd underline them in the article and I would appreciate just presenting them.

The title of it is "A Contrarian View of Colonialism," and among other things, Paul Johnson states Hong Kong demonstrates the anti-exploitation point of view, because when the British flag was first raised on the island there was virtually nobody living here to be exploited. During the century and one-half in which the colony existed, the millions of Chinese, who came here or sought, sometimes in vain, to gain entry, clearly did not see it as a place where they would be exploited. The vast majority shared the view of the veteran Chinese newspaperman Sang Ky-phan, who died in 1989, just before the Tiananmen Square Massacre, and who wrote of Hong Kong, "this is the only Chinese society that for a brief span of 100 years lived through an ideal never realized at any time in the history of Chinese societies. A time when no man had to fear a midnight knock on the door."

The creation of Hong Kong has been grotesquely misrepresented by anti-colonist mythology. It has been presented as part of a campaign by the greedy British to impose the curse of opium on the Chinese people. He then goes on to point out that the Opium Wars basically were caused by an existing opium habit of the Mandarins, and they would accept nothing but opium in trade or in bribes for their silk and their products. And interestingly Mr. Jardine and Mr. Matheson became the greatest traders in opium. But this was the only thing the Mandarins would accept in trade for silk and the like.

Herschensohn: I think he's absolutely right. If I may add this: it does make me so sick about the complaint about the Opium Wars and what's called the century and a half, 156 years, of humiliation. The humiliation of the People's Republic of China is due to what the Chinese people were able to do without the P.R.C. having jurisdiction and the contrast between Hong Kong and the cities on the mainland. Also, please keep in mind that the lease of the New Territories had nothing to do with the Opium Wars. Nothing. Also, I'm very sick of what I consider retroactive morality. You know, Margaret Thatcher didn't sell opium to anyone, and Chris Patten didn't sell opium to anyone, and I didn't have any slaves, and my folks didn't have any slaves, and I didn't sign treaties with the American Indians. I mean a lot of things happened that have made us now engage in what I call retroactive morality. Dump it. End it. I have no feeling of revenge when I go to Germany, Italy and Japan. It's a new generation, there are new governments, they're all new people. The old governments are out. Once you start demanding retroactive morality—and the People's Republic of China is so guilty of doing that about the Opium Wars—once you start doing that, you never end conflict, the conflicts then go on forever, and you're paying for those things that other people did that you had absolutely nothing to do with. Ernie?

Ernest Scherer, Jr.: Ernie Scherer from California. I was here in '95, and I was struck, the other night, by Martin Lee's comment when he said that everything he feared two years ago has happened. What struck me is that nothing I feared two years ago has happened. I think this transition has gone as well as anyone could reasonably expect from a democracy standpoint. I was just reading *The Economist,* the issue that came out just before we left the U.S., and it has the famous picture from Tiananmen Square: a little guy standing up in front of tanks, and in this depiction, he's holding up the scales of justice in one hand and a bag of money in the other, and the article asks the question, will Hong Kong take over China instead of vice versa? I'm very optimistic, I have to say. I think these people here are going to lose a certain amount of their freedom, I think they have. I don't think they care particularly, and I think that's why they will lose it. I think economically this place can prosper very well. I'm very optimistic here about the economic prospects, and very distressed about the freedom loss that the people are going to have here. But again, I think people get the governments in many cases—in many senses—that they deserve, and I don't sense that the people here are as concerned about their freedoms and liberties as we are, frankly.

Herschensohn: If they're not, then I can't respect the people of Hong Kong any longer—if that's true. I don't respect people just because they're going to get rich. That doesn't mean anything to me, and that isn't what I have found in Hong Kong. I've found people, by and large over the past number of decades, who risked their lives to get here because they wanted to be free. In my first decade of trips here this wasn't a rich place. In fact it was depressing; it was a real cultural shock the first time I got here, because of the immense poverty. There was also a very thin top layer of extreme wealth, like you'll find in almost any underdeveloped country, and there was no middle class. The first time I came here I got sick, I had never seen poverty like that before. I loved what God had done; the harbor, the mountains, but it wasn't what Man had done. Man hadn't done much. There had been no collaboration between God and Man at that time. The way in which this place has grown from people fleeing across that border, and going on junks, and risking their lives has made it what it is. If it's only money, if that cover on the magazine with the dollar sign, or the pound sign, or whatever it is, is accurate, then it's all futile. And I don't believe that. I don't believe that at all. What Martin Lee meant, when he said it's all come true, is that the Legislative Council is out of business, and a Provisional Council has replaced it. I have a copy of the Joint Declaration and the Basic Law, and in it there's no room for a Provisional Council. The first legislature was to be elected, but it wasn't. Then to have the main provisions of the Bill of Rights abrogated is something that he feared, and it happened. As long as we continue to care, and I think as long as we don't say, "Well, it's going to be okay," we can help sustain Hong Kong's freedoms. That's if we continue to really care and be critical when criticism is called for. I think the reason that the transition went as smoothly as it did, and the idea that demonstrations are continuing, I think that is a—look we'll never know, you don't know what other people are thinking—but I believe it to be a direct result of the fact that so many cared so much. That's the way that we can make this place remain free, and maybe in the long run China will be free. But if we didn't care so much, you can bet that they would have done what they would do in any other Chinese city. That government isn't one of great compassion for its citizens. So I think that's what caused it. I believe it was the Martin Lee's and the Szeto Wah's and the British and the Americans who really care enough that Jiang Zemin and Li Peng took notice and said, "Let's do this psychologically right." As I said, I'm not a mind reader, but I certainly believe that it had its effect. As soon as we start saying all anyone cares about is money, I'm afraid were going to bring about a tragic future for this place because the P.R.C. will say, "we can go much further and further," and they will.

Victor Childers: Victor Childers from Indianapolis. I need a little more information on the history of this electoral arrangement, because the young man from the P.R.C. yesterday put the blame on the British for messing with the electoral process, and I'm not fully aware of the background on that. We've heard a bit about functional representation, which really raises some questions about how broadly democratic it is. Can you help me on that?

Herschensohn: Yes, I think so, or I hope so. Prior to Tiananmen Square, 1989, this place was about as apolitical a place as I've ever seen in my life. No one cared about politics. The fact that the governor was appointed was irrelevant. The fact that there was no free election was irrelevant, because they were free in daily life. The people here were so grateful for the freedoms that they enjoyed, and in all honesty, more freedom than we have in the United States right now. I mean that in terms of regulations and taxation and just a way of life. No crime on the streets. I'm sorry it's raining, but if you went out at 3:00 in the morning, you wouldn't be looking over your shoulder. It is a place of real Libertarian freedom. So prior to '89, I saw only one demonstration once in Hong Kong, and I just happened to be here, but this was a demonstration against the P.R.C. and against the governor at that time, I think it was Governor Youde, but I don't remember, and they said, "You're going to go home in 1997 and have tea and crumpets, and we're going to be here and we want our freedom." It wasn't a big demonstration. Hong Kong was largely apolitical because people didn't care. I have never known one person from Hong Kong who was afraid of the government. Then came Tiananmen Square, and then everybody got worried about what's going to happen in 1997, and there was that demonstration that Szeto Wah organized, over a million people went, that was over one-sixth of the population, and everyone cared. But still Great Britain didn't have—I don't think—the guts to make any great changes until Chris Patten got here in '92. When Chris Patten got here he wanted to bring about democracy as quick as he could. He had fear of what would happen in '97. The images of Tiananmen Square were real, and he knew it could happen here. So he felt he couldn't do it all just like that, and quickly make it one man, one vote, as it's called. But he tried to make changes of significance. One of them was that in '95 he would have no appointed representatives anymore. Everyone was going to be elected, but he retained the functional constituencies. That means, as example, that if you're a lawyer, in effect you have two votes, you vote in your congressional district as we would call it in the U.S., and also vote in the A.B.A. "district," putting it, again, into U.S. terms. The system of sixty representatives had twenty elected by direct geographical constituencies, thirty by functional constituencies, and ten by an election committee. But at least it was all elected, there wasn't any appointed by the government. There wasn't anyone appointed in the Legislative Council by him—by Great Britain. Even this step was terribly criticized not only by the People's Republic of China, but even by Great Britain. Governor Patten was on a tightrope. He was balancing himself, getting in trouble with the democrats, with the People's Republic of China, and with his own government. It was real tough. He did what he could, when he could do it. So from an American standpoint you say, "Gee, what a strange thing to have these functional constituencies," but in fact it was all he could do—he wanted to move it as fast as he could, but if he did everything overnight, he felt his own government would come down on him, the P.R.C. would come down on him, and he'd create nothing. So what he did create was as near to a free election as has ever happened here. He's a better man than some of the people we've elected.

Question: I don't really think you answered Victor's question, and I had the same question I think that he has, although we haven't talked about this. From what the young man said yesterday and from other things I've read, it appears as though in that original document that was signed by Thatcher, or something that was developed afterward, that there was some provision for an electoral process at some point down the road. And it seems as though the Chinese objected to what happened with Chris Patten, that he in effect overstepped the bounds of that document. Are you aware, Bruce, of exactly what the process was for having a later election?

Mr. Herschensohn: Yes. Originally, at the time of the Joint Declaration in '82, elections were not as direct, not as democratic. That was '82. These dates are important. The Joint Declaration was completed in '84. Tiananmen Square was '89. Chris Patten came here in '92 and made the elections more democratic. When Chris Patten came here he felt that he better make quick changes while Great Britain still had jurisdiction over Hong Kong. Now, it is true that there were less democratic rules in effect prior to the Joint Declaration, which came out in '84. It's true that it was perceived that nothing would change in the interim. And it is true that there were changes in the interim. The changes weren't illegal, but they were surely unexpected, and they wouldn't have happened if it wasn't for Tiananmen Square and for Chris Patten saying, "We still have five more years of rule—I'm going to do everything I can to ensure that" what he called "a through-train gets through." So in a legal sense there's an argument here. In a moral sense there's no argument. But going back to legalities, please recognize that, in fact, what the P.R.C. signs is going to mean whatever the P.R.C. says it means. The Constitution of the P.R.C., Article 34 guarantees free elections—this is for the mainland—Article 35 guarantees free press, free speech, free demonstrations, Article 36 guarantees freedom of religious belief. None of it's come true. So whatever the documents say, it's whatever the P.R.C. says they mean.

Paul Hoff: I'm Paul Hoff from Las Vegas. There's one subject that I haven't heard much about. As you realize, when Mao died and when Deng died, both times, there was turmoil within the leadership as to whose ideas were going to prevail. I haven't heard a lot about that here, and I think that's a very important aspect of this, and I doubt if anybody speaks about it openly, but there must be an awful lot of Chinese around here that have some feel of what's going on back there in Beijing as to who is likely to prevail.

Herschensohn: When Mao Tse-tung and Chou En-lai died, their coming leadership was not yet handpicked, so there was a power struggle. Deng Xiaoping did hand pick Jiang Zemin. Li Peng had served Deng Xiaoping and is serving Jiang Zemin and so it seems to be a more predictable continuity than before, because it was handpicked. This was Deng's guy. He had had other guys prior to Jiang Zemin but when they did him wrong, they were out of business. I think the leadership—although you never know what's going on—something could happen today, and you don't know why or how—but it seems as though the leadership is Jiang Zemin and Li Peng. It appears that way.

By the way, just one of the oddities of the government of the People's Republic of China: Deng Xiaoping, in his later years, held no office at all. He was paramount leader, whatever that means, and the only office he retained was "bridge commissioner," and "bridge" not meaning bridges over rivers, but the game of bridge! That was it, that was it, that's what he held. And the reason he died at such an early age of ninety-two was because he smoked. (Laughter)

Question: Just some insight: I had a meeting with a client of mine this morning. He has a factory in Shenzhen, with an office here. They're two Frenchmen. They have about 400 people working in Shenzhen, and I asked him about his feelings on what was going on, and he said that he's so amazed how fast that mainland China has changed. He said it's beyond words. He said that he couldn't even explain it, but within less than ten years the south of China has become a masterpiece. He said there are cities and buildings going up everywhere. He says as fast as you can see, it's going up, and he says the south of China has really, really changed. He says the attitude in mainland China has changed. He feels the influence that Hong Kong is going to have on mainland China is going to be quite profound. He didn't know whether the P.R.C. would have much effect on the freedoms here. I guess nobody has a crystal ball to know what's really going to take place here, but he's very optimistic and he says his people are.

Herschensohn: I understand that, and I hear that very often. I'm sure he believes things will be good. Some believe it, some don't. And some, because of the inevitability of the action that took place a couple nights ago, some want to make the best of it, and I think that's human nature. What are you going to do, keep on bashing your fist against the wall? I just know that in the United States, if I thought a government I fled from was taking over, and no matter how good it looked and no matter what they promised, I would be terribly apprehensive, I would be terribly worried.

Any more questions?

Then there are just a couple of things I want to clear up. I gave a very incomplete answer earlier regarding the British law and it's something that you ought to know, and I don't want to think about a crummy answer while going home on the plane. The British law books have been here for 156 years, and some laws in them are authoritarian. They give the right of the British to do a lot of authoritarian things. They never did them except once. In 1967 when the Cultural Revolution was going on across the border, Red Guards, three hundred of them, came into the New Territories and into Kowloon and onto the island. Red Guards, guns, the whole thing. It was such a scary time that the governor went to the Peninsula Hotel and had an aircraft waiting at Kai Tak airport to take him out of here. It was a very frightening time, and so, indeed, they enacted some of those authoritarian acts, and added more. At that time you couldn't demonstrate, you couldn't do a lot of things, because I would say that the definition of danger to national security, even though this isn't a nation, was truly met. So in '67 Great Britain did take those authoritarian actions that they hadn't taken before. After '67 it went back to the way that it was before. When Chris Patten came in, he wanted to get rid of those things that were on the law books, he wanted to change them and it was very, very tough. I know what you think of the—because I did too—about the functional constituencies and things that aren't really one man, one vote, but he physically couldn't move any faster. It's similar to the criticism that's given of Margaret Thatcher because she negotiated with Beijing. I don't think she had any choice because of those fifteen-year leases and because of the fact that she had just exhibited such strength in the Falkland Islands. The major point regarding democracy is that the Provisional Legislature is not part of the Joint Declaration, and it is not in the Basic Law. The first legislature was to be elected, which is why they call this new legislature a Provisional Legislature. It isn't Legislature Number One, it isn't Legislature Number Two, it's a Provisional Legislature. But that was not in the Joint Declaration of '84, it wasn't in the Basic Law of 1990.

Another thing that I want to add before we leave is this: There were some questions asked of Frank Shakespeare and Ed Fulner—really good questions about the future in regard to the Islamic Fundamentalist Revolution. And someone asked a question in regard to the importance of India. I just want to tell you what I think could be a possibility for the future. I wish it would be high on our contingency list in the United States, and apparently it is not. You can write a hundred different scenarios of what could happen in the future, and you never know what's going to happen, but this is plausible and this entails both questions—all three questions that were asked about the P.R.C., about the Islamic Fundamentalist Revolution, and about India, which were awfully good questions:

There have been two major wars between India and Pakistan over Kashmir, I think you know that, 1947 and 1965. It looks like there could be another war. The conflict has been enlarging over the last three years. So many say that it's going to be like '47 or it's going to be like '65. Not a chance. In '47 and '65 neither side had the bomb, neither side a missile delivery system, China was not a great power at all, and there was no such thing as an Islamic Fundamentalist Revolution. If India and Pakistan went to war today over Kashmir, which is certainly possible, I think it is entirely probable that there would be an alliance between the People's Republic of China and the Islamic Fundamentalist Revolution, and you would have half the people of the world on one side of a conflict. They would join Pakistan. I don't know what Russia would do. Russia, when it was the Soviet Union, went to the side of India. But you could have a major world confrontation over something like Kashmir. That is just one of the scenarios of possibility. It's one of the reasons that the United States, even in peace time, has to have the kind of quality and quantity of defense that we had in the 1980s under President Reagan. By spending a lot, the worst thing that could happen is that we waste money. But if we spend too little, the worst thing that could happen is that we waste the United States, and a lot of other free people around the world.

I tremble when I hear debates about cutting defense. We simply cannot afford to do that. I'm giving you a scenario. Someone else could give you another scenario that could happen. We simply don't know what's going to happen in the world. There's close to 200 countries in the world, and we don't have jurisdiction over the events of countries other than our own. So the only thing that we can do, and the thing that will always keep free people free, is when governments that are not democracy-loving—are scared to death of us. The greatest weapon in the world is fear, and I've got to tell you we sometimes seem to be afraid of the P.R.C. In the Bush Administration, after Tiananmen Square, President Bush said that he was cutting off all high level meetings between the United States and the P.R.C. The next day, Brent Scowcroft, who was national security advisor, and Assistant Secretary of State Larry Eagleburger went to Beijing, and that immediately told the leaders in Beijing that these guys are scared, that they didn't really mean what they said, that what was said was only for domestic consumption. And that was not a good thing to do.

Anyway, I just wanted to clear the thing up, too, about the British law books because they were pretty bad, they still are. But they didn't use those things other than in 1967. It's also just my hope that because I've been fortunate enough to live in the twentieth century, which has been the Century of America, that I want to be sure that the next generation lives in a Century of America, or better yet, the Century of Liberty throughout the world. And the signals right now, the signals are that it's going to be the Century of the People's Republic of China or the Century of the Islamic Fundamentalist Revolution or the Century of a new hegemony from Russia or the Century of the United Nations Organization. None of those are good. Those are the possibilities because we don't seem to care enough about foreign policy anymore. We continually say, "Well, the Cold War is over." Practically every time you hear someone in politics they're talking about one domestic policy or another. That's fine, because they're all important, but it isn't fine when you exclude those things that could mean the choices between war, peace, liberty, and slavery.

And so The Claremont Institute's interest in foreign policy, I believe, is tremendously important, and it's one of the reasons why I'm so glad that you're all here, and why it's so important that you contributed so much to this conference. Thank you.

Leaving Hong Kong

To say that now "they have Hong Kong back" is inaccurate. The government of the People's Republic of China never had Hong Kong until July 1, 1997.

It was because of the introduction of that government in 1949 that millions of Chinese left the homes they had and risked their lives to enter Hong Kong, where they found the freedom to make it what it became.

Now that its jurisdiction has been transferred, the world should carefully watch the governing of Hong Kong to see that not one freedom of its people is violated. Too much is at stake to ignore Hong Kong. It's for sure that it will not be ignored by those who have governed China with such a heavy, totalitarian hand.

Epilogue

One Year Later: Hong Kong

Robert Elegant
May 1998

Editor's note: Robert Elegant was originally scheduled to address the conference in Hong Kong, but due to illness was unable to do so. We are especially pleased, therefore, to include an epilogue by him that covers events since the handover. He is an award-winning best-selling author of historical fictions on Hong Kong and China, such as *Dynasty* and *Last Year in Hong Kong*. He has written nonfiction works on China and Asia and was for many years the Asian correspondent and foreign affairs columnist for the *Los Angeles Times*, living in Hong Kong for twenty-five years. He is fluent in both Mandarin and Cantonese.

HONG KONG—In the fifth decade of the nineteenth century, Britain took the island called Hong Kong from China at gunpoint. In the last decade of the twentieth century, China took back from Britain at gunpoint not only Hong Kong Island, but the small Kowloon Peninsula, which had been seized later, and the broad New Territories, which had been leased for ninety-nine years in 1898.

In no case was the indigenous population asked its view. Nor were its interests seriously considered. In the first and last cases the transfer of sovereignty ran counter to the wishes of the majority of the inhabitants.

The few thousand part-time fishermen part-time pirates using the island in 1840 would surely have preferred to remain under the nominal rule of the Manchu Dynasty in far distant Beijing. The decadent Chinese Empire exercised no effective control over its remote extremity, leaving the fishermen/pirates unhampered by either taxes or interference in their unlawful ways. Nor in 1898 were the tens of thousands in the farming villages of the New Territories eager to exchange loose and ineffectual Chinese rule for British efficiency and intrusiveness.

In 1997 well over six million persons of Chinese blood living in the Crown Colony of Hong Kong were by and large not pleased at falling under the harsh and invasive government of their presumed Motherland. They were happy with the highly effective and low tax administration that had made Hong Kong outstanding for its prosperity even in economically buoyant Asia. The Colony was also remarkable in disorderly Asia for civil order based upon general consent, rather than coercion; further for intellectual freedom, as well as freedom of expression in authoritarian Asia; and for relatively limited corruption in universally largely corrupt Asia.

Opinion polls and the belated introduction of a measure of democracy by the Colony's last British governor revealed beyond any doubt that most of the people of Hong Kong were quite content with the status quo. In 1995 they elected legislators sworn to resist Communist tyranny. Three years later they were to humiliate Beijing's candidates in the first legislative election under China's sovereignty, indeed the first free election on Chinese soil since the Communists established the People's Republic in 1949.

Naturally, their wishes were not decisive, in fact played no part whatever in the decision to deliver Hong Kong to China.

In the nineteenth century motivations and decisive factors were simple. Militarily negligible, China had to yield to British demands backed by the cannon of the Royal Navy and the Royal Artillery. British merchants in Asia knew just what they wanted: a secure base under British rule from which to smuggle opium into China in contravention of Chinese law and thus redress the highly unfavorable balance of trade between the two nations. Britons yearned for China's tea, silks, furs, and porcelains, but Chinese believed they already possessed all possible goods that made for happiness within their own borders. Except, sadly, for the cheap opium grown in India.

In the twentieth century everything was more complicated. Britain knew it could not, if it came to the test, repel a greatly superior Chinese army. Therefore, no serious attempt was made to distinguish the return of the leased New Territories from the return of Kowloon and Hong Kong Island, which had been ceded in perpetuity. For a time Prime Minister Margaret Thatcher insisted: "A treaty is a treaty!" But a powerful group in the Foreign and Commonwealth Office was determined from the moment the issue arose that the transfer of the entire Crown Colony must proceed smoothly. British cupidity was again a decisive factor, just as it had in the nineteenth century.

The professional diplomats naturally wished to avoid conflict. That was their trade.

They further contended that Britain's trade with China would suffer gravely if London thwarted Beijing's wishes in any way, however minor. Imagine then the effect on Beijing if London duly surrendered the New Territories at the expiration of the lease, but retained Kowloon and Hong Kong Island, which had been ceded in perpetuity by treaty. Some of the diplomats were to have a direct personal interest in British trade and investment in China.

Yet the Foreign Office had originally not expected Beijing to ask for the return of even the leased New Territories. The Crown Colony was an ever-flowing Fortunatus's purse for Beijing, a very busy entrepot between China and the outside world, as well as China's chief source of foreign capital and foreign expertise. Its nominally Communist autocrats had in 1979 finally recognized that they could not retain power unless they gave up stringent centralized control of the economy, allowed enterprises to utilize their own profits, and offered workers material incentives. Thus they could produce goods consumers truly wanted in the quantities truly required, rather then goods arbitrarily selected in fixed quantities by bureaucrats. Only thus could they significantly better the lot of the restive masses.

Because of that radically new emphasis in Beijing's policy and, further, because Hong Kong was vital to the success of that new policy, British diplomats simply assumed that Beijing wanted Hong Kong, even the New Territories, to remain under British administration. They therefore set out to secure Beijing's agreement to extending beyond 1997 private leases on government-owned land in the New Territories. They were taken aback when paramount leader Deng Xiaoping told them in 1979 that not only the New Territories, but Hong Kong Island and Kowloon must be returned to China on July 1, 1997, when the head lease on the New Territories expired.

Ever resilient, the diplomats in 1982 assured Beijing that there would be no obstacles to a smooth transfer of sovereignty. The flat guarantee they offered before Prime Minister Margaret Thatcher had been persuaded to go along. Later, at least one of them, perhaps more, tried hard to convince the Chinese that it was he above all who had persuaded her. Even greater personal advantage could be expected from a grateful Beijing, which never forgets its enemies and hardly ever forgets its friends.

When Beijing knew it wanted, it fact needed, was not what the Foreign Office believed Beijing required. Most Communist leaders would have preferred a Hong Kong that continued to serve their economic interests by providing financial services and large sums of money. But, above all, they wanted a Hong Kong that would not imperil their hold on power by its constant example of a more relaxed, more free, and much happier political entity.

Hong Kong was—and still is—El Dorado, the golden city, a promised land overflowing with rice wine and roast duck to hundreds of millions in Mainland China. Beijing will, therefore, not be satisfied until it reduces Hong Kong to something like the same gritty and apprehensive state as the rest of China.

A further imperative impelled Beijing. The sting of the humiliation and depredation inflicted on China by the foreign powers from the early nineteenth century onward could only be salved by reclaiming each inch of territory that had once been Chinese. Minuscule Portuguese Macau was the only other foreign enclave remaining; since it was effectively under Chinese rule already, formal reversion was slightly postponed. Taiwan was s different kind of challenge. It was already under Chinese rule, although it did not acknowledge Beijing's suzerainty.

But Hong Kong was the very first and the most conspicuous of the territories Britain had stolen from China, the others already having been retaken. Hong Kong *had* to be reclaimed to restore China's self-respect by that splendid victory and wipe out the shame of the past. And Hong Kong had to be reclaimed no later than July 1, 1997, lest it appear that Beijing was truckling to London.

While bowing gracefully to the inevitable and looking to Britain's interests, the diplomats were not overly concerned about the well-being of the people of Hong Kong. They did not turn a blind eye, but simply assumed what they wished to believe. A very senior and very influential British diplomat assured me years ago that Hong Kong would not suffer as a result of the disorder he correctly foresaw in China, but would remain prosperous and happy after it came under Chinese rule.

His optimism was not justified. The mood in Hong Kong nowadays is sour and pessimistic. The Crown Colony was cheerful and optimistic. Transformed into a Special Administrative Region of the People's Republic of China, it is glum.

The diplomats would insist that such dejection is largely the fault of Chris Patten, the last British governor, who was not one of them, but a politician. Patten, they say, aroused false expectations by introducing a measure of democracy, whereas the autocratic rule of previous London-appointed governors had nurtured a populace that was contented, docile, and "not interested in politics." If Patten had not interfered, they contend, Hong Kong would today be a happy land untroubled by the discontent and political demonstrations that regularly test the authority of the Beijing-appointed government of the Special Administrative Region.

Anyway, the diplomats would add, the depressed state of the Hong Kong economy is due not to Beijing's rule, but to the fiscal crisis that has shaken all of East Asia from South Korea to Indonesia. That contention is in part true, but by no means wholly. The Hong Kong economy was depressed even before the spectacular Asian downslide.

The proprietor of a shop selling linen and embroidered garments replied forthrightly when I asked how his business was doing: "I haven't made the smallest profit since July 1, 1997. Just losses all the way—and getting worse. I can't even cover the rent."

A campaign to reduce greatly inflated business rents by 40 percent has been overtaken by events. He added: "Forty percent reduction wouldn't be enough. I'd still go broke."

His unhappiness was matched by everyone I asked the same question. In good part that dejection is due to the fall in tourism in the former shopping paradise, which is now rather expensive. The number of visitors has fallen by 50 percent since July 1, 1997. That abrupt slump is due primarily to the change in Hong Kong's status, as witness the many empty hotel rooms the week of the handover, whereas hotel managers had earlier been rubbing their hands and raising their prices, anticipating an overflow of guests. Also a major factor is the Asian recession, which is keeping tourism at home.

The old Pedder building houses, factory outlets, and other cut-rate shops. All now display signs offering even greater bargains, which literally translated from the Chinese is *Great Price Cutting.* By changing one of the three words, one shop has made its come-on read *Great Bloodletting! Eighty percent off!*

General depression is due not only to deteriorating business conditions and the consequent falling standard of living, but also to a peculiar Hong Kong psychology. Most people still repose greater confidence in Great Britain, now a small, far away, third-rate power entangled with European Union, than they do in their presumed Motherland, so called People's China, a colossal resurgent power on their doorstep.

That paradox arises from the fact that a majority of Hong Kong men and women are either themselves refugees from oppressive People's China or descendants of refugees. During the decades I lived in the Crown Colony I found it hard to discuss China with such persons. They automatically disbelieve Beijing's every statement and discount Beijing's every achievement, saying: "The Communists only know how to lie!"

Manifestly, the people of Hong Kong are not only different from their presumed compatriots across the border, but are alienated from China. The two groups are anything but the same, though they may look alike.

Once in Shanghai I fell into conversation with two men whose features were wholly Chinese, although their clothing, their confident demeanour, their command of English, and their obvious prosperity set them apart. Both were from Hong Kong. I realized after exchanging a few sentences that they were referring to the Shanghailanders as "they" and to the three of us from Hong Kong as "we" regardless of my not being Chinese at all.

In an oddly upside-down way, I recently encountered similar scorn. The language of Hong Kong is a dialect, virtually a separate language, called Cantonese. To my shame my Cantonese is poor despite all the time I've spent in Hong Kong. I therefore spoke to a non-English speaking salesman in Mandarin, which is known as *Putunghua,* the common language of all China. He retorted in Cantonese: "Don't talk that language to me. I'm not Chinese. I'm a Hong Kong man!"

The alienation, all but antagonism, between mainlanders and Hong Kong people has been aggravated, rather than allayed, by the Colony's transformation into an integral part of People's Republic that is, in effect, ruled directly from Beijing, but still enjoys quite different economic and social conditions from the rest of China. Immigration policy is one clear indicator.

The border between the New Territories and Guangdong Province was for five decades closely guarded to keep out refugees from China, who were "illegal immigrants." Yet many slipped across, in good part because the heart of the largely British-officered Hong Kong Police was not really in the assignment. Today the border is even more closely watched—and is much less permeable.

Understandably, Beijing does not want an influx of mainlanders seeking a better standard of living and greater freedom in Hong Kong. The SAR is tense enough without such an influx's heightening tension and perhaps inciting clashes. Above all, Beijing does not want large numbers of mainlanders visiting

Hong Kong and returning to compare conditions at home with the exotic territory that is legally part of China.

Before the transfer, tourists and businessmen from China were readily distinguishable from the locals. Their clothing was shabby and badly cut, and their complexions were rather muddy. They were also quite uninhibited, released, albeit temporarily, from harsh discipline at home. Even in free, easy, and very rude Hong Kong, the mainlanders were notably uncouth.

They still are.

Looking for a particular trinket in one of the many gold shops that line Queens Road Central, I was jostled by twenty or so men and women who were obviously mainlanders by their clothes, complexions, and behavior. All wore plastic tags reading: *Guangdong Province Tour Group.*

All could afford the small gold objects they were eagerly pricing—and buying. Gold does not change in value as abruptly as fundamental situations can change in unstable China.

The group was shepherded by three older men wearing dark-blue, high-buttoned Mao Zedong tunics, which are rarely seen even in China nowadays. When I began talking with a young man, one of those shepherds gently shouldered me aside. He was clearly not worried about my learning more about conditions in China. I can go to Guangdong and talk freely with most people any day. Although the authorities there would like to stop such spontaneous conversations, they cannot do so entirely without affecting trade, investment, and tourism, all big money spinners. Rather, it appeared, was the man in the Mao suit anxious to prevent his charges learning more about Hong Kong through conversation. Still, he could not keep them from seeing prosperity unrivalled anywhere in Mainland China.

Hong Kong in recession glitters with riches and throbs with commerce compared even with go-ahead Shanghai. But Hong Kong is undeniably suffering a recession that is sliding towards a depression. The woes are by no means limited to the merchants who depend on tourist dollars. Everyone is singing the blues.

Other realities show what is happening. Little is manufactured in Hong Kong today. Almost all industry has migrated to China itself, lured by much lower wages and by even greater latitude regarding working conditions. The chief money-maker in the SAR is money itself. Investment, insurance, banking, finance, and speculation bring in the bucks. But employment in finance has fallen some 20 percent recently, and those who hang on to their jobs have been taking salary cuts as large as to almost appear punitive.

Rents for luxury flats have not yet dropped decisively. Too many foreigners and well-to-do locals are still competing in a limited market. But domestic rents are already faltering, instead of rising 20 to 40 percent on each renewal of a lease, as they did only recently. Firms that happily paid $12,000 a month or more for an employee's flat are now radically reducing such benefits or cutting them off entirely. Former beneficiaries of such largesse are now looking for cheaper housing on offshore islands like little lama, which had been virtually a hippie colony—by staid Hong Kong standards at least.

Not by chance, overall property values are also falling, particularly commercial property. Hong Kong's formerly buoyant economy floated on inflated property values that allowed low taxation that in turn attracted investment and the all-Asian headquarters of foreign firms. Taxes have so far only increased slightly. But the pledge by Tung Chee-hwa, Beijing's appointed Chief Executive, to build eighty thousand new flats for the under-privileged every year, however meritorious, will certainly drive down rents and will probably increase taxes. Good for the less well off, the promised expansion of housing will, sadly, not be good for the economy in general *if* it really happens. Property values are already down some 30 to 40 percent from their peak, and, to repeat, overvalued property has been the foundation of prosperity.

Trade is also down for firms that cater to locals, except of course for those providing essentials like food and funerals. Newspaper and magazine advertising has fallen sharply. And so it goes: a long, slow, funereal drumbeat.

Optimists contend that the present shakedown will make Hong Kong much more competitive when the general Asian recovery occurs. That recovery is inevitable, though none can say when it will start or how far it will go. It will, of course, help Hong Kong greatly, but it will not heal the territory's fundamental malaise.

Non-economic woes also beset the government of the Special Administrative Region. The heart of that government is the old Hong Kong Civil Service. Stripped of all but a few of its British members, it is, first, encumbered with an appointed executive arm that is inexperienced, impractical, and slavishly obedient to Beijing, despite the pledge that "Hong Kong people will rule Hong Kong!"; second, encumbered with a timid judiciary that has ruled itself out of cases presenting issues that could affront Beijing, the highest court specifically forbidden to try any case involving politics, which can mean anything Beijing wants to do; and, third, has been encumbered with an appointed legislature that was hardly representative, although Tung Chee-hwa and his sycophants have repeatedly asserted that Hong Kong for the first time enjoys real democracy, since the chief authority is no longer a governor appointed by Britain.

He might just as well say as did most British governors: "Hong Kong people aren't interested in politics, only in making money!"

That reiterated justification long comforted those Britons who felt a twinge of guilt at the arbitrary, indeed despotic, way Britain ruled the Crown Colony for most of its 155 years. By and large, the virtually absolute British governors were benevolent, but they were still despots.

That assertion of lack of interest in politics was in fact true—for a small minority of the population. The rich, the very rich, and the super-rich really didn't care who ruled Hong Kong or how it was ruled, just as long as they were left free to make money. They were left free, virtually untethered by law, for the

Colony practiced almost perfect economic laissez faire—and profited greatly thereby. However, efficient execution of the vital functions the government reserved to itself and impartial administration of British justice by independent courts provided the secure legal framework on which the ingenious, hard working, and risk taking native Chinese population built a major commercial and financial center on the "barren rock with hardly a house on it" that was Hong Kong Island in 1840 according to Lord Palmerston.

All the people were very much interested in making a living, a good living. But the mass of the people were also vitally interested in politics: the emerging middle class, the managers, the professionals, the shopkeepers, the artisans, and also the workers. It was precisely that vital concern with politics that first alarmed Beijing, which in its doctrinaire ignorance had thought the people of Hong Kong little difference from the people of China.

Ironically, the political event that put Beijing on it guard demonstrated strong sympathy between the people of Hong Kong and the people of the mainland, as well as their mutual concern with critical political events. That was just the kind of interest in politics that Beijing sought to crush in mainlanders and feared equally in Hong Kong people.

Profoundly moved by the massacre in Beijing in 1989 of students and workers campaigning for democracy and by the persecution of all dissidents, however mild, throughout China, a million men and women gathered in a candle-lit vigil in Hong Kong. Such vigils on a smaller scale have continued every year since. Hong Kong was until July 1, 1997, also a haven for refugee dissidents and provided funds for their movement. Naturally, Beijing is determined to crush that independent spirit.

The people of Hong Kong proved themselves deeply interested in politics in 1955, when the second legislative election in its history took place. Twenty of the sixty seats were to be filled by direct public election, twenty by the governor's direct appointment, and twenty by 'functional constituencies,' which meant groups demarcated by occupation. That election was only a further small step towards democracy, not a great lead towards democracy. Patten, who would have liked to make that election far more democratic, was constrained by the diplomats' prior agreement with Beijing that only a third of the legislators would be directly elected.

Regardless, some 35 percent of those eligible came to the polls—and voted overwhelmingly for the Democratic Party of barrister Martin Lee, which stood for increased democracy and for vigorously resisting the encroachment on freedom Lee foresaw when a Beijing-controlled regime took power in July 1997. The Democrats could do nothing about the handover. That was an irreversible fait accompli, although the people had clearly shown that they did not want Chinese rule.

That election and the legislature is produced were the centerpiece of the democratic innovations introduced by Governor Chris Patten over the vehement protests of the Foreign Office clique, protests echoed by both British and

Chinese *taipans*, the very big businessmen who accumulated hundreds of millions, even billions. Among the paradoxes of Hong Kong, the rich are for Beijing, while the mass of the people would like to see Beijing's rule vanish.

Regardless, both the Foreign Office and the *taipans* are now chipping away at Patten's solid reputation in retaliation for his reforms, which they still contend have impeded Hong Kong's chief business, which is, of course, business. Both those groups had wanted a smooth transfer of sovereignty because they believed their own interests were best served by truckling to Beijing.

Neither the Foreign Office clique nor the *taipans* could imagine that Beijing's suzerainty would signal an economic decline. And they believed—or professed to believe—that the mass of Hong Kong's people would be just as well off under Chinese rule, if not better off. Freedom and dignity for the people did not bulk large in their estimation.

From the beginning the new regime was dogged by unforeseen problems that in the long run severely impeded further economic development and profits.

The first was simply credibility. Even before the takeover, the government-to-be had declared the 1995 legislative election invalid and had appointed its own legislature in waiting. An elaborate and intricate process handpicked committees to select committees to chose committees that finally elected the legislators. That complicated mummery convinced no one that the legislature that took its seat on July 1, 1997, reflected the popular will. No more did the layers of committees that selected Tung Chee-hwa as chief executive carry conviction.

Everyone knew that Tung had been chosen by President Jiang Zemin of the People's Republic, who confirmed his choice by ostentatiously shaking hands with Tung under the lenses of television cameras a long time before the charade of committee selection began. Tung was selected because he would do Beijing's bidding without question. In any event he was in debt to Beijing. He had mismanaged his father's shipping fleet into near bankruptcy—and had survived by borrowing some $200 million through friends of Beijing.

Nor did the procedure for electing a new legislature in May 1998 enhance the regime's democratic credibility. There were still sixty seats, and again only twenty were filled by popular election. The rest were either appointed directly, as had been a minority under Patten's reforms, or were chosen by "functional constituencies," trade associations of, say, gold traders, doctors, bankers, lawyers, and the like. So too had they been under Patten because the Basic Law drafted by Beijing and the Foreign Office so provided. Thus harking back to Benito Mussolini's corporate state was either not recognized as such or failed to disturb the architects of the new Hong Kong, which was to be ruled by democracy Beijing style—essentially a more efficient and more invasive totalitarianism than Mussolini's fascism.

Nonetheless, the first legislative election after the handover was a stunning repudiation of Tung Chee-hwa's reign, despite his rigging the voting against the anti-totalitarian parties. Despite torrents of rain and winds of near typhoon violence, a remarkable 53 percent of the general electorate, the highest ever, turned out to choose the twenty legislators representing the general public.

They returned fifteen candidates of Martin Lee's Democratic Party and its close allies. The remaining five came from the Democratic Alliance for the Betterment of Hong Kong, a mildly leftist, old line labor union party that does not truckle to Beijing. Although the voting pattern had been altered to favor pro-Beijing candidates, not a single one was elected by the general public. In the functional constituencies, five more Democrats were chosen, although the number eligible by occupation to vote had been reduced from some 1.15 million to less than a hundred fifty thousand.

It was a smashing victory for the advocates of democracy and independence, a stinging repudiation of Tung Chee-hwa and his puppet-masters in Beijing. In immediate practical terms it was something less. A majority of the sixty legislators will vote as Beijing directs, for twenty were appointed directly and the functional constituencies, largely the realm of big business, returned some fifteen pro-Beijing candidates.

Martin Lee is now all but literally the leader of the opposition in Communist China, since nowhere else in the sprawling nation is any opposition party tolerated. Of course, the SAR will continue to run as Beijing direct. Nonetheless, a spark of democracy will glow in Hong Kong until either Beijing stamps it out or Beijing itself changes even more radically than it is changing at the moment.

In the year 2002 a committee of eight hundred is to select the next chief executive, either Tung Chee-hwa or another equally subservient to Beijing. In 2007 the successive chief executive is to be popularly elected, but Tung has said he feels that may be too soon. He has also decried Hong Kong's excessive Westernization and has restricted teaching in English, a measure originally planned by the outgoing colonial administration to facilitate the Sinicization of Hong Kong. Yet today switching to Cantonese as the language of instruction seems downright silly. Not only will graduates of the newly restricted schools not know the international language, English, well. They won't even be adept in *Putunghua*, China's common national language.

The press, radio, and television are already under pressure, nonetheless effective for arising from the fears of reporters and editors under pressure from proprietors. Such self-censorship is probably more effective that outright censorship, since it knows no bounds. Direct censorship has not been imposed— and may never need be. The Chinese-language media are, however, harassed. The frankly oppositionist *Apple Daily* has been charged with violations of terms of employment and other non-journalistic offenses.

The English-language press, the barometer by which most foreign observers assess Hong Kong's political weather, is however reasonably free of interference. Only a few regularly read the English press. They are predominantly foreigners who, in any event, are mostly transients and thus don't really matter. But Radio Television Hong Kong, an editorially autonomous public entity rather like the BBC, which broadcasts in English and Cantonese, has been fiercely attacked for failing to present government policy "positively." Hong Kong's new regime really cannot see the difference between a quasi-independent broadcasting service financed by the government and a wholly government-controlled service—no more than can Beijing.

Deng Xiaoping, China's paramount leader, who died a few months before the handover he had enforced, made several promises to sweeten the pill. He did so in part to save British face by fostering the illusion that London had successfully negotiated modifications of Beijing's original conditions, all for the benefit of the people of Hong Kong. His chief purpose was to reassure the people so that they would, as he advised, "set their hearts at ease." Deng did not want a frightened populace that could be difficult to govern and would certainly not make for a prosperous SAR that would spin money for the People's Republic.

Despite Deng's reassurances, tens of thousands of the emerging middle class fled each year from 1984 onwards. More would have fled if they could. They were quite right to doubt Deng's promises.

The paramount leader had guaranteed that Hong Kong's social and economic system would not change for at least fifty years after the handover. He had encapsulated his guarantees in a simple formula: *One country—two systems.*

Yet Tung Chee-hwa himself recently declared that *one country* took absolute precedence over *two systems* whenever the two principles clashed. They clashed repeatedly during the first year of Tung's term. Tung also assured his own followers that dissenting voices on Radio Television Hong Kong would be silenced—all in good time. So would public demonstrations protesting government actions.

Such demonstrations, reasonably free at the beginning, are now much restricted. Four men have been convicted for demonstrating, two of them for defacing the scarlet flag of the People's Republic of China. Neither defacing the Union Jack nor public protest was an offense under "oppressive colonial rule."

Beyond doubt, Beijing is gradually making Hong Kong a little totalitarian state under cover of apparently moderate policies. We should have expected nothing else. Above all, as already noted, Hong Kong cannot be allowed to become a threat to Beijing's absolute rule of China by its example of a happier people under a more lenient government. But absolutism will be enforced "slowly, slowly," as Tung Chee-hwa observed of the ultimate suppression of the media and all freedom of expression.

Foreign influence has slowed that inexorable process—and could slow it further. Paramount is American influence, since President Jiang Zemin needs the public approval of the Clinton Administration to enhance his personal prestige, as it already has, and, he hopes, it will in the future. American goodwill is also vital to China's industrial progress. But such influence can only show the process. It cannot stop the totalitarianization of the SAR.

Non-economic and non-political events have also made Hong Kong uneasy, for they show that Heaven itself does not look favourably on the new government. Traditional Chinese belief held that a dynasty reigned because it had been vouchsafed divine approval, which was knows as the Mandate of Heaven. Extensive natural catastrophes traditionally demonstrated that the Mandate of Heaven had been revoked, and the reigning dynasty would, therefore, soon fall. Natural catastrophes began the instant the regime appointed by Beijing took office.

It rained continually for months. Landslides swept away buildings and imperiled lives. The people slipped into dejection under the seemingly endless rain pelting down day after day after day. The business slump had already begun and was soon to dip further because of by monetary and commercial crises throughout Asia. But it was initially the weather, not the economy, that depressed the people of the new Special Administrative Region of the People's Republic of China.

That was not a good start. Neither was it the end.

A month of two later, Hong Kong was afflicted by a virulent influenza carried by a virus that could leap from its normal habitat in chickens or ducks to human beings. Naturally fearful, the government ordered millions of fowl destroyed. The mass slaughter, which all but impoverished poultry breeders and traders, was not carried out adeptly. Stray dogs and cats gnawed and clawed at black refuse sacks containing some dead chickens and some that were not quite dead. Highly efficient under British control, the Hong Kong Civil Service made a mess of that essential execution under Tung Chee-hwa's aegis.

Still another natural disaster struck early in 1998. Hong Kong's inshore fishing had already been curtailed by noisome pollution and by competition from Japanese, Taiwanese, and Korean boats. Nonetheless, Hong Kong's trawlers and motorized junks were still finding good catches not too far away. Then came the red tide, a flood of scarlet algae that poisoned innumerable fish.

What then, Hong Kong's people asked, of the Mandate of Heaven?

Tung's Chee-hwa's administration has further been marred by a general rise in crime, as well as public and private corruption. To be fair, both armed robbery and bribery were already increasing under Chris Patten's administration. Both were then fuelled in good part, as they are now, by the virtual immunity from prosecution of Beijing-owned corporations and by the alliance between the criminal secret societies of Hong Kong, the so-called Triads, and the officers of the People's Liberation Army in the nearby city of Guangzhou, also called Canton in English. The military would, among other transactions, send thugs from Canton to Hong Kong to carry out crimes the Triads wished to subcontract.

Crime with roots in China is evidently so widespread is that the Independent Commission Against Corruption refuses to discuss cross-border issues. But, then, it refuses to discuss any matter at all regarding its crusade, preferring to issue self-congratulatory press releases. Nonetheless, the ICAC, created decades ago, is now very large—and still growing. There is self-evidently a growing need to fight corruption.

The ICAC's reticence may also be due to fear of the servants of the new regime of any revelation regarding any sensitive matter. Many matters are now sensitive that were not sensitive under even the most discreet British governor.

It is also whispered among those in the know that the Civil Service itself has now been corrupted, encouraged, perhaps, by the example of totally corrupt Chinese officialdom. Yet those who talk knowingly of such bribery may only believe they are in the know. Nonetheless, the fact that they believe and repeat such rumors is in itself significant. To say the least, the Beijing-appointed regime and its servants are not well regarded.

In China itself the absolute authority of the Communist Party Centre at Beijing is being continually undermined by the personal economic interests and the assertiveness of the officials and entrepreneurs in the provinces amid continuing economic liberalization. And, of course, Hong Kong money and Hong Kong expertise are vital to China's continuing economic development.

Martin Lee of the Democratic Party therefore avows long-term optimism, perhaps to counter unavoidable short-term pessimism regarding the future of Hong Kong. He believes the changes already effected on the mainland by Hong Kong's influence will grow greater and will in time make the rulers of China less tyrannical and, thus, less inclined to impose tyranny on Hong Kong.

He could be right. No one can deny the sweeping changes occurring in China owing to the daunting dilemma its ruler's face. As already noted, if they are to remain in power, they must placate the masses by at least fulfilling their basic material desires. Whipped up patriotism and the artificial idealism of Marxism-Leninism-Maoism, even general suppression of all freedoms and the threat of "reform through labour" or still harsher punishment like the constant drumfire of executions for crimes that are often political—not all those deterrents can any longer keep the masses in line. Civilian officials as well as army officers are now members, even leaders of extra-legal secret societies, and every new measure of economic liberalization effectively undermines the authority of the central leadership. Beijing is now extending such relaxation, yet simultaneously intensifying ideology-based civil discipline. In the long run that self-contradictory policy simply will not work.

Nonetheless, the prospect of China's changing so radically as to affect its rule of Hong Kong benignly is still far distant. In fact, the necessity to exercise iron control over the SAR will grow as Beijing tries in vain to beat out the wild fire of domestic discontent.

Beside China, Hong Kong is much smaller than, say, a mouse beside an elephant. Presumably a mouse could in time induce an elephant to eat cheese if it were not trampled in the interim. But how long would it take?

While we wait for that moment, the Communist Party closes its mailed hand ever tighter on the Special Administrative Region of Hong Kong. Relentlessly, albeit gradually, the people are being deprived of the opportunity, the objective education, and, above all, the dignity and freedom they previously enjoyed. Regardless of all else, such erosion of human rights is reason enough to deplore the present trend and to fear for Hong Kong's future.

Glossary

Basic Law

The Mini-Constitution for Hong Kong established by the People's Republic of China, somewhat based on the Joint Declaration (April 4, 1990).

BDTC = British Dependent Territories Citizen Passport

Used by those living in Hong Kong for travel. Does not give the right of abode in Great Britain.

Bill of Rights Ordinance

1991 local law based on the International Covenant on Civil and Political Rights (ICCPR) and the International Covenant on Economic, Social and Cultural Rights (ICESCR).

BLDC

Basic Law Drafting Committee which composed the Basic Law. There were fifty-nine members; thirty-six from the PRC, twenty-three from Hong Kong. In the end, all decisions had to be approved by the PRC.

(BNO) British National Overseas Passport

Authorized by Great Britain to replace all BDTC's by July 1, 1997. Does not give the right of abode in Great Britain.

British nationality (Hong Kong) Act of 1990

Gives 50,000 heads of households in Hong Kong the right of abode in Great Britain (with dependents, app. 225,000 people.) The PRC says they will not recognize those passports.

CFA

Court of Final Appeal

CP

Communist Party

District Boards

Provides a forum for public consultation. Also provides some local recreational and cultural activities. Nineteen members.

EXCO

Executive Council
Similar to a Cabinet. Five of its sixteen members must also be members of Legco.

Guangdong

The province surrounding Guangzhou

Guangxhou = Canton

Pinyin for the same city

Hong Kong Alliance in Support of the Democratic and Patriotic Movement in China

A group, including Martin Lee and Szeto Wah, organized to support the students who demonstrated in Tiananman Square in 1989 and continues to protest human rights violations in China.

Hong Kong Macau Working Group

Advisory group appointed by the PRC. Xu Ze is the head of the Political Department.

Joint Declaration on the Future of Hong Kong, Signed by Great Britain and the Peoples Republic of China.

Establishing all of Hong Kong's transfer to the PRC on July 1, 1997, as a Special Administrative Region for fifty years under "One country—two systems."
(Initialed on September 26, 1984, and signed on December 19, 1984.)

JLG

Joint Liason Group (Sino-British)
September 26, 1984, through January 1, 2000, group of representatives of both Great Britain and the People's Republic of China meeting in Beijing, London, and Hong Kong at least once a year in each of the three locations, for liaison and consultation without being an organ of power. Each side has a senior representative of Ambassadorial rank and four other members with a staff of twenty. Their proceedings are confidential unless otherwise agreed by both sides.

LEGCO

Legislative Council
Prior to the elections of 1985, all Legco members were appointed by the governor. In 1985, the first indirect elections for twenty-six of the members to the Legco took place through functional constituencies and electors. In 1991 an addition was made of the first direct elections for eighteen of its sixty seats.
On September 17, 1995, for the first time there was a fully elected Legco as a body of sixty with twenty elected by geographical constituencies, thirty elected by functional constituencies and ten by an electoral college.

MFN

Most Favored Nation Trade Status

OMELCO

Office of Members of the Executive and Legislative Councils
Secretariat for members of both groups.

PAP

The People's Armed Police of the PRC, which is a paramilitary force under orders of the Communist Party's Central Military Commission.

Peking = Beijing

Same city. Peking was used pre Pinyin, which was instituted in 1979.

Pin-Yin

New spelling and pronunciation for Mandarin, instituted in 1979.

PLA

The People's Liberation Army of the PRC.

PRC

The People's Republic of China

Preparatory Committee

Establishment in January 1996 using PWG's recommendations and dealing with how Hong Kong will be run by the PRC.

Provisional Legislature

Interim body to be established by the PRC in July 1997, likely to replace the currently elected Legislative Council.

PWC

Preliminary Working Committee
Closed at the end of 1995. Operated as a shadow government for the PRC and never recognized by Great Britain. Replaced with the Preparatory Committee for 1996-97.

Regional Council

Providing local services to the New Territories. The counterpart of the Urban Council which is used for Hong Kong Island and Kowloon. Thirty-six members.

Right of Abode

The right to live in a particular country or territory. In Hong Kong generally referred to as the right to live in Great Britain.

S.A.R.

Special Administrative Region
The designation of Hong Kong by China as of July 1, 1997, and Macau as of
December 20, 1997. It provides the basis of "One country—two systems."

S.E.Z.

Special Economic Zone
Chinese cities given special tax breaks. Shenzhen is the one closest to Hong
Kong, and Zhuhai is the one next to Macau.

The Three Treaties

Treaty of Nanking (1842) = Hong Kong Island ceded in perpetuity to Great
Britain.
The Convention of Peking (1860) = Kowloon and Stonecutters Island ceded
in perpetuity to Great Britain.
The Second Convention of Peking (1898) = The New Territories leased to
Great Britain for ninety-nine years from July 1, 1898, through June 30,
1997.

Urban Council

Providing local, municipal services in urban areas of Hong Kong Island and
Kowloon. (Garbage collection, parks maintenance, recreation, and culture,
etc.) forty councilors.

Xiang Gang

Pinyin for Hong Kong.

Xinhua News Agency

The de-facto "embassy" of the People's Republic of China prior to the
handover.

Names:

Aung San Suu Kyi

Winner of election in Burma, placed under house-arrest by coup.

Deng Xiaoping

The "paramount leader" of the People's Republic of China

Jiang Zemin

President of the People's Republic of China after the death of Deng
Xiaoping

Emily Lau

Democracy advocate who was an Independent on the Legislative Council
and became a member of the Frontier Party.

Lee Kwan Yew

Leader of Singapore

Christopher Francis Patten

The last British governor of Hong Kong

Li Peng

Prime Minister of the People's Republic of China

Christopher Francis Patten

The last British governor of Hong Kong

Tung Chee-Hwa

The first chief executive after the handover of Hong Kong to the People's Republic of China.

About the Author

Bruce Herschensohn has been a television and radio political commentator for the last two decades. After service in the U.S. Air Force he began his own motion picture company and then was appointed Director of Motion Pictures and Television for the United States Information Agency. During his tenure the USIA received more awards for film and television productions than all other departments and agencies of the U.S. government combined, including the Oscar from the Academy of Motion Pictures Arts and Sciences. In 1969, he was selected as one of the Ten Outstanding Young Men in the Federal Government. He received the second highest civilian award, the Distinguished Service Medal, and then became Deputy Special Assistant to President Nixon. His travels to over ninety countries gave him unique insight of worldwide political and governmental affairs. Herschensohn taught "The U.S. Inage Abroad" at the University of Maryland, occupied the Nixon Chair at Whittier College teaching "U.S. Foreign and Domestic Policies" and was Chairman of the Board of Pepperdine University. He was appointed a member of the Reagan Transition Team. Herschensohn was the 1992 Republican nominee for the U.S. Senate in California and was defeated while winning over one million votes more than the national ticket of the Party. He was a Fellow at the John F. Kennedy Institute of Politics at Harvard University for the spring 1996 semester teaching "U.S. Foreign Policy." He is currently teaching "The World Leadership Role of the United States" at Pepperdine University's School of Public Policy, and is a Non-Resident Associate Fellow of the Nixon Center for Peace and Freedom, and is a Distinguished Fellow at The Claremont Institute.